BINAH VOLUME 1

Studies in Jewish History

The BINAH Series is a publication of
THE INTERNATIONAL CENTER FOR UNIVERSITY TEACHING OF JEWISH CIVILIZATION, Jerusalem

Academic Chairman	Moshe Davis
Associate Editor	Priscilla Fishman
Editorial Consultant	Shulamith Nardi

co-published with

THE OPEN UNIVERSITY OF ISRAEL, Tel Aviv

President	Nehemia Levtzion

BINAH VOLUME 1

Studies in Jewish History

Edited by
JOSEPH DAN

BINAH: Studies in Jewish History,
Thought, and Culture

PRAEGER

New York
Westport, Connecticut
London

Library of Congress Cataloging-in-Publication Data

Studies in Jewish history / edited by Joseph Dan.
    p. cm. — (Binah ; v. 1)
    Articles originally written and published in Hebrew, have been
adapted from scholarly journals into English.
    Bibliography: p.
    Includes index.
    Contents: The death of Joab / Ephraim E. Urbach—Tacitus on the
Jews / Jochanan H. Lewy—The concept of history in hekhalot and
merkabah literature / Joseph Dan—The origins of Jewish communal
organization in the Middle Ages / Yitzhak F. Baer—The generation
of the Spanish exiles considers its fate / H.H. Ben-Sasson—From
apostasy to return to Judaism / Joseph Kaplan—The dispute between
Jacob Berab and Levi ben Habib over renewing ordination / Jacob Katz
—Jewish diplomatic activities to prevent expulsion of the Jews
from Bohemia and Moravia in 1744–45 / Barouh Mevorah—On the
return of Moses Hess to Judaism / Michael Graetz—The
"Kulturkampf" and the Jews of Germany / Uriel Tal.
    ISBN 0–275–93035–1 (alk. paper). ISBN 0–275–93036–X (alk.
paper)
    1. Jews—History. 2. Judaism—History. I. Dan, Joseph, 1935–
II. Series.
DS102.4.S78   1988
909' .04924—dc 19   88–5813

Library of Congress Catalog Card Number: 88–5813
ISBN: 0–275–93035–1 (loose-leaf)
      0–275–93036–X(hb)

First published in 1989

Praeger Publishers, One Madison Avenue, New York, NY 10010
A division of Greenwood Press, Inc.

Printed in the United States of America

The paper used in this book complies with the
Permanent Paper Standard issued by the National
Information Standards Organization (Z39.48–1984).

10 9 8 7 6 5 4 3 2 1

The revitalization of the Hebrew language and culture during this century has led to a florescence of Jewish scholarly activity in Israel, in the United States, and in academic centers throughout the world.

Over the years, Israel's institutions of higher learning have produced a sizable corpus of scholarly monographs in Hebrew. These works have appeared in academic journals, but because of the linguistic barrier, this exciting material has largely been inaccessible to the educated reader in other countries.

The BINAH Series has been developed to bridge this gap. Its focus on Jewish history, thought, and culture seeks to make available to a broad, interested public the fruits of these scholarly studies in Jewish civilization.

R. Hanina ben Dosa: When deeds
extend beyond learning, learning
endures.

Pirke Avot 3:12

The beginning is the most
important part of the dream.

Plato, The Republic, II, 377b

CONTENTS

INTRODUCTION

The studies in Jewish history presented in this collection, originally written and published in Hebrew, have been adapted into English in an attempt to bridge the language gap between the English-speaking student of Jewish civilization and the large group of scholars who write and publish in Hebrew.

When European scholars in the early nineteenth century laid the foundations for the scientific, philological approach to Jewish history and culture, the language used for this modern, scholarly, systematic study was German. Later in the last century, a growing number of Jewish scholars began to publish their studies in Hebrew and in English, establishing new centers for Jewish scholarship in England, the United States, and Eretz Israel. The mass emigration of Jews from Europe to America and Israel encouraged this process in the twentieth century and, after the Holocaust, Israel and the United States emerged as the largest centers of Jewish scholarship.

When The Hebrew University of Jerusalem was founded in 1925, it incorporated the Institute of Jewish Studies that had been founded the previous year to serve as a center for scholarship in Jewish civilization. This institute grew rapidly, and in the last sixty years some of the most prominent scholars in Jewish studies have taught therein. Graduates of the Hebrew University played a major role in the establishment of the other universities in Israel—in Tel Aviv, Ramat Gan, Haifa, and Beersheva.

Today, Israel has become the major center of Jewish scholarship and publications in the academic world. At the same time, studies in Jewish civilization have assumed a growing role in the life of the vast Jewish community in the United States. In the last generation the importance of these studies has been recognized within the general academic world, and courses in Hebrew and in Jewish civilization are being taught in hundreds of institutions of higher learning in North America and throughout the world.

Thus, two great communities of scholars in Jewish civilization emerged,

one publishing mainly in Hebrew, and one publishing mainly in English—
not to mention the developing scholarship in other areas of the world and
in other languages. While the scholars are familiar with each other's languages, their students often are not. An ongoing effort to translate scholarly
books and articles from Hebrew to English and other languages has become
necessary. The collection presented here is one detail in this large picture.

The BINAH Series is designed especially for the university undergraduate
student who is taking a general 'Introduction to Judaism' course or studying
a more specialized area of Jewish civilization. The articles are all adapted
from scholarly journals and have not previously been available in English.
They are not parts or chapters of books, but present a thesis in its entirety,
as intended by the author.

The term 'adapted' should be explained. The articles presented in this
collection were published in first-rate scholarly journals; they were written
by scholars, for scholars. Because the authors intended them to be read by
experts in the field of Jewish studies, the articles often lack explanations of
important terms, names, and dates that were assumed to be well known
to the readers of the original Hebrew version. On the other hand, the authors
often included, especially in the notes, detailed discussions of related scholarly problems which are not directly connected with the main thesis of the
article. A straight translation of these papers would present the undergraduate student with so much detail and discussion that the effort of
assimilating its contents would be disproportionate to such a student's
needs. It was, therefore, decided to present the articles in an adapted form,
adding explanations and clarifications where necessary in the body of the
paper, and omitting notes and references to side issues. It should be emphasized that each article was carefully read either by the author or, in the
case of scholars who are no longer with us, by an expert in the field, to
ensure that the adaptation was accurate and true to the content of the
original Hebrew text. The experience accumulated in using this material in
the classroom will enable us to refine this approach in future volumes.

The articles included in this volume merely hint at the wealth of scholarly
studies published in Hebrew, and should serve to indicate the important
potential available for the teaching of Jewish civilization on the undergraduate level. To aid dissemination of these materials, the International Center
for University Teaching of Jewish Civilization, Jerusalem, the authors of the
articles (or their literary estates), and the translators/adaptors grant permission to photocopy these articles for teaching purposes, without further
permission or fee.

It is hoped that the following BINAH collections will continue to enrich
the material at the disposal of those teaching Jewish civilization.

Joseph Dan

1

EPHRAIM E. URBACH

The Death of Joab: A Midrashic Interpretation of Political History

The literature of the midrash is our main source concerning the history of the Jews and their ideas and attitudes toward their own problems and toward the world around them, for the period between the second and seventh centuries. Most midrashic material does not deal with contemporary problems directly; many sections interpret biblical stories and verses, and only indirectly present the author's attitude toward the issues of his own times. One of the most difficult tasks of the historian is to discern within the midrashic material the historical significance of the sage's statements. Such an attempt is presented in the following study.

Ephraim Elimelech Urbach is professor emeritus of Talmud at The Hebrew University of Jerusalem. He served for many years as the President of the Israeli Academy of Arts and Sciences, and is the President of the World Union of Jewish Studies. Among Professor Urbach's major works are the history of the Tosafists in Western Europe (twelfth and thirteenth centuries), the four-volume edition of Arugat ha-Bosem *(a thirteenth-century commentary on the* piyyutim) *and, best known, his study of ancient Jewish religious beliefs,* The Sages.

BACKGROUND

The first two chapters of the First Book of Kings, describing the transition of power from a dying King David to his youngest son, Solomon, are

---

This article originally appeared in Hebrew, in *Dov Sadan Memorial Volume*, Jerusalem, 1977. The translation/adaptation is by Moshe Aumann.

The International Center for University Teaching of Jewish Civilization, Jerusalem, the author of the article, and the translater/adaptor grant permission to photocopy this article for teaching purposes without further permission or fee.

regarded in literary and scholarly circles as an unsurpassed work of art—because of both the historicity of their content and the profound insight they provide into the characters and personalities of the persons involved, their literary style, and their dramatic impact.[1]

In relating to these chapters, our sages, authors of homiletical writings in the midrash and the aggada, made no attempt to assess them as a literary creation. Their main concern was to ferret out the inner truth contained in them. They were aware that the biblical narrative frequently leaves much unsaid, accentuating the highlights of a story, the most important or significant element in the chain of events, and remaining silent about the rest—or, at most, hinting at them. Such hints may be found in words or phrases that, on the surface, appear superfluous in the overall framework of what is otherwise a bare, concise statement. In approaching such a text, the rabbis also make use of phrases whose presence in the text may be adequately explained in a variety of ways, but which serve them as a hook, so to speak, on which to hang the important additional details that are missing in the biblical story and that we would like to know.

THE PURPOSE OF MIDRASH

Our sages did not regard themselves as producers of literature, but as interpreters or exegetes. The task they undertook was not to write a somewhat expanded paraphrase of the biblical text but, rather, to dig up and expose to the light of day the information hidden behind the bare words. Quite often this exposure involves criticism of some of the personalities in the story, or of their actions. The supplementary material thus presented to us may not derive inexorably from the text, but neither is it merely a figment of the imagination.

What is this homiletical material? In many cases, it may simply provide a searching look into the past—not from a stationary vantage point allowing only a limited, one-dimensional view of a given situation, but through movement to the distant past, and then forward toward other events that were chronologically later, but which, for the viewer, have also become part of the past. This shifting vantage point provides a depth of background and perspective that make it possible to note the connection between separate events and to understand their reasons. "That which they were not told—they saw; and that which they did not hear—they looked into" is a good way, perhaps, to describe the attentive scrutiny which our sages directed toward biblical texts. Although the premise underlying this method is that Divine Providence governs the progression of human events, the sages' methodological approach remains well within the bounds of the empirical historian's rationalism.

Let us take a closer look at these two chapters in the Book of Kings, a narrative of high drama involving a rich variety of figures.

THE PRETENDER

Chapter one of the First Book of Kings opens with a description of King David's old age. The atmosphere is thick with fatigue, languor, and apathy. Adonijah, the oldest of David's surviving sons (two of whom, Amnon and Absalom, had earlier met untimely deaths), decides to fill the void by pressing his claim to the about-to-be-vacated throne ("I will be king!"). The king's passivity is emphasized in the verse, "His father never scolded him; Why did you do that? He was the one born after Absalom and, like him, was very handsome."

Based upon the seemingly superfluous allusion in this verse to Absalom, the midrash (Tanhuma Shmot 1) criticizes David for not having disciplined and reprimanded his sons, as a result of which they fell into bad ways and caused their father "unending anguish," for "bad ways in a man's home are worse than the wars of Armageddon." All the wars that David fought and all the dangers that he had faced did not have the negative impact on him that was generated by the deeds of his wayward sons.

David's hypertolerance and passivity vis-a-vis his sons' activities made him reluctant to play an active role in the transfer of power in the kingdom. David refrains from any kind of reaction or response even when Adonijah makes his unauthorized move. It is only through the energetic intervention of the prophet Nathan—and of the queen, Bathsheba, acting on Nathan's initiative—that David is finally aroused from his lethargy and induced to forestall Adonijah's plans by having Bathsheba's son Solomon anointed king. Actually, all that was required of the aged and tired regent was that he agree to Nathan's plan, and this he did. In the words of the Tanna, Rabbi Judah, "and when Bathsheba and Nathan came before David, he gave his consent" (Ecclesiastes Rabbah 4,9).

THE CHARGE TO SOLOMON

Once Solomon was anointed king, all that remained for David was to instruct him before his death, as he does in Chapter Two of the First Book of Kings. The harshest of these instructions was that concerning David's erstwhile trusted chief-of-staff, Joab son of Zeruiah:

Further, you know what Joab son of Zeruiah did to me, what he did to the two commanders of Israel's forces, Abner son of Ner and Amasa son of Jether; he killed them, shedding blood of war in peacetime . . . So act in accordance with your wisdom, and see that his white hair does not go down to Sheol in peace. (I Kings, 2:5,6)

The justification for this order is clear: It is Joab's guilt as the slayer of Abner and Amasa. But what is the meaning of the words, "what Joab . . . did to me"? Indeed, the midrash asks precisely this question. The answer offered

I.1.3

by the midrash is the following: When David wrote to Joab, "Place Uriah in the front lines where the fighting is fiercest" (II Samuel 11,15), Joab did so, and Uriah was killed.[2] Then, the midrash continues, all the officers of the army assembled around Joab, and Joab showed them the writing, wherefore it is said, "what Joab son of Zeruiah did to me, etc.," for they realized that David had ordered Joab to kill Uriah.

Needless to say, the biblical text can be understood easily and it contains no reference to Joab's role in the death of Uriah. However, the rabbis felt that Joab's seemingly senseless act in sending Uriah to a certain death at the front could not be allowed to go unquestioned. Thus the midrash states that the officers, Uriah's comrades-in-arms, demanded an explanation. In an attempt to defend his action, Joab produced the missive that the king had sent him, containing the terrible order. It is not surprising that Joab's revelation of the king's role in the Uriah affair gave rise to whispers and rumors that also pointed in the direction of Joab's murder of Abner son of Ner, long before the Uriah episode. Had this also taken place with David's prior knowledge—perhaps at his instigation?

The problem of whether the words "what Joab . . . did to me" are merely an introduction to the charge that follows, concerning the killings of Abner and Amasa, or whether they should be understood as a separate charge, was resolved by some commentators in favor of the second interpretation, with the interpolation of the word 'and' after the first phrase; but even then we do not find any hint here of the act ascribed to Joab in the Uriah episode. One exegete, in fact—Ralbag—while subscribing to the separate-charge thesis, maintains that "what he did to me" refers to the killing of Absalom, a theory that finds a certain amount of support in other sources. It is a little difficult, however, to accept the view that, in David's legacy to his son Solomon, the killing of the rebel Absalom should have been recorded on the liability side of the king's ledger.

The counterpart of the midrash establishing the motivation for David's charge to Solomon in earlier political events is another midrash that is apologetic and eschatological in character. Christian exegesis has adopted this interpretation, in total disregard of the other. On the other hand, we have evidence that, among the Jews, the politically motivated midrash enjoyed wide currency. The *Melokhim Bukh* (Book of Kings), a poetic adaptation in Yiddish of the biblical text, first printed in Augsburg in 1543, mentions David's letter to Joab in these words:

The letter about Uriah the Hittite was in his hands. I had to be very much afraid of him . . . He kept pushing the letter in front of my eyes; I had to do what he wanted.

SOLOMON'S RESPONSE

Solomon is in no hurry to execute his late father's will. It is only after an innocent action on the part of his mother Bathsheba gives him grounds to suspect that Adonijah has not abandoned his plan to take over his father's throne, that Solomon orders his execution.

Having removed his archrival from the scene, Solomon proceeds to act against members of the Adonijah camp: first, against Abiathar the Priest—who was not even mentioned in David's will. For the time being, Solomon spares the priest's life and only sends him into exile with this explanation: "... you deserve to die, but I shall not put you to death at this time, because you carried the Ark of my Lord God before my father David, and because you shared all the hardships that my father endured (I Kings 2:26).

Then came Joab's turn: "When the tidings reached Joab, he fled to the Tent of the Lord and grasped the horns of the altar ... "[3] When, at the king's behest, Benaiah arrives on the scene and tells him to come out, Joab replies, "No, I will die here!"

In the biblical account, these four words (*lo, ki fo amut*) are all that Joab utters at this point. This paucity of speech on Joab's part puzzled our sages. How are we to understand Benaiah's message to his king upon his return to the palace: "Thus spoke Joab, and thus did he answer me." Does this message not hint at a lengthier exchange than the four words reported explicitly? Furthermore, what is one to make of Solomon's long and eloquent speech giving Benaiah a new order to strike down Joab—if not as a detailed reply to a detailed plea by Joab? Three verses (I Kings 2:31–33) are devoted to King Solomon's charge to Benaiah:

... strike him down and bury him, and remove guilt from me and my father's house for the blood of the innocent that Joab has shed. Thus the Lord will bring his bloodguilt down upon his own head, because, unbeknown to my father, he struck down with the sword two men more righteous and honorable than he—Abner son of Ner, the army commander of Israel, and Amasa son of Jether, the army commander of Judah. May the guilt for their blood come down upon the head of Joab and his descendants forever.

Then Benaiah did his king's bidding and struck down Joab.

In both of these chapters, the narrator refrains from making judgments. He lets the characters speak for themselves, leaving the assessment of their words to the reader.

JOAB IN ANOTHER LIGHT

The biblical narrative concerning Joab ends with the words "and he was buried at his home in the wilderness." But that is not the end of the story in rabbinic literature. There, the figure of Joab emerges in all its tragic grandeur. The Bible's sparse and measured words on Joab's demise conceal a myriad of untold details of a stormy life, and of the turbulent annals of David's fledgling kingdom. Joab's death is not understood solely as a penalty for his transgressions; the brief depiction of his burial does not evoke a grim rabbinic postmortem justification of divine judgment. Rather, it seems to be a poignant lamentation, a eulogy and a paean of praise. "And he was buried at his home in the wilderness," says the biblical verse, and the third-generation Amoraim[4] of Eretz Israel comment: Surely Joab's home was not in the wilderness!? Rather, when Joab, the commander of Israel's forces, died, Israel was turned into a veritable wilderness. Why? Because of his deeds which were deserving of praise—by some accounts, the highest praise. And what were his deeds? According to Rav, who took a special interest in the story of Joab's life, his home was always open to the poor whom he supported, nor was it tainted by stolen goods or by illicit personal relations.

THE SOLOMON-JOAB DEBATE

Having begun with the end of the story, let us return now to its beginning. A question arises regarding Joab's flight to the altar. Two Amoraim, Rav and Rabbi Johanan, express different opinions on this question, but are agreed that there is no validity to the view that, under the circumstances, the act of taking hold of the horns of the altar entitled Joab to immunity from the death penalty. The midrash says that the altar was on the premises of the high court, the Sanhedrin;[5] and it was to the Sanhedrin that Joab fled, with this calculation in mind: Better they slay me in court and have my sons inherit me, than that the king slay me and inherit me. His motive, then, in fleeing to the altar was not to find a haven and save his life, but (as is indicated in other midrashim as well) to prevent his earthly goods from falling into the hands of the state. Joab's quoted words, "for I shall die here" support this interpretation.

Joab's concern, however, was not only for his property and his heirs. He who, on more than one occasion, had known how to stand up to King David does not look like a person who would take his leave of this world without responding to the accusations that had been leveled against him. And, indeed, in the midrashim, Joab comes across not only as a hero in battle but also as a hero in Torah. The midrashim have Joab assert that he had been well within his rights in killing Abner, and that he had killed him lawfully, since Abner had previously slain Joab's brother Asael; therefore Joab was now acting in the legitimate capacity of a blood redeemer. King Solomon replied that Asael had been in pursuit of Abner, to which Joab retorted that Abner could have saved himself without, in the process, taking Asael's life. Solomon finally was compelled to concede that, in the matter of Abner, Joab was not at fault.

Nor was Solomon able to find a convincing reply to Joab's argument that his second target, Amasa, had been a rebel and a traitor. Solomon, in other words, lacked legal proof of Joab's guilt in the two slayings—proof that would have provided the juridical grounds for his execution. Joab's joining the Adonijah camp before Solomon was crowned certainly is insufficient ground for putting him to death—yet that, in the last analysis, was the only reason given in the Bible: " . . . for Joab had sided with Adonijah, though he had not sided with Absalom" (I Kings 2:28). The words "though he had not sided with Absalom" appear both superfluous and puzzling for, after all, what had Joab to fear for not having joined the rebel Absalom?[6] Rav Judah, a disciple of Rav's, finds a hint in this added phrase that Joab wished to but actually did not join Absalom. Rashi elucidates this interpretation:

Scripture tells us here that he [Joab] wished to side with Absalom as well, but was unable to carry out this thought . . . for fear of David, who was then still strong and robust; now, however, in David's old age, he changed course and sided with Adonijah.

This recital of Joab's attitude toward Absalom constitutes neither an assignment of blame nor an exoneration; it simply stresses the gravity of the first-mentioned act of joining the Adonijah camp, which had to be regarded as an act of rebellion against David. As one of the commentators said, it is inconceivable that Joab should be condemned to death for having merely thought about doing something he never really did! After all, the people of Israel sided with Absalom in their thousands, and Amasa also joined his camp, without being considered traitors for having done so.

In sum: A stalwart army commander like Joab would not have fled to the Tent of the Lord simply to seek refuge there, nor did he remain silent when confronted with the charges against him. As indicated between the lines of Benaiah's message to the king, he spoke and he responded and offered proof that Abner and Amasa were not better and more righteous than he, arguing that in a court of law—in the Sanhedrin—he would have been acquitted of the charges against him. In the end, his fate was sealed for one reason alone: because he sided with the would-be usurper of the throne, Adonijah, while David was still alive. The young Solomon wanted to make certain that Joab would not, at some future occasion, threaten his own reign.

MIDRASHIC APPROACHES

The midrashim we have cited on the biblical story of Solomon and Joab have a double purpose: to render the story more plausible, and to underscore its realism by placing it in the setting of earlier events—the past serving as a guide to a better understanding of the present. David, in his old age, is still troubled by the Uriah episode and by the letter bearing his signature that Joab possesses; Joab, in turn, recalls details connected with the deaths of Abner and Amasa.

Most of these interpretations are attributed to the Amoraim Rav and his student Rav Judah; Rav is known as one who undertook a realistic scrutiny of the past, and as an outspoken opponent of the apologetic approach. Of Rabbi,[7] who sought to defend David's conduct in the Bathsheba-Uriah episode, Rav had this to say (Tractate Sabbath 56a): "Rabbi, who is descended from David, turned things around in his defense." Rav went even further, and accused David of having committed the sin of listening to slander in the affair of Mephibosheth and Ziba (II Samuel 19), although the biblical narrative does not treat David's role in the affair as a sin; besides, Mephibosheth's conduct is not above suspicion—and, indeed, Rav's colleague, Samuel, justifies David for this reason. The Talmud cites this strongly worded pronouncement by Rav Judah, who spoke in Rav's name:

Had David not lent an ear to evil talk, the Kingdom of the House of David would not have been split asunder [after Solomon's death], the Israelites would not have indulged in idolatry, and we would not have been exiled from our land (Shabbat 56a).

The very fact that a passage like this was allowed to remain in the talmudic text, despite the biblical apotheosis of David, and despite all the messianic hopes connected with David and the Davidic dynasty, is overwhelming proof of the esteem in which rabbinic circles held the realistic study of the past.

The midrash is replete with instances of divine justice in the form of 'measure for measure': When David said to Mephibosheth, you and Ziba shall divide the field, a heavenly voice proclaimed: Rehoboam and Jeroboam will divide the kingdom (Sabbath 56b). In a similar fashion, Rav held that the execution of Joab had other dire consequences as well—notably, the harsh fate of several of the kings of the Davidic dynasty. When King Solomon sent a message to Joab calling upon him to submit to his fate, Joab replied: You cannot afflict the same man twice over: If you kill him, be prepared to accept the curses which your father laid upon him; and if not, let him be, that he may receive the curses which your father laid upon him. The fact is that all the curses pronounced by David against Joab came to fruition against David's own descendants (Sanhedrin 48b): 'one that has an unclean issue' (Rehoboam); 'a leper' (Uzziah); 'one that leans on a staff' (Asa); 'one that falls by the sword' (Josiah).

Rav's interpretations, it appears to me, substantiate what we wrote above, about scrutinizing the past from a vantage point that, on the one hand, offers a look into the more remote past and, on the other, reveals what the future holds in store for the characters in the story—a future that, for the interpreter who views the entire historical process, has also become part of the past.

I.1.8

POPULAR LEGENDS ABOUT JOAB

These interpretations, and others like them, do not possess the characteristics of the popular aggadah and its customary flights of fancy and
hyperbole. There are, it is true, a number of aggadot and stories dealing
with Joab's courage, his wisdom, and his guile,[8] but they did not originate
in the academies of Rav and the Amoraim. On the other hand, the material
we have cited from these sources, which casts a new and different light on
the biblical narrative in the Book of Kings, helped form the popular legend
or aggadah. The rabbinic interpretations were widely disseminated; the
versions that have reached us in later sources include additional elements
and embellishments, some of which, the evidence indicates, have their
origins in very early sources that are no longer extant.

The execution of Joab son of Zeruiah is also the exclusive subject of a
poetic introduction, in Aramaic, to the Seventh Commandment—"You shall
not kill"—in the *Mahzor Vitri* produced in Rashi's academy, as well as in
many of the manuscripts of the Ashkenazi Mahzor also dating to the Middle
Ages. It is one of a series of such poems introducing each of the Ten
Commandments. In this poem, Joab boasts of his good deeds, his conquests,
and his favors to King David; the poem also contains Joab's last will to his
son Joel. Here it transpires that Solomon ordered his son Rehoboam to
execute Joab, but Rehoboam recoils from the deed when the people turn
out in their masses, weeping and in great agitation.

These popular themes are interwoven with halakhic-juridical argumen-
tation. Joab exclaims: Woe to this world if this be justice![9] There is a brief
exchange between the king and Joab, in which the latter appears to have
the upper hand. King Solomon: Say not that it is anger or hatred that has
caused me to put you to death, for it is under the law that I slay you; and
I am not overwrought, as people are in their hour of anger, for my mind
is unperturbed. To which Joab replies: I am greater in Torah than you are
... and you cannot bring proof as to why you must slay me. As for the
killing of Abner and Amasa, that is between me and my Maker, and I had
rather die at my own hands than have others strike me down. Joab, in other
words, does not try to justify the killing of Abner and Amasa; he merely
argues that, in the absence of witnesses and prior warning, which are
required by Jewish law to convict a man of murder in a court of law, his
fate is in the hands of God, not of man. The poem ends with the following
words:

When the nations heard that Joab was slain, they rejoiced in public, but in their
hearts they wept; and the Children of Israel wept long and bitterly over the death
of Joab ben Zeruiah.

I.1.9

DISSEMINATION OF MIDRASHIM ON JOAB'S DEATH

The very fact that a connection is made between the biblical warning not to kill and the slaying of Joab, and the way that episode was depicted and interpreted in rabbinic literature, indicates the wide currency enjoyed by the midrashim. Further support for this thesis may be found in the previously cited *Melokhim Bukh*. This medieval work, like the poems introducing the Ten Commandments, was designed for a wide audience desirous of hearing biblical texts. These texts were spread by word of mouth, and embellished with a wealth of midrashim, to the enjoyment of readers and listeners alike.

Not unexpectedly, the style of the *Melokhim Bukh* reflects the atmosphere prevalent in the feudal society of the Middle Ages, with appellations such as 'Herzog Joab' (the Duke Joab) and 'Hauptmann Benaiah' (Captain Benaiah), and expressions of the chivalrous relations between them. Yet the major motifs in the narrative are those we find in the midrashim and in the Aramaic poem and its interpretation—with a tendency to expand on the more popular among them. At times, however, one cannot help but wonder whether the author of this work did not have a version of the poem different from that available to us. The verses describing the reactions to the slaying of Joab are particularly instructive in this respect:

When the nations heard that Joab was slain, they rejoiced in their hearts and cried with their eyes, doing this as a show for King Solomon. They were compelled— all the nations in equal measure—to serve him. And they wept bitterly that his [Joab's] life had been taken, thinking that they were thus ingratiating themselves with the king.

It would seem that what is written here is precisely the opposite of what is in the poem, which says, "When the nations heard that Joab was slain, they rejoiced in public, but in their hearts they wept." This response of the nations is puzzling—until we note the commentary on the text of the poem: "When all Israel heard they rejoiced in public, but in their hearts they wept." What has happened is the inadvertant omission of a phrase because of similar wording. The reaction of the people of Israel is thus attributed, in the poem, to 'the nations'. Indeed, we find this version in the well-known *Mahzor Nuremberg* manuscript:

When the nations heard that Joab was slain, they wept in public, but in their hearts they rejoiced. When the House of Israel heard that Joab was slain, they rejoiced in public, but in their hearts they wept.

Let us now look at the continuation of the text in the *Melokhim Bukh*:

I.1.10

... But Israel did the reverse: They laughed outwardly and wept in their hearts. Out of fear of the king, they refrained from weeping too much, but they could not avoid it altogether. One could write much about this ... the lips overflow when the heart is full. The Israelites began to weep ... that such a prince and scholar should be lost to Israel! May God bestow His grace upon this pious and honest man; the fact that we were unable to prevent this caused us much pain.

CAUSES NEAR AND REMOTE

It is a long way from the interpretations of Rav and other Amoraim, through the Aramaic poem, down to this popular medieval work. But they all have one thing in common. All of them present an interpretation of the events related in the Book of Kings that differs from that which appears to emerge from the biblical text itself. In these interpretations, King David's last will has been consciously ignored. At most, what is left of it are the words, "Act in accordance with your wisdom" (I Kings 2:6)—and that wisdom manifests itself in the removal of all the potential opponents to the consolidation of Solomon's kingdom, among them Joab, who had sided with Adonijah.

In the final analysis, then, it becomes a matter of the Solomonic realpolitik, revealed to us in the biblical narrative, versus the rabbinic interpretation inviting us to view these events in their broader historical perspective. The danger here lies in going overboard in one direction or the other.

One may have one's doubts, from the halakhic-juridical point of view, about Joab's attempts (in the rabbinic literature) to justify the killing of Abner and Amasa by invoking past events; but this does not give Solomon the right to justify his murder of Joab by citing those killings. The rabbinic interpretations of the biblical narrative detract from, rather than add to, that narrative. They reveal the king's subjective motives for his acts, as they are presented by Solomon himself—who not only manages to stay alive but, as the biblical narrative reports (I Kings 2:46), "Thus the kingdom was secured in Solomon's hands." The rabbinic interpretation reveals that this objective fact was not only the result of these events, but also the motive for the web of occurrences.

This realistic view of the chain of events, as we have described it, exposes the true motivations of our cast of characters; but it still does not fully explain the significance of these events. The question arises: Is it possible, by intellectual effort, to discover a meaningful plan in the march of history? It appears that even those rabbis who looked for such a plan came up with a negative answer to this question. The limitations of human understanding could lead to a different succession of events emerging from the interplay of conditions, motivations, decisions, efforts, and failures. In the rabbinic view, a meaningful plan in history could be discovered only by means of the belief in Divine Providence. The Mishnah elaborates on the verse, "And if a man lie not in wait, but God deliver him into his hand" (Exodus 21:12) as follows: One man killed a person unwittingly, another killed deliberately; came the latter and fell into the hand of the former . . . Or, in the words of the ancient proverb: "Evil is generated by evil-doers" (I Samuel 24:13).

Indeed, this is the interpretation followed by the Amoraim whose views we have presented. And it is on this level that we may find the explanation for Joab's fate. It was rooted in his own behavior, in precisely the same way that Rav found the explanation for Abner's demise: Why was Abner punished? Because he should have spoken up against Saul in the matter of the priestly city of Nob,[10] and he did not do so. Other rabbis found other reasons, but none of them provided adequate justification for Joab's deed in taking Abner's life. And, in truth, Joab's arguments in his own vindication—as Rav presents them—make no mention of any of these reasons.

There is something pretentious, even a certain lack of faith, in the attempt to explain and justify events that occurred in the course of political history entirely in terms of a long-range Providential plan. In the last analysis, this blurs human responsibility for such acts. In point of fact, however, to posit a causal linkage between earlier and later events does not, by any means, lessen this responsibility. Thus, to explain the division of David's kingdom (in Solomon's day) by means of David's statement, "You and Ziba shall divide the field" (II Samuel 19:30), merely reveals the weakness of the united monarchy from the very outset—since David never overcame his suspicions of the House of Saul and of the tribes that professed loyalty to him. David's deeds, however, did not constitute an irrevocable decree of history. What happened was that Solomon did not live up to his obligations, and so he was told: "Because you . . . have not kept My covenant and the laws which I enjoined upon you, I will tear the kingdom away from you . . . " (I Kings 11:11).

The exposure of human foibles and motivations should make us aware that they do not necessarily exhaust all the possibilities and that, beyond them, there exists another set of factors and causes that may have been forgotten or lost sight of by those who study past events. And even then, the attempt to discover the hidden elements in the historical drama does not entitle us to lay at their doorstep exclusive responsibility for the deeds and events under consideration.

NOTES

1. See R. N. Whybray, *The Succession Narrative*, London: SCM Press, 1968, p. 10, and its bibliography; also *The Jerome Biblical Commentary*, London: 1968, p. 182.

2. Uriah was the husband of Bathsheba, whom David wished to make his queen.

3. In Jewish biblical tradition, one who killed another accidentally had immunity from seizure and punishment as long as he grasped the horns of the altar

in a sacred site of sacrifice. However, one who schemed to kill another was to be taken from the altar and put to death (Exodus 21:14).

4. Rabbis of the talmudic period.

5. The conceptual world of midrash has its own inner logic that does not necessarily have a basis in historical reality. (See J. Dan, "The Concept of History in Hekhalot and Merkabah Literature," in this volume.) Thus, for the midrashic sages, the institution of the Sanhedrin existed in the period of the kings of Israel.

6. The Septuagint and, in its wake, other translations of the Bible render this phrase: "and he did not side with Solomon"—a deliberate modification of the biblical text.

7. Rabbi Judah Hanassi, editor of the Mishna.

8. See M. Gaster, *The Exempla of the Rabbis*, London: Asia Publishing Co., 1924, p. 8.

9. The same exclamation, with minor changes, appears in the Berlin Manuscript (British Museum), the Oxford Manuscript, and the Nuremberg Mahzor.

10. Nob was wiped out of King Saul's order because he suspected its inhabitants of having conspired against him with David.

2

YOCHANAN H. LEWY

Tacitus on the Jews

One of the most meaningful of the problems which face the historian of Judaism in general and of anti-Semitism in particular is whether anti-Semitism is the product of Christianity's hatred of the Jews following the Church's description of the death of Jesus, or whether it was a powerful force in the Hellenistic and Roman world even before the spread of Christianity. The most extensive material dealing with the Jews, their history and beliefs, by a Roman historian is to be found in Tacitus's work, and its analysis is essential to the understanding of attitudes to Judaism in the non-Christian ancient world. The following study is dedicated to such an analysis.

Prof. Yochanan H. Lewy was one of the earliest scholars of classical literature and history, in Latin and Greek, at The Hebrew University of Jerusalem. He published a series of studies dedicated to the use of classical sources for the understanding of Jewish history, mainly through a detailed comparison between the testimonies of Jewish and non-Jewish sources.

BACKGROUND

The observations of the Roman historian Tacitus on the origins and customs of the Jews rank among the best-known writings on the Jewish people in classical literature. It is not stylistic grace or depth of thought that accounts for this fame but, above all, Tacitus's wild accusations against the Jews,

This article first appeared in Hebrew, in *Zion* 8 (1943). The translation/adaptation is by Aryeh Rubinstein.

The International Center for University Teaching of Jewish Civilization, Jerusalem, the literary estate of the author of the article, and the translator/adapter grant permission to photocopy this article for teaching purposes without further permission or fee.

which have no parallel in the entire literary tradition of the ancient world. His malevolent writings have been used by 'enlightened' anti-Semites as unassailable proof of the age-old hostility of civilized nations toward Judaism, serving as a treasure trove for polemicists and apologists alike; some of his barbs are used by anti-Semites to this very day.

The sources upon which Tacitus drew for his chapters on the Jews have not been preserved, but it is clear that a good many views and tales were derived from Greek writers, with some motifs to be found in the ancient literary tradition going back to the time of Alexander the Great. But what these Hellenistic writers reported differs in significance from the words of Tacitus. A formulation first employed by a Greco-Egyptian writer necessarily assumed different political and intellectual connotations when expressed by a Roman statesman of Trajan's day, who advocated a world empire and observance of the ancestral tradition. The extended searches for the Greek origin of Tacitus's views are thus rather pointless.

Like most of the great ancient historians, Tacitus sought to understand the nature of his times. The purpose of describing past events was to enable the reader to make a correct evaluation of the current situation, and an educated guess as to what the future might hold in store. Hence, any interpretation of Tacitus must consider the intellectual background of his ideas.

Many scholars have ignored Tacitus's writings on the origins and customs of the Jews because so many of his observations are questionable. Instead of describing the early history of Israel, he presents an assortment of legends and fabrications, for most of which there is no solid basis. His remarks on the nature of Judaism are similarly replete with serious errors and crude distortions. Jewish scholars have therefore permitted themselves to dismiss these chapters completely, leaving them to 'folklore enthusiasts' for whom they had slight regard. The error in this rationalistic approach will be clarified. Contempt for such falsehoods is unacceptable, even from the historical-pragmatic viewpoint.

It should be borne in mind that Tacitus was both a member of the Roman senatorial class and a representative of the national culture. This invests his remarks with the weight of a document faithfully reflecting the attitude of the Roman leaders toward the Jews. It is true that his writings reflect only the views of the conservatives, but these opinions decisively influenced Roman politics. His conjectures, fabrications, and distortions are thus no less instructive for us than official documents bearing the royal seal, for they are part of the body of Roman tradition regarding Israel's practices.

TRANSLATION OF TACITUS'S TEXT

The following translation of Tacitus's chapters on the antiquities of the Jews are to be found in his *Histories*, which describe events in Rome between the years 69 and 96. In the fifth book of that work, Tacitus discusses the wars of Vespasian and Titus against the Jews (V, 1–13). In the manner of classical historians, he injects into the narrative a general survey of the Jews' origins, history, land, and customs, adding to this excursus a short account of the beginning of the siege of Jerusalem. Since Tacitus writes about events annalistically, proceeding year by year, he interrupts his description of the siege at the end of the year 69, and goes on to another event that occurred that year. He continued the story of the Jewish war in the later books, which are not extant.

Here is the translation of the chapters dealing with the origins and manners of the Jews (*Histories*, V, 2–5; Loeb Classical Library translation by C. H. Moore):

However, as I am about to describe the last days of a famous city, it seems proper for me to give some account of its origin.

It is said that the Jews were originally exiles from the island of Crete who settled in the farthest parts of Libya at the time when Saturn had been deposed and expelled by Jove. An argument in favor of this is derived from the name: there is a famous mountain in Crete called Ida, and hence the inhabitants were called the Idaei, which was later lengthened into the barbarous form Iudaei. Some hold that in the reign of Isis the superfluous population of Egypt, under the leadership of Hierosolymus and Iuda, discharged itself in the neighbouring lands; many others think that they were an Egyptian stock, which in the reign of Cepheus was forced to migrate by fear and hatred. Still others report that they were Assyrian refugees, a landless people, who first got control of a part of Egypt, then later they had their own cities and lived in the Hebrew territory and the nearer parts of Syria. Still others say that the Jews are of illustrious origin, being the Solymi, a people celebrated in Homer's poems, who founded a city and gave it the name Hierosolyma, formed from their own.

Most authors agree that once during a plague in Egypt which caused bodily disfigurement, King Bocchoris approached the oracle of Ammon and asked for a remedy, whereupon he was told to purge his kingdom and to transport this race into other lands, since it was hateful to the gods. So the Hebrews were searched out and gathered together; then, being abandoned in the desert, while all others lay idle and weeping, one only of the exiles, Moses by name, warned them not to hope for help from gods or men, for they were deserted by both, but to trust to themselves, regarding as a guide sent from heaven the one whose assistance should first give them escape from their present distress. They agreed, and then set out on their journey in utter ignorance, but trusting to chance. Nothing caused them so much distress as scarcity of water, and in fact they had already fallen exhausted over the plain nigh unto death, when a herd of wild asses moved from their pasturage to a rock that was shaded by a grove of trees. Moses followed them, and, conjecturing the truth from the grassy ground, discovered abundant streams of water. This relieved them, and they then marched six days continuously, and on the seventh seized a country, expelling the former inhabitants; there they founded a city and dedicated a temple.

I.2.3

To establish his influence over this people for all time, Moses introduced new religious practices, quite opposed to those of all other religions. The Jews regard as profane all that we hold sacred; on the other hand, they permit all that we abhor. They dedicated, in a shrine, a statue of that creature whose guidance enabled them to put an end to their wandering and thirst, sacrificing a ram, apparently in derision of Ammon. They likewise offer the ox, because the Egyptians worship Apis. They abstain from pork, in recollection of a plague, for the scab to which this animal is subject once afflicted them. By frequent fasts even now they bear witness to the long hunger with which they were once distressed, and the un-leavened bread is still employed in memory of the haste with which they seized the grain. They say that they first chose to rest on the seventh day because that day ended their toils; but after a time they were led by the charms of indolence to give over the seventh year as well to inactivity. Others say that this is done in honour of Saturn, whether it be that the primitive elements of their religion were given by the Idaeans, who, according to tradition, were expelled with Saturn and became the founders of the Jewish race, or is due to the fact that, of the seven planets that rule the fortunes of mankind, Saturn moves in the highest orbit and has the greatest potency; and that many of the heavenly bodies traverse their paths and courses in multiples of seven.

Whatever their origin, these rites are maintained by their antiquity: the other customs of the Jews are base and abominable, and owe their persistence to their depravity. For the worst rascals among other people, renouncing their ancestral religions, always kept sending tribute and contributions to Jerusalem, thereby increasing the wealth of the Jews; again, the Jews are extremely loyal toward one another, and always ready to show compassion, but toward every other people they feel only hate and enmity. They sit apart at meals, and they sleep apart, and although as a race, they are prone to lust, they abstain from intercourse with foreign women; yet among themselves nothing is unlawful. They adopted circum-cision to distinguish themselves from other peoples by this difference. Those who are converted to their ways follow the same practice, and the earliest lesson they receive is to despise their parents, children, and brothers as of little account. However, they take thought to increase their numbers; for they regard it as a crime to kill any late-born child, and they believe that the souls of those who are killed in battle or by the executioner are immortal: hence comes their passion for begetting children, and their scorn of death. They bury the body rather than burn it, thus following the Egyptians' custom; they likewise bestow the same care on the dead, and hold the same belief about the world below; but their ideas of heavenly things are quite the opposite. The Egyptians worship many animals and monstrous im-ages; the Jews conceive of one god only, and that with the mind alone: they regard as impious those who make from perishable materials representations of gods in man's image; that supreme and eternal being is to them incapable of representation and without end. Therefore they set up no statues in their cities, still less in their temples; this flattery is not paid their kings, nor this honour given to the Caesars. But since their priests used to chant to the accompaniment of pipes and cymbals and to wear garlands of ivy, and because a golden vine was found in their temple, some have thought that they were devotees of Father Liber, the conqueror of the East, in spite of the incongruity of their customs. For Liber established festive rites of a joyous nature, while the ways of the Jews are preposterous and mean.

I.2.4

Tacitus's chapters on the Jews are written in the best tradition of the ethnographic writers before him who described the attributes of foreign nations. He considered all the points demanded by that tradition, organizing his material in the customary manner; the construction of his sentences is simple, in contrast to the grandiloquent language of his other books. The ethnographic pattern served as a general background against which he highlighted the unique character of Judaism.

ETHNOGRAPHIC MOTIFS

Scholars who have investigated the literary style of ethnographic studies maintain that the rules of form laid down in this tradition affected the content of those studies. Certain ethnographic motifs come up again and again in connection with different peoples, and these 'mobile' motifs, they say, often serve to divert attention from real differences between peoples and to blur their unique characteristics. Scholars have found signs of the influence of ethnographic typology in Tacitus's observations on the Jews, and they have concluded that there are so many of these motifs as to call into question the credibility of the work.

This view is unacceptable for a number of reasons. Although traces of ethnographic typology are evident in the works of the Roman writers from whom Tacitus borrowed some of his abstruse formulas, there is no proof that with these details he also accepted their general outlook on the Jews. We must distinguish between the historian's information and his views. Not all that Tacitus knew about the Jews was learned from books. During his lifetime the Jewish community in Rome reached its peak, and for many years he served as a member of the committee on state cults in the capital. Thus he was not obliged to rely solely on literary tradition when he sought to learn about the character of the Jews. Above all, Tacitus was a contemporary of Vespasian and Titus, whose battles had aroused great interest among the Romans and led many of their writers to study the defeated nation of Judea and its customs. There is no reason, therefore, to assume that Tacitus copied blindly from his sources without reflecting on the import of the borrowed material; indeed, even a cursory reading of his chapters on the Jews proves the opposite. The man who wrote them has a definite opinion about the subject he discusses. If he erred, he did so deliberately.

There is support for this judgment among the scholars who have studied Tacitus's attitude toward the sources he used in writing the *Histories*. It is accepted that he did not get his information at first hand, but rather from the writings of Roman authors who had personally witnessed the events related or who relied on the testimony of eyewitnesses. Tacitus then copied or omitted, emphasized or condensed, the material in accordance with his own historical predilections. His critical approach to the sources and the preeminence of his own views are recognizable in every chapter of his narrative; there is no reason to believe that his attitude to the sources was any different in the chapters devoted to the Jews. One must then conclude that, while those chapters were based on literary sources (which have not been preserved), he selected and edited the details in accordance with his prejudices.

Hence, in trying to clarify the nature of Tacitus's observations on the Jews, investigation of the formal rules of the genre, or of the nature of his sources, is of limited value. His observations, like those of any writer worth his salt, can be interpreted only in their own terms. After a rigorous examination of his views, one may consider the possible influence on him of other writers with similar opinions, but such an investigation should be conducted only after the writer's own standpoint has been determined.

One of the gems of ancient ethnographic literature is the work *Germany* which, scholars now agree, Tacitus wrote with a political motivation. He believed that the Germans constituted the most dangerous threat to the survival of the Roman Empire, and decided to investigate the roots of their might. This led him to study the causes of the rise and decline of nations in general. The course of his own people's history taught him that Rome's greatness was the result of its observance of the virtues and mores of its ancestors. Thus, for Tacitus, the principles of government and the moral values of the early Romans became the touchstone of the political virtues of all nations. It was by this criterion that he measured the qualities of the Germans, and he found the roots of their strength in the similarity of their ways to those of the early Romans.

Tacitus took from the diverse ethnographic material on the Germans only those items that he considered relevant to his ideal image, saying little about ethnographic data that he thought lacking in institutional content. This explains the omissions, the blurring of facts, and other faults criticized by scholars who regarded the book strictly as an ethnographic work. He did not assess the Germans as a scholarly historian who records a multitude of facts and shows equal scientific interest in each, but as a statesman who spies out the enemy's forces and exposes the hidden sources of its strength. His main purpose was to enable his countrymen to understand the enormity of the danger they faced: While they themselves were renouncing the customs of their ancestors, from which their strength derived, another nation was emerging that was observing the ancient Roman virtues. This conception also explains the literary form of *Germany*. The hypothesis that a nation's mores are the source of its strength led Tacitus to cast his proofs in the form of an ethnographic description. The rules of that literary genre enabled him to examine the enemy's customs and to utilize its behavior to explain the secrets of its success.

When we compare Tacitus's observations on the Germans with his remarks on the Jews, we find that he approached the two tasks from opposite standpoints. Whereas he highlighted customs of the Germans that seemed to have some resemblance to those of the ancient Romans, he evinced interest only in the characteristics and practices of the Jews that differed from those of other peoples in general and of the Romans in particular. The principle that the Jews "regard as profane all that we hold sacred, and they permit all that we abhor," which he says Moses followed in instituting his "new religious practices," was the very principle followed by Tacitus himself when, from the wealth of Greek and Roman traditions, he selected examples dealing with Jewish ways.

Most customs of the Jews, in his view, were adopted simply in order to distinguish them from the Egyptians. In the course of time, he emphasizes, this urge to be unique also produced institutions opposed to those of all mankind. Examination of the various customs described by Tacitus reveals that each one differs in some respect from a particular custom of the Egyptians or the Romans. He emphatically opposes all the attempts made by other ethnographers to explain the laws of the Jews on the basis of a source common to them and some other nation. The self-segregation of the Jews and their aloofness from the rest of the human race, Tacitus believed, characterized them from their very beginnings.

Tacitus's second objective in his choice of Jewish practices was to explain both the strength and the weakness of the Jews as a collective body. He makes no mention of the Jews' language, clothes, weapons, economic system, or many other matters described by the ancient ethnographers. What mainly interests him are those points that can help explain the powerful unity of this people and, in particular, the strength of its military opposition to the Romans. He mentions the commandment to "be fruitful and multiply" (Genesis 1:28), and the prohibition against abandoning one's children, which may explain the increasing numbers of the Jews; their belief in the immortality of the souls of those who fall in battle, which may explain their courage in war; their physical health and willingness to work hard (in which they differed from the other peoples of the East), which prepared them to persevere in war; and their devotion to their Temple, to which proselytes made monetary contributions, which provided funds that were used to build the fortifications that the Roman legions faced when they laid siege to Jerusalem.

Tacitus writes not only of the strength of the Jews but also of the shortcomings of their system. The commandment to observe the Sabbath served as an excellent example. The seventh day was devoted to rest because that day ended their toils, "but after a time they were led by the charms of indolence to give over the seventh year as well to inactivity." Tacitus sees the Sabbath law as an invitation to a life of idleness, which saps the vigor of the people; he likens the Jewish way of life to that of many 'barbarian' peoples, whose laziness the Romans found contemptible.

As a statesman who weighs the spiritual and material forces of the enemy, Tacitus examines the history of the Jews and arrives at certain conclusions

I.2.7

regarding their political behavior. He finds that they are not a people skilled in war or ready for political independence. He bases his conclusion on the following historical facts. When the East was under the dominion of the Assyrians, the Medes, and the Persians, the Jews were regarded as "the meanest of their subjects" (*Histories,* V, 8). True, they dared to revolt against Antiochus, but they were successful only because the Syrian king had his hands full warding off an attack by the Parthians. They established a monarchy, which lasted only a short time, at a period "when the power of Macedon had waned, the Parthians were not yet come to their strength, and the Romans were far away." When their kings proved incapable of ruling, civil wars broke out, and the kings tyrannized the people and even the members of their own families. Then Pompey appeared, and put the Jews under the Roman yoke. Even afterward, short periods of peace alternated with revolts, until the last uprising in the year 66.

In writing this historical survey, Tacitus had two aims: to teach the Roman reader the highlights of Jewish history and, at the same time, call attention to certain Jewish traits. The first is that the Jews never excelled in either deeds of heroism in war or in establishing a state of any worth. When international circumstances enabled them to establish an independent government, they showed political immaturity by shifting sharply from a position of subjugation to a regime of tyranny—which inevitably led to civil wars. This explains why Tacitus nowhere mentions the Jews' public institutions or battle tactics; he did not think they were noteworthy features of the Jewish character.

The second evaluation emerging from Tacitus's historical overview is that the Jews are a rebellious people by nature. The revolts against the Romans were not motivated by a political objective (an inclination to liberty, or for domination over other peoples) but, typically, by religious zeal. Tacitus was of the opinion that the root of Jewish existence, the Jews' independence— and their destruction—was religion. Their religion made them a nation and determined their character and way of life. For this reason, Tacitus places the Jewish religion at the center of his interest.

Even here Tacitus does not deviate from the statesman's perspective of judging other nations according to the benefit or the damage they have brought to his own country. A striking example of this method is the conclusion Tacitus reached regarding the Jewish concept of monotheism. After mentioning the Jewish idea of the unity of God and the Jews' rejection of gods and idols, he adds: "Therefore they set up no statues in their cities, still less in their temples; this flattery is not paid their kings, nor is this honor given to the Caesars." Tacitus regards Judaism's concept of one God not solely as a spiritual virtue, but also as the source that nurtured the rebellious souls of its adherents. It was the prohibition against idol worship that led to the Jews' refusal to honor the emperors (required of all Roman subjects), and to fulfill their obligation to their rulers.

I.2.8

We find another application of this approach in his discussion of converts. He does not see fit to consider the reasons why converts were attracted to the Jewish faith. As far as he is concerned the people who embraced Judaism were the dregs of mankind, since they were disloyal to the gods of their former nation and supported those of its enemies. He weighs their deeds in relation to the foundations of the Roman state and society, the gods, the fatherland, and the family: "The earliest lesson they receive is to despise the gods, to disown their country, and to regard their parents, children, and brothers as of little account." Tacitus undoubtedly knew that proselytes also learned other things, but he derided those teachings as well, since it was clear to him that they were antithetical to the institutions of the Roman state.

TACITUS'S VIEWS ON THE ORIGIN OF THE JEWS

Tacitus does not content himself with stating that the laws of Israel were directed against the institutions of Rome. He delves into an investigation of the roots of the conflicts between Israel and Rome, and he finds them in the special circumstances that determined the founding of the Jewish state. In his opinion, the tradition of the Jews' origin also explains the source of the hostility between the two peoples. His detailed description of early Jewish history seeks to prove that the destruction of the Jews' polity was inherent in their early deeds.

This was not uncommon. The ancient ethnographers regarded the study of the origin of peoples as essential for an understanding of their customs. They considered it axiomatic that the character of a nation was formed and influenced by the special circumstances of its origin. In many cases historians carried out their research with the deliberate intent of tracing certain attributes of a people they liked or disliked back to their early history. They would ignore the accepted tradition of the people, and their study of a nation's origins often served as an instrument of polemics or apologetics.

Greek and Roman tradition regarding the origin of the Jews was full of defamatory legends; Tacitus drew his knowledge of Jewish antiquity from the writings of those authors. One of them, apparently, was the Greek philosopher and historian Posidonius. In describing the conquest of Jerusalem by Antiochus Sidetes, this author puts in the mouths of the king's councillors a variety of reasons for sacking the holy city and exterminating the Jewish people. They argued that Israel's history from the very start proved that it denied the fundamentals of religion and was hated by the gods. The ancestors of the Jews were lepers who were expelled from Egypt at the behest of the gods, and after they developed into a nation

they imposed on their children and their children's children the commandment of hating the rest of humankind. This is also the reason why they instituted laws

I.2.9

different from those of other nations, such as the prohibition against sitting down at the table of a gentile or acting kindly to him in any way.

Explaining the characteristics of nations on the basis of those of their earliest ancestors was a standard formula for speeches in praise or denunciation of peoples and states. Since the political, cultural, and moral worth of nations was measured by the honor of their race, the Greek writers, and the Romans after them, turned the legendary traditions of their peoples into testimonies to their noble origins. There thus emerged an almost standard list of praiseworthy traits (a nation's antiquity, the purity of its race, the gods' love for it, its contribution to human culture, the superiority of its laws, etc.) that served as the framework for many accounts of the early history of nations. This typology also laid down reprehensible qualities that served to disparage the character of a despised people. The orator Quintilian, a contemporary of Vespasian and his sons, illustrated this formula when discussing the history of the Jews, a subject then of particular interest to the Roman public. He said: "We also hate the ancestors of the evil ones, and it is to the disgrace of the founders of the cities that they united with a people that brings destruction upon all other nations, as did the founder [Moses] of the superstitious Jewish religion."

Tacitus, then, was hardly original in using a nation's origin for an immediate purpose. Nevertheless, his description of the antiquities of the Jews differs substantively from other accounts of the origin of nations that we find in Greek and Roman literature. Other historians and rhetoricians mention bits of legends only in passing and with the object of deprecating the character of the nation they hate. Tacitus, on the other hand, employs pseudohistorical, calumnious arguments to establish his central thesis. He cites many details as a justification for his conclusion regarding the Jews' unsavory traits and the reason for their being disliked. Ethnography here wraps itself in the cloak of etiology. It will repay the effort to trace the method followed by Tacitus in order to direct the details of his narrative toward his main idea.

The first illustration is the opening sentence of his survey of the origins of the Jews: "However, as I am about to describe the last days of a famous city, it seems proper for me to give some account of its origin." Unlike other historians, who inserted their ethnographic interpretations at the point where they first mention a foreign people, Tacitus links his excursus on the Jews with a description of the destruction of their state. Reference to the Jews' origins is not his introduction of the foreign nation to the reader, but an afterword to the end of its state or, more precisely, an epilogue on its holy city. This juxtaposition lends special significance to his tales about the beginnings of the city and the nation. He alludes to the end at the very beginning in order to arouse thoughts in the reader about the metahistorical decree that is fulfilled in the history of this doomed nation. In his conception, the devastation of Jerusalem was an atonement for an ancient sin committed by the generation of its founder, Moses. This view is clearly evident even in the details of Israel's origins.

In general, histories of nations open with an inquiry into their place of origin. The first five legends in Tacitus's chapters on the Jews deal with the nation's various names, its land, and its holy city—explanations that ordinarily preceded the basic narrative of a nation's early history. Although Tacitus does not say so explicitly, each of the six legends he records on the Jews' geographical origin is also designed to ascertain whether they were aborigines or migrants from elsewhere.

The indigenous origin of a people was regarded as an incomparable mark of honor. From the days of Socrates and Plato, the glorifiers of Athens never tired of praising the birth of its first inhabitants on the soil of Attica. Emigration was considered justified only when it was undertaken voluntarily, or at the behest of the gods, or when the leader of the emigrants and the founder of their new state was a hero whose deeds were recounted in Greek legend. Thus the Romans acquired a testimonial of nobility by tracing their ancestry to Aeneas and the other heroes of Troy. The story that the Jews originated from the Solymi nation, mentioned by Homer and cited fifth by Tacitus in his series of legends on the possible origins of the Jews, belongs to this type of mythology.

No less honored by the Greeks and Romans were those nations which abandoned their homelands due to economic necessity. The Jews belonged to such nations, according to Tacitus's second and fourth legends, which relate that the Jews had emigrated from Egypt to Assyria. For the Greeks and Romans, it was an irreparable defect if a nation's ancestors had been banished from their original habitat for uncomplimentary reasons. This is the supposition of the third Egyptian legend. At the bottom of the scale were those nations whose ancestors were ejected from their homeland by the curse of the gods. According to the defamatory legend of the plague of Egypt, the Jews fell into this category.

Tacitus employs every means of persuasion to inject in the mind of the reader a negative impression of the Jewish people. He arouses certain auxiliary thoughts: The Jews were Saturn's 'cold and hard' nation, feared by all because of the influence of their unlucky star; they were the nation exiled by the Assyrians, rulers of the ancient world; 'fear and hatred' had always separated them from the community of nations. The only legend that offered a respectable explanation of the Jews' beginnings was the fifth, which cites the Solymi origin, and it is characteristic of Tacitus to minimize its value. Immediately following this legend, he recounts the story of the lepers to the very last detail, emphasizing that this is a true account. The dark shades of the Egyptian legend were meant to overshadow the illustrious pedigree bestowed on the Jews by the Homeric epithet.

Tacitus makes it clear in a number of ways that he prefers the sixth legend

I.2.11

to all the others: by leaving it for last, by highlighting the nature of this tradition, by the precision and length of the description, and by using it to explain laws observed to his day. To be sure, he makes a show of approaching all six legends with the same degree of objectivity. He cites the source for each and refrains from expressing an outright opinion in favor of any one of them. In truth, however, he again employs every means at his disposal to lead the reader to the conclusion that the last legend is the version closest to the historical truth of the beginnings of the Jewish people.

Tacitus spices the last tale with the choicest ingredients of his literary art. He mentions a famous pharaoh of ancient days, pestilence—'the plague of Egypt'—the temple of the god Ammon and his oracles, and the great and fearful desert with its horrors and wonders. Just as the splendor of Egypt enchanted the imagination of the Romans in the period of the empire, so Tacitus is intrigued by its darkest secrets.

The legend of the lepers also reminded Tacitus of his own people's legend of Aeneas, as recounted in Virgil's epic. Both stories tell of the flight and adventures of a hero banished from his place of birth together with a company of friends, who in their wanderings witness miracles that are impressed in their memories and later become the basis for permanent rules and customs.

The original Egyptian legend of the lepers underwent many changes before it reached Tacitus. Hellenistic writers clothed it in the wraps of an etiological legend, designed to explain the nation's customs on the basis of the history of its ancestors, and they added various motifs (including a few borrowed from the Book of Exodus) in order to adapt it to its new role. With its transfer to Roman soil, the legend entered the sphere of influence of Roman epic literature, changing both its outward appearance and its inner nature in accordance with that sublime example. The influence of the narrative rules of the Roman epic is apparent in Tacitus's dramatic arrangement of the events. His story is composed of two 'acts': the unification of the masses by Moses, and their being saved from dying of thirst. The plot progresses at a rapid pace and ends with a surprising turn. Twice the masses despair and twice they are saved at the last moment by their new leader, whose bold energy and ability stand out in contrast to the despair of the multitude. Tacitus organized the two scenes of his story around their highest point, disposing of the other details of the plot in a few words.

The hero of the tale as recounted in the legend was Moses. In accordance with the custom of historians of the day, Tacitus avoids any explicit description of his qualities, depicting his character by means of his words and deeds alone. Just as Moses created his nation in his image, the nation's qualities were reflected in his person. His character personifies his people's hatred for gods and men. After he was cut off from the congregation of his former nation, Egypt, by the command of the gods, he decided to chart his future without their assistance. He turned to the aimless wanderers, explained their situation to them without deception, and unified them through recognition of the naked truth: *Una salus victis nullam sperare salutum*, the only solution for the defeated is not to hope for salvation. From this point on, he himself assumed the role of divine leadership.

In accordance with this nihilistic intention, Moses also laid down the laws his people were to observe after they settled in their new land. Since he had attained power by teaching hostility to the gods and to men, he decided to strengthen his position by perpetuating this belligerency. His hatred was primarily directed at Egypt, his original homeland. Egypt's inhabitants and cults served him as examples of gods and men in general, and for this reason he based his constitution on doing what the Egyptians considered abominable. He commanded the Jews to slaughter their sacred animals (the ox because the Egyptians worshipped the sacred bull Apis, and the ram in derision of the god of Ammon). Moses's other regulations were likewise designed to plant in the hearts of the banished people the memory of the hardships they had suffered as a result of their forced flight from Egypt, thereby intensifying their hatred for those who expelled them.

Even Israel's belief in one God comprehensible only to the mind was an outgrowth of the hostility Moses's followers bore for commandments of their forefathers. The spiritual principles of the religion of Moses were the exact opposite of the materialistic principles of the Egyptian religion. In contrast to the multiplicity of Egyptian gods, the Jews established the belief in one God; in contrast to the images of animals, a God apprehendable by the mind alone; and, in contrast to the perishable material of idols, the eternity of their deity. The conclusion that emerges is that it was not purity of heart or depth of conception that gave rise to the sublime idea of one invisible God, but blind hatred. The aim of this explanation was to deny to Israel's Torah any claim to a superior moral code, and to present it as an expression of the basest envy of the human heart.

Moses promulgated his laws and regulations in order to implant the memory of the exodus from Egypt in the hearts of his flock. These laws were not meant to remind his people of the heavenly signs and wonders that had helped them in their time of need, but of the malevolence of the hostile gods and the cruelty of men which would have brought about their annihilation. Tacitus leaves it to the intelligent reader to ponder how inordinate was the contempt for the gods and the hatred of man evinced by this people, who laid down as an eternal law the remembrance of their travails at the hands of both deity and man. Their feeling of "hate and enmity toward every other people" was a result of the hostile behavior of their former fellow Egyptians. As a result of a cruel fate, the fundamental values of human society became the forces of destruction for the Jewish people. It was only natural for a band of people, banished from their home-

I.2.13

land by the curse of the gods and the superior strength of their own countrymen, to nurse an eternal hatred for that which caused them trouble from their beginnings as a people.

Tacitus was not content with merely reporting events, but dug deeper in an effort to discover the secrets of the national soul that gave rise to them. For him, the events of ancient times were the embodiment of the inner aspirations of the nation and manifestations of its character. The myth became the mirror of the mores.

The first Roman writer who used myth as a means to understand a people's soul was the poet Virgil. It was he who tapped this new source which enabled the Romans to better understand both their own nature and that of other nations. Tacitus inherited not only Virgil's artistic tools, but also his metahistorical approach to the content of ancient legends. His description of the antiquities of the Jews is in the genre of a pejorative myth. Like the legend of the founders of Rome, the story of the lepers reflected the 'ideal reality' of the nation. The deeds of Moses were the prototype of the misanthropic acts of his followers; their laws and customs were the pattern of their souls, and their hardships were the signs of fate which made them bear the curse of their hatred for mankind until their exit from history.

To what extent did Tacitus regard the Egyptian legend of the origins of the Jews to be historically reliable? From other parts of his writings we know that he was skeptical of the stories about the origins of nations; in concluding his story of the lepers, Tacitus even admits that its historical credibility is questionable. However, his own conviction of the legend's essential truth was strong enough to overcome his doubts about its literal testimony.

TACITUS'S USE OF HISTORY

Tacitus delved into the history of the past in order to explain the events of the present. His stories on the origins of the Jews and his explanation of their customs were also intended to provide a reason for the destruction of their Temple, and to justify it historically as well as morally. It is safe to assume that Tacitus, after concluding his description of the Jewish revolt, went on to discuss in detail the reasons that led Titus to destroy the Temple. While the original text of these chapters is not extant, an excerpt from them has been preserved in a chronicle by the Christian writer, Sulpicius Severus. The latter copied from Tacitus a summary of the views expressed by the leaders of the Roman council of war before their legions' final attack on the Temple. According to his rendering, several commanders were in favor of sparing the famous edifice, "but others, including Titus himself, argued that the Temple must be destroyed, mainly in order to root out completely the religion of the Jews." This was certainly not Titus's true reason, but it undoubtedly was close to the viewpoint of Tacitus. We have seen that he tried to prove that the religion of the Jews was the reason for their rebelliousness. This conception necessarily led to the conclusion that the only way to cope with the threat of future rebellions was to wipe out the center of the religion.

In the eyes of the Greeks and Romans, the destruction of any sanctuary in the world was sacrilege; their polytheistic belief in the sanctity of a god's holy place ruled out its destruction. This applied to the temples of all peoples. However, the Romans invented a special ritual which enabled them to strike at the seats of the foreign gods without desecrating their honor. Before their final assault, they would adjure the gods protecting the besieged cities of their enemies to come out of their temples and join the Roman gods, solemnly pledging to build them a new home in their city. Another stratagem for nullifying the sanctity of a foreign temple was to find fault with its system of worship, thus justifying its desecration on moral grounds. This was the method followed by Antiochus Epiphanes when he spread the slanders that human beings were sacrificed at the Temple in Jerusalem and that an ass was worshipped there.

Tacitus found justification for the destruction of the Temple in the fact that the Jewish religion lacked both moral content and religious basis. It was a faith deliberately created in order to deny the fundamental precepts of the religions of all other nations. This basic premise determined the ways of the Jews from their earliest days, when the curse of the gods of Egypt brought about their downfall. Their leader united them by a proclamation repudiating the gods, handing down his laws without seeking the blessing of heaven and without the help of the gods, for he knew they hated him. He cunningly based his code on the commandment to desecrate all that was holy to other nations. Even his followers' adherence to a single invisible and eternal God did not stem from their pious reverence of heaven, but from their hatred of man. In this way, the destruction of the Temple was interpreted as a divine punishment for the sin of showing contempt for the basic values of true religion.

According to this conception, Israel's religion lacked a god. Traces of Divine Providence were not detectable either in its history or in its laws. Hence, its ritual was unable to influence the will of heaven. Tacitus expresses this view explicitly when he speaks of portents of the Jews' war against the Romans: "Prodigies had indeed occurred, but to avert them either by victims or vows is held unlawful by a people which, though prone to superstition, is opposed to all propitiatory rites" (*Histories*, V, 13). This observation has its origin in the Romans' belief in the efficacy of ritual. The object of all sacred worship, whether prayer or sacrifice, was to win the grace of the gods, to avert their wrath in advance, or to propitiate them after the event. The gods made their anger known by means of portents in order to spur their worshippers to atone with sacrifice and vows. The Roman historian Livy, for example, relates that before the conquest of Rome by the Gauls a divine voice was heard, prophesying a calamity, but the inhabitants of the city ignored the warning and the wrath of heaven was poured out on them; when the danger subsided, the Romans recalled the omen and hastened to atone for their sin.

A nation that acted faithlessly toward the gods was unable to mollify them. When Cicero, the greatest orator of Rome, tried to prove that the Gauls were irreligious, he said that they did not act like other people who seek peace and forgiveness from the gods. Rather, they fought against the gods, destroyed their holy places, and desecrated their names by sacrificing human beings. Similarly, because of the Jews' evil deeds and thoughts, Tacitus denies them what Cicero denied the Gauls—the blessings of heaven.

However, contradicting the opinion that Israel was not blessed with divine protection is the tacit interpretation of the omen that Tacitus mentions among the prodigies that heralded the destruction of Jerusalem: "Of a sudden the doors of the shrine opened and a superhuman voice cried: 'The gods [note the plural!] are departing'; at the same moment the mighty stir of their going was heard" (*Histories*, V, 13). According to this vision, the Temple in Jerusalem was a seat of the gods and its sanctity came to an end only because they departed from it. Not unlike other religions based on the worship of a god who dwells in the temple of his country, Judaism, too, was originally under the protection of a god in its temple, until he left it.

The belief that the gods abandon the city of their domicile after it is captured was widespread among the Greeks and Romans. According to Virgil, Aeneas was forced to flee Troy after it transpired that "the gods, under whose protection its kingdom stood, had departed from it." The gods of Jerusalem, on the other hand, abandoned their temple voluntarily before the Romans began their siege. Hence, the Temple at the time of its conquest was entirely devoid of sanctity. The rumor of the omen signifying the departure of the gods from Jerusalem seems to have been spread by the Romans to give currency to this claim.

The remarks of the historian Dio Cassius on the conquest of the Temple in Jerusalem point to a practical aspect of the portent. When the Roman legions broke an entry into the Temple, "they hesitated in their assault because of their awe and they did not go within until after being forced by Titus." The fear of the troops is evidence that they regarded the Temple as a holy place, even though they hated its defenders. The rumor that the gods had abandoned the Temple reassured its conquerors that they were not desecrating a holy place.

The leaders of Rome adopted a third stratagem to justify the destruction of the Temple. Josephus expressed the opinion that the God of Israel in His wrath concealed His face from His sinful people and relinquished the city and its Temple to the Roman enemies. According to a Greek contemporary of Josephus, but one who did not parrot his views, Titus expressed almost the identical idea to the emissaries of countries bordering Palestine. When they came to honor him with a victory wreath for his conquest of Jerusalem, he proclaimed that "he did not deserve the honor, for it was not he who had accomplished this, for he had only given his hand to God, who manifested His wrath." The similarity between this view and that of Josephus can only lead to the conclusion that Titus deliberately repeated the opinion of the pro-Roman Jews who regarded the victory of the Romans and the destruction of the Temple as a decree from Heaven.

It was the same Josephus, of course, who wrote a book on the Jewish wars in Aramaic, in order to disseminate his view among "the Parthians, the Babylonians, the most remote tribes of Arabia, the Jews beyond the Euphrates, and the inhabitants of Adiabene," in other words, among those nations, more or less, that wished to praise Titus. There is solid basis for assuming that Josephus carried on his literary work with Titus's approval, perhaps even at his initiative. The emperor was helped by the Jewish writer in his grand plan to stabilize Roman rule in the east, and one way of achieving this was to calm the feelings of the nations neighboring Palestine. Titus knew that many Jews living in those countries had joined the rebels, and that many non-Jewish inhabitants of those lands had been impressed by the oracle that "at that time one from their country would become ruler of the world." Just as Titus promoted the interpretation that his father, the Emperor Vespasian, was the king hinted at in the prophecy, in order to remove the nationalistic element from the messianic tidings, he also adopted the Jewish view that attributed the destruction of the Temple to God's wrath against His people.

Tacitus did not make use of the various artifices then in vogue to concoct a religious reason for the destruction of the Temple. The origin and customs of the Jews sufficed, in his opinion, to justify the Romans' all-out war against the Jews and their Temple. When he recounts for his contemporaries the events of "the last day of the famous city," there is not a trace of any sense of horror. The tragic pathos comes not from any feeling of sorrow or pity over what the city and its inhabitants had suffered, but from the belief that in his day the curse of the gods overwhelmed the nation he despised and that their verdict was executed.

This teleological explanation of the destruction of Jerusalem suffers from a serious contradiction. According to Tacitus, Titus intended to strike a death blow at Israel's religion by sacking the Temple. The course of history thereafter proved that his scheme had failed. Not only did the Jewish people survive, but their religion did not lose its drawing power in the gentile world. Is it not reasonable to suppose that it was the failure of the plan to 'destroy the root' that aroused the historian's ire against the Jews?

Scholars who have dealt with Tacitus's writings on the Jews have ignored a cardinal rule in the study of sources, namely, that a historian's account must be considered in the context of the period in which he wrote. They have disregarded the fact that Tacitus wrote his observations on the Jews around the year 100, about thirty years after the razing of the Temple. During

I.2.17

these thirty years, some of the ramifications of the destruction of Jerusalem became clear to the Romans, including the influence of that decisive event on the continuing existence of the Jewish people. It would have been impossible for Tacitus to ignore this. His principal goal, after all, was to correct the views of earlier historians in accordance with the experience and viewpoints of his own generation, and to speculate on the course of future developments from a knowledge of the trend of events up to his day. Examination of the writings of Greek and Roman authors on the condition of Judaism from the sack of Jerusalem until the beginning of the reign of Trajan shows that the developments of those thirty years could have had considerable influence on shaping Tacitus's retrospective conception of the destruction of the Temple.

All the sources testify, directly or indirectly, to the intensification of Jewish religious propaganda in countries under Roman rule after the destruction of the Temple. In the year 95 or thereabouts, Josephus wrote the famous words:

The masses have long since shown a keen desire to adopt our religious observances; and there is not one city, Greek or barbarian, nor a single nation, to which our custom of abstaining from work on the seventh day has not spread, and where the fasts and the lighting of lamps and many of the prohibitions in the matter of food are not observed (*Contra Apion*, II, 282).

The increase in proselytes is also attested to by the decree of Domitian regarding the poll tax imposed by his father Vespasian on all Jews of the empire. Domitian ordered that the tax also be paid by all those who "observed the customs of the Jews without admitting this publicly." Since the emperor's intent was to increase state revenue, the number of such unofficial converts must have been great enough to warrant the issuance of the new decree.

In this period Judaism acquired friends even among persons of high station. A delegation from Alexandria complained to the Emperor (Trajan) that they were unable to obtain justice because the Senate was 'full of Jews', a patent exaggeration employed by enemies of the Jews down through the centuries, but which undoubtedly had some partial basis in fact. A midrash mentions a 'God-fearing' senator in Domitian's day who gave his life for the sanctification of his faith. Even more suggestive was the Senate's decision, after the murder of Domitian, to mint a special coin with the inscription *Fisci Judaici calumnia sublata* (abrogation of accusations with regard to the Jewish tax), indicating that the Jews had many friends in the Senate, some of whom may have been suspected of being sympathetic toward Judaism. In sum, the cohesion of the Jews in the lands of the Diaspora, particularly in Rome, and the spread of Judaism there, were not at all affected by Roman religious persecution in Palestine. Judaism continued to capture the hearts of gentiles, although its national and religious center was destroyed.

Undoubtedly, Tacitus's angry sentences bespeak his disappointment over the confutation of the hopes attached to the destruction of the Temple. This is reflected in his remarks about the institutions of the Jews, which he evaluates from a Roman standpoint. Not only does he point to the depravity of Jewish customs, but he notes their evil influence on the proselytes. Tacitus opens and closes his description of Jewish customs with a mention of the proselytes, whom he disliked even more than the Jews. When Tacitus discusses the proselytes, a sudden change of writing style is apparent. Up to that point, he pretends to be a disinterested historian who reaches his conclusions on the basis of evidence. Now, however, he removes the mask of objectivity, and his sentences express unrestrained hostility. Not only does he accuse the proselytes of shamefully desecrating all that is holy to the Romans, but his antipathy leads him to distort the facts. He writes that the wealth of the Temple in Jerusalem came mainly from the contributions of proselytes. The shekel tax levied on every Jew and the numerous contributions given by wealthy Jews are relegated to second place, even though they accounted for the bulk of the revenue of the Temple treasury.

It is quite obvious that Tacitus is particularly incensed by the success of the Jews' religious propaganda. His sharp words hint at his feeling of helplessness when confronting the spread of 'the vanquished religion'. The irritation expressed in his reaction constitutes additional historical testimony to the rise in the status of Roman Jewry in his lifetime, and indicates that the conversion activity struck at a weak spot in the Roman body politic. Tacitus himself lists the values that were undermined by the proselytizers: faith in the gods, love of country, respect for one's parents and other family members, and reverence for the ancestral traditions. In short, Tacitus paints the Jews as a band of conspirators who undermine the very foundations of society. Not only do they shirk their own duties as members of the human race, they influence those who join them to do the same.

The fact that Tacitus links the customs of the Jews with those of the proselytes indicates that his observations relied on the Jews' status in the Diaspora. His list of 'crimes' is based on the assumption that the Jews were living in a land where respect for the gods and observance of the traditions of the founding fathers were incumbent upon every citizen without distinction; we may deduce that the Jews Tacitus had in mind were mainly those living among the subjects of Rome. Two examples from Roman literature will suffice to substantiate this conclusion. When Cicero tried to prove that his enemy Claudius was unworthy of being considered a member of Roman society, he charged him of having sinned against 'the parents, the gods and the fatherland'. And Cato, in his vituperative oration against

Catiline, accused him of having rebelled against 'the fatherland, the ancestors, the altars, and his own family.' To Tacitus, the Jews were similarly evildoers who waged war against the foundations of Roman society.

THE JEWS AND THE STATE

In describing the practices of the Jews, Tacitus also sought to show that they were damaging to the laws of the state. This outlook would seem to contradict the official view, for the Jews enjoyed the status of a 'permitted religion' (*religio licita*) in the empire. They were allowed to observe the precepts of the Torah, celebrate their holidays, gather in their synagogues, organize within their communities, raise funds, and the like. These rights were protected by the state. Even after the destruction of Jerusalem, when the Jews were required to pay the half-shekel previously collected for their Temple to the Roman temple of Jupiter Capitolinus, no restrictions were placed on the religious authorities of the Diaspora communities. The principle of religious toleration was not violated by the Roman authorities until the absolute victory of Christianity.

By its nature, however, this principle had two faces. The authorities granted the Diaspora Jews the right of religious autonomy on condition that they refrain from any offense against the state religion. Proselytizing was considered a violation of this condition because it estranged Romans from the worship of their gods. Thus the same writers of Tacitus's day who spoke favorably of the Roman tradition of religious toleration became enemies of Israel as a result of the spread of Judaism within Roman society, for fear that it would weaken the hold of the laws of their fathers.

Seneca the philosopher called the Jews 'a wicked nation' (*gens sceleratissima*) because the Jewish Sabbath had won many adherents throughout the empire: "The conquered have imposed their customs on the conquerors." As used by Seneca, the adjective *sceleratus* refers to a crime against the state; he regarded observance of the Sabbath as an affront to the laws of Rome. Quintilian similarly reviled the Jews as "a people that brings ruin upon other nations," referring to the proselytizers who alienated citizens of various nations from the laws of their fathers, thus undermining their institutions. Juvenal, the greatest Roman satirist, denounced Roman proselytes to Judaism because "they tended to despise the laws of Rome."

The complaints of these writers about the vulnerability of Roman law to the activity of the proselytizers parallel a general development of Roman jurisprudence on the subject. Conversion in itself was not regarded as a crime, but a Roman citizen who embraced Judaism could be found guilty of heresy toward the gods of the state. The clash between the laws of Israel and the laws of Rome centered on the conversion of Roman citizens. The Roman writers we have mentioned used Judaism's influence on non-Jews as an opening for their criticism of its customs. They regarded the Jews as a religious community bent on ensnaring the souls of their fellow citizens, and they reacted with nationalistic hostility. For Tacitus, too, it was Judaism's activity within the surrounding society that changed his attitude toward the character of the Jewish people in general. He saw that, with the penetration of its beliefs among the public, Judaism had become a functioning organ in the body of Roman society. This realization led him to the conclusion that the Jewish people were to be judged by the social standards of the Roman state. Tacitus then examined the laws of the Jews and found that Judaism belonged to a class of foreign religions which endangered the legal and social structures of his country.

To understand the train of thought that led Tacitus to his definition of the nature of Judaism, we must consider the official position of foreign religions in the Roman social system in the period of the empire. Judaism belonged to the group of alien religions that had been placed under the supervision of the state authorities. As noted above, once these religions were granted approval their members were permitted certain privileges. The authorities scrupulously checked on the observance of all regulations and punished all violations.

Livy gives a detailed account of the spread of the Greek cult of Bacchus in Rome to demonstrate that it constituted a public danger, whereupon the authorities decided to stamp it out. His description throws light on the attitude of the Romans to foreign religions in general. True, the events he describes took place in the year 186 B.C.E., but they were given wide currency in the religious circles of the state, and the action of the authorities on that occasion served as a precedent for similar cases. According to Livy, the mysterious cult of Bacchus, which originated in Greece, spread to Rome and other Italian cities like a contagious disease. Thousands of residents of Rome were secretly inducted, sworn not to reveal the secret of their cult, and to do all that they were commanded. They assembled for nocturnal orgies, and shamelessly sealed their pact with carnal acts. The degeneration of their morals led the members of the secret cult to commit serious criminal acts, "for it was a principle of their religion to regard nothing as forbidden."

When the Senate learned what was going on at the secret gatherings, it decided to act immediately and with the utmost severity. It banned Bacchanalia, put the members on trial, and executed many of them. In addition, one of the consuls explained to a mass assembly the danger to the public interest inherent in this cult. He began by proclaiming the principle of the Roman religion which commanded that only the gods of the fathers be worshipped and not gods "who capture the hearts of men by corrupt and foreign practices and lead them to crime and licentiousness." He then explained that the secret convocations of cultists attacked the law of their ancestors, and he hastened to depict the consequences of the spread of this false religion. People whose morals had been subverted by the evil cult could not maintain internal peace or defend the state in war. Hitherto, the cultists had been content to commit their crimes as individuals, but with their increase in numbers they would try to gain control of the state. The consul closed by enjoining the populace to remove from their hearts any false belief in the sanctity of the foreign cult, "for there is nothing that can mislead the heart like a flawed religion."

The Roman authorities gave four reasons for prohibiting Bacchanalia: (1) alien worship of any kind clashed with the obligation to observe the religion of the fathers of Rome; (2) any unauthorized assembly of citizens was forbidden; (3) the cultists were conspiring to seize control of the state; and (4) the customs of this cult were incompatible with the Roman code of morality and were liable to corrupt the morals of society. Of the four objections, only the first is religious in nature. The next two are political, while the last is moral. The worshippers of Bacchus were put on trial for the political crime of rebellion against the state, but, according to Livy, the authorities were moved to act mainly from their concern over the possible subversion of the morals of the citizenry. They regarded the alien cult as a source of debauchery and crime, and each of its adherents as a criminal.

The combination of religious, political, and moral reasons served as a basis for the actions of the authorities against foreign cults in general; but numerous documents indicate that the moral reason, *cura morum*, was uppermost in the discussions of the authorities. For example, the Roman authorities expelled the worshippers of the Thracian god (a cult associated with libertine practices) because they sought to ruin the morals of the Romans. The decree expelling the Jews and the Egyptians from Rome in the time of Tiberius was also issued because of moral and criminal transgressions committed by some of the followers of these foreign religions. The emperor Diocletian explained the ban on the Manichaean sect in terms of their intention "to ruin the Roman people and our entire kingdom as if with the poison of a predatory snake."

Christianity was also considered a licentious religion that should be persecuted because of its harmful influence on the morals and customs of the Roman people. The slanders spread about the Christians—that they assembled in utmost secrecy at night and sanctified themselves by slaughtering children and drinking their blood, as well as by fornication—were believed even by some of the heads of the Roman state. These base allegations had a decisive influence on the activity of the state against the believers in Jesus. Pliny the Younger, Tacitus, and Suetonius were among those who believed in the evil of Christian customs, and concluded that the authorities must exterminate this vile sect.

In short, the Romans entertained a certain image of a base religion (*prava religio*) which imposed on its members evil deeds that impinged on the ways of Roman society. Such a religion constituted a public menace and its adherents were regarded as violators of criminal law. In the eyes of the Romans, Christianity was an example of a base religion that sought to spread its dissolute customs among the Romans. The numerous bits of evidence of the Christians' transgressions, as delineated by the Roman writers, provide us with an understanding of the concept *prava religio*.

After Christianity was outlawed by an explicit decree of the Senate, it was sullied by all the slanders ascribed to separatist sects. The Christians were deprived of the right of assembly which was enjoyed by the Jews and members of the other authorized foreign religions. They were regarded as a political organization that sought to disturb public order, and participants in their meetings—not unlike the worshippers of Bacchus—were treated as insurrectionists.

Tertullian, the most formidable defender of Christianity about a century after Tacitus, tried to show how greatly the special rites of the outlawed organizations differed from the Christian practices, and how similar the latter were to the customs of authorized religions. He had harsh words for those Romans who looked askance at the spiritual and emotional unity of the Christians and who suspected them of conspiring to overturn the existing order. He quoted a typical denunciation of the Christians: "See how greatly they love one another and how ready they are to die for one another"; and he countered: "To whose misfortune do we assemble?" Tertullian's remarks indicate that Christianity was not only regarded as a political conspiracy but was compared, in its nature and aims, to a band of criminals (*coetus nefarius*) that sought to violate public order.

Christianity was apparently not the only religious association suspected of abusing its privileges. According to a later historical source, Augustus Caesar was urged to require all his subjects to worship the gods in accordance with the tradition of the Roman forefathers, and to ban foreign religions since they "entice many people to live by foreign laws, and thence arise plots, conspiracies, and revolts." For this reason, the emperors in the second century imposed a strict prohibition on any association that sought to pursue political goals "under the guise of holy worship."

Christianity differed from the other religious associations mainly in its adherents' belief in a sacred teaching recorded in holy scriptures. "We assemble in order to read the divine writings," Tertullian replied to the conspiracy libel. In contrast, the Pythagoreans were an example of a religious community founded in order to realize a particular doctrine, which then turned into a political conspiracy that attempted to dominate the state. According to tradition, Pythagoras organized his disciples into an association whose members swore to observe the religious and moral codes of their master and to keep his teaching secret. The sons of the well-born in his city joined his order, but manipulated the association for political purposes. They gained control of the state and enslaved the populace, which then rose up against the Pythagoreans, killed some of them, banished the rest, and set their assembly halls afire. Antagonistic demagogues incited the masses by spreading the slander that the disciples of Pythagoras were keeping secret a 'holy oration', which called on them to worship their cohorts as if they were gods and to bridle other people as they would animals. The agitators held that the members of the association had turned philosophy into a plot against the masses. The tradition of the Pythagorean conspiracy is a blatant example of the tactics employed to discredit societies that espoused esoteric doctrines. The 'holy oration' guarded assiduously by the Pythagoreans was actually a collection of mystical aphorisms which the demagogues charged with political meaning in order to turn the general populace against the members of the sect.

The conspiracy charge was also leveled against the Jews. The infamous libel of Apion—that the Jews killed a human being every year and drank his or her blood, and sanctified their covenant by swearing to hate the Greeks and to love only their coreligionists—was based on a calumny often used against political conspiracies. Quintilian portrayed Moses as the leader of a conspiracy bent on destroying the general public. Similarly, Juvenal described Moses as the founder of a mysterious sect whose members preserved a 'secret scroll' in which Moses instructed them to hate mankind and to aid only their fellow Jews. He turned the doctrine of Moses into a clandestine teaching similar to the secret covenant of the Pythagorean circle.

Examination of the Roman concept of the nature of foreign cults that were to be outlawed helps us to understand Tacitus's purpose in discussing Jewish customs. It is obvious that he delineated the nature of Judaism in accordance with the accepted formula of a 'base religion'. The first sign of this intention is his use of the term *pravitas*, 'corruption', in the opening sentence of his description of Judaism. This corruption, Tacitus contends, was embodied in its specific appeal to the Roman rabble and in its adherents' contempt for the laws of public morality. One of Tacitus's claims is that Jewish men and women copulated without shame. To all his other indictments of Judaism, Tacitus adds this moral defect in order to make it fit the standard image of *prava religio*.

As Tacitus saw it, Judaism's threat to Roman society lay in the organizational power of the Jews. A community united by institutions that rejected the conventions of Roman society and that attracted traitors to the national tradition must be determined to destroy the foundations of public morality. Tacitus compared Judaism's practices to those of the forbidden associations and found them similar. Like the associations which rejected the existing order, the 'association' of the Jews maintained a common treasury whose funds were used to increase its influence and to prepare for the rebellion. The loyalty and compassion the Jews showed for their coreligionists was also an unacceptable trait. We must recall that Tacitus leveled similar accusations against the Christians and sought to nurse the suspicion that they banded together because of their antipathy toward the general public.

As used by Tacitus, 'loyalty' and 'compassion' were not moral virtues. He held that these traits were adopted by the Jews as a tactic to strengthen their internal ties and to attract non-Jews. Similarly, he suggested that the commandment of circumcision had been invented only to widen the gulf between Jews and other people. Even the Torah, in its content and nature, resembled a conspiratorial constitution. Tacitus emphasizes that the abrogation of fundamental moral codes was the first indoctrination lesson for proselytes to Judaism, an initiation ceremony designed to impose the precepts of the sect on the new adherents of the perfidious covenant. It follows that acceptance of the teachings of Judaism was tantamount to the signing of a collective pact of rebellion against public morality.

Tacitus utterly disregarded the true Torah of Moses, for its laws and ordinances were not consonant with the treasonous tendencies of the Jewish people; he followed the accepted contention that the laws of Judaism must be in accord with the social character of its community. Thus, like Juvenal and like the enemies of Pythagoras, he resorted to the typical slanders that were spread about political associations united by a sanctified doctrine.

Hence, Tacitus's remarks about Judaism's moral corruption were not a random collection of invectives, but a deliberate combination of details which add up to a unified picture of a religious association that endangered the survival of Roman morality. From the abundant Roman tradition of Jewish traits and customs, Tacitus chose precisely those motifs which would portray to his readers the image of a 'base religion' with which they were already familiar and which would engender detestation for the laws of Judaism. From his description, it followed that these laws should be prohibited by the state, as had been done with respect to the laws of Bacchus and Jesus.

Although Tacitus evaluates the laws of Israel by Roman standards, he says explicitly that they are in conflict with the laws of all nations; the Jews thus constituted a threat not only to Roman morals, but to the morals of all peoples among whom they dwelt. Since the area in which the Jews were living practically coincided with the domain of Roman rule, the 'covenant of Abraham' assumed the image of a universal conspiracy against the world order established by Rome. *Pax Romana* not only ensured domestic peace to the peoples united under its protection, but also nurtured a belief in their cultural unity. The concept *genus humanum*, 'mankind', changed in that period from an abstract ethical term to a real force in Roman policy. In Tacitus's generation it denoted the amalgamation of peoples subject to the political and cultural control of Rome. Hatred of mankind, *odium generis humani* (according to Tacitus, the sin of the Jews and Christians), was a malicious offense against both the political and the cultural aspects of the concept of *pax Romana*, and justified the extermination of the criminals.

The power of the Jewish people's unity was first revealed to the Romans at the end of the reign of Caligula when it appeared certain that the Jews throughout the Roman world would rise to a man against the emperor's command to set up his image in the Temple in Jerusalem. An echo of this

I.2.25

event reverberates in the warning of his successor, Claudius, to the Jews of Alexandria not to join together with their brothers in the neighboring countries, lest he be compelled to punish them "as though they were people inciting to rebellion against the inhabited world," that is, against the Roman Empire. A Stoic philosopher who preached the idea of a model human society under the rule of the Caesars advised Vespasian to exclude Palestine from the domain of Roman rule since the Jews had proved by their separatism that they had "betrayed not only the Romans, but all of mankind."

Tacitus was undoubtedly aware of these arguments. The conviction that the Jews had deliberately entered the domain of other peoples in order to interfere with their way of life led him to view them as a people that conspired against all the members of the family of nations comprising the Roman Empire. Tacitus held that the Roman Empire was a unified political body whose members belonged to this world state. By expanding the unit of the state into the concept of an alliance of states within the empire, Tacitus was able to present the Jews as a brotherhood of conspirators (*coniuratio*) whose area of activity coincided with the boundaries of the empire.

THE JEWS AND THE ROMAN MORES

Tacitus rejected the laws of Israel out of concern for the observance of *mores Romani*. He regarded the spread of Judaism's laws among the subjects of Rome to be a result of a general decline in morality which made people more susceptible to the harmful influence of every wanton custom. For this reason he stressed that proselytes joined the foreign sects after they had begun to despise the religions of their fathers. Juvenal, too, said that proselytes accepted the laws of Moses since they had learned from their fathers to loathe the laws of Rome. Similarly, Fronto the rhetorician attributed the success of Christianity to the general moral corruption "which embraced the entire world like a contagious disease." For these three Romans, 'the Jewish problem' was an important element within the more serious crisis of *mores Romani*.

This explains Tacitus's interest in the laws of Israel and the excessive severity by which he judged them. We shall return here to our observations on the purpose of his book on the Germans. Tacitus's basic thesis was that Rome had risen to greatness by virtue of its forefathers' high moral standards. Like the best men of his generation, Tacitus was seized by fear as he witnessed the disintegration of traditional practices. He understood that in the first century of the empire's history an internal revolution had taken place, leading to the attrition of the moral forces of his nation. This erosion could bring about the destruction of the state itself, whose source of vitality was *virtus Romana*. Recognition of the role of *mores* in his people's history spurred him to investigate the agents of this moral disease.

The concept *mores* encompasses a broad sphere in the life of the Roman state. The public sense of the early Romans was constituted of a number of values pertaining to the life of the individual. Abiding by these standards was as important as obeying written laws. A special senior official with the title of 'censor' was charged with the supervision of public morals. The Senate itself saw fit to oversee these morals and to take steps against those who would scorn them. Augustus Caesar took upon himself the supervision of laws and morals, in order to improve the condition of the state whose inhabitants were shedding those restraints. After his efforts failed, some outstanding individuals sought to extol the spiritual heritage of the great censors in the days when Rome flourished, in order to prevail upon their own generation to mend its ways. Tacitus, too, became an arbiter of his people's morals, because he recognized the inability of the Roman institutions to cope with this moral degeneration. His concern for bolstering the traditional institutions explains his hypersensitivity to anything liable, in his opinion, to contribute to their collapse.

The search for weak spots in the structure of Roman society led Tacitus to a serious study of the phenomenon of Judaism in general and the spread of its beliefs among the subjects of Rome in particular. He saw their disloyalty to the gods of the fatherland as a denial of one of the sublime principles of *mores Romani*. To properly appreciate the gravity of this charge, it should be remembered that the customs of Rome encompassed not only the precepts of private and public morality, but also the preservation of religion. The religion of the Romans was political in nature, and faith in the gods' superiority was an expression of confidence in the state. The gods of Rome blessed their worshippers with dominion over the nations of the world and ensured the stability of their kingdom. A Roman who sinned against the gods aroused their wrath against the state. More than once, Tacitus expressed the view that the decline of the state was a punishment from heaven for its citizens' turning away from the ways of their fathers. Thus, the observance of the religious customs of Rome was a prerequisite for the existence of the state itself.

The annulment of family ties by proselytes was a transgression against the principles of *mores Romani*. The unity of the family, which was a legal entity subject to the rule of *pater familias*, and the purity of its morals, were considered to be at the foundation of Roman society. Augustus used his authority as 'inspector of morals' to correct defects in the family system of Rome in a legal manner. Roman writers with a tendency to preach considered these defects a decisive factor in the decline of Roman society. A major portion of Tacitus's discussion of the reasons for the disintegration of Roman society dealt with ways in which the family had lost its authority. In contrast to the Roman situation, he noted that the purity and rigid structure of German family life was a source of the Germans' strength.

Tacitus discovered a new threat to family unity in all proselytizing activity. Support for his contention can be inferred from two well-known cases in which the wives of two senators were judged by their husbands, in family courts, for 'alien superstition' and violation of *disciplina domestica*. Tacitus no doubt related the charges against these women to those against Roman proselytes to Judaism—they "regard their parents, children, and brothers as of little account." For such an infraction against *mores Romani* there was no atonement.

Tacitus's 'moral' approach also explains his indifference toward the legal status of Judaism. Not only does he remain silent about the fact that the religion of Israel was recognized by the Roman authorities as a 'permitted religion', but he does not find it necessary to mention the 'book of laws' on which the system of Judaism was based. The reason for this twofold omission was neither pretentious ignorance, as has been suggested by one scholar, nor a refusal to adapt the Torah of Moses to his own prejudices, as described above. Rather, his was a basic decision not to go into the matter of legislation as such, and to concentrate his inquiry solely on moral factors. Tacitus's disregard for the constitutional aspect of the history of his and other peoples stemmed from his awareness of the rift between the domain of laws and the domain of morals which had developed during the period of the empire, and from his disbelief in the stability of any legislation lacking a firm moral basis. From the repeated revolutions, which changed the ways of the Roman state so profoundly, he learned that all legislation is transitory, and that the force that moves events in states is the moral character of their citizens. In accordance with this assumption, Tacitus focused his discussion of Judaism on a criticism of its ethics, and paid little attention to its legal status in the Roman state and to its internal legislation.

Tacitus uses the term *mos* (in singular or plural) four times in his discussion on the laws of Israel: when he mentions the persecution of the Jews by Antiochus Epiphanes who endeavored "to abolish Jewish superstition and to introduce Greek civilization (*mores*) in order to cultivate this most ignoble of peoples"; when he speaks of "those who are converted to their ways (*morem*)"; when he villifies their religious rites as "ways (*mos*) preposterous and mean"; and when he explains that the fortifications of Jerusalem were built because "the founders of the city had foreseen that there would be many wars, because the ways (*morum*) of their people differed so greatly from those of their neighbors." In these contexts *mos* signifies conduct that is at one and the same time religious, moral, social, and political. Tacitus does not distinguish between these aspects because it was their combination that, in his opinion, constituted the very foundation of all states. Based upon his study of Roman institutions, he measured the qualities of Judaism by the criteria of his own nation's concept of the state, and judged Judaism's character from the system of social arrangements that determined the outward form of its regime.

This secular approach was undoubtedly one of the chief reasons that prevented Tacitus (and the Roman and Greek intellectuals in general) from giving due appreciation to the practices of the Jews. These critics did not regard Judaism as a sanctified institution that created the nation's customs and determined its tastes and values, but as a political institution established to buttress the social edifice and make the people increasingly dependent on its immutability. Even those who approached this monolithic structure in order to study its nature at close quarters came up against an iron wall of customs designed—so they thought—to distance them from those who had fortified themselves within. In their anger, they refused to investigate what was taking place behind 'the fence built around the Torah'.

When Tacitus expounded on the ways of the Jews, his eyes were always focused on Rome; the phenomenon of Judaism served as a touchstone for examining the condition of his own country. This led him to disregard completely those historical factors that were unconnected with the criticism of his own nation's habits. An example of the narrowness of his approach is his description of Roman rule in Palestine from the reign of Claudius until the outbreak of the rebellion:

The princes now being dead or reduced to insignificance, Claudius made Judea a province and entrusted it to Roman knights or to freedmen. One of the latter, Antonius Felix, practiced every kind of cruelty and lust, wielding the power of a king with all the instincts of a slave. He had married Drusilla, the granddaughter of Cleopatra and Antony, and so was Antony's grandson-in-law, while Claudius was Antony's grandson. Still the Jews' patience lasted until Gessius Florus became procurator: in his time war began. (*Histories*, V, 9)

Tacitus tries to give the impression that it was the excesses of the procurator Felix that led to the Jewish rebellion against Rome. He mentions no other reason for the war which, in fact, broke out only during the rule of the third procurator after Felix. His rationalization for the delay is that the oppressed people were in such despair that they did not dare try to throw off their yoke until some time had elapsed.

We are surprised to hear this hostile historian provide a reason that may be taken as a moral justification of the Jews' revolt. This deviation from his normal approach can be explained by his dislike for Felix, which surpassed even his contempt for the Jews. Felix's conduct symbolized for Tacitus one of the greatest disgraces in the annals of Roman society: the influence of the freedmen from emperors' households on the administration of the state. The power of the *liberti Caesaris* expanded in the time of Claudius and continued until the reign of Domitian, to whom Pliny the Younger was referring in particular when he wrote: "The Caesars are the rulers of their citizens and the servants of their freed slaves." The freedman Pallas, who actually ran the state during the reign of Claudius, was the brother of Felix who thought, according to Tacitus, that "all his evil deeds would go unpunished as long as he could depend on such an authority." Tacitus indignantly remarks that the former slave not only dared to act with 'royal' impunity, but even rose by marriage to the rank of a relative of the emperor himself. Just as Felix's tyranny led to the outbreak of rebellion during his procuratorship, the avarice of the other freedmen in Claudius's court paved the way for the uprising. Tacitus accuses them of having permitted the Jews, in return for bribes, to build high walls around Jerusalem—walls which later obstructed the legions of Titus in their conquest of the city.

Following the general principle that the internal situation of the conquered provinces depended on the nature of its rulers, Tacitus examined the reasons for the failure of Roman rule in Palestine and found the root of the problem in the disorder of Roman society. The rebellion of the Jews served as another indication of the crisis of *mores Romani*. This conviction satisfied him regarding the causes of the uprising; he therefore did not delve deeply into the internal motives that incited the rebels to act.

Tacitus shrewdly discovered in the rise of slaves to power a decisive factor in the internal revolution that undermined both the peace and the moral standards of the state. Felix's capricious behavior served Tacitus as an example of the tyrannical practices infecting the Roman government once the 'slave mentality' began to dominate the leadership of the state. No less a threat to Roman society was posed, he thought, by the domestic slaves of the capital's upper crust. In the first century of the empire, slaves in Rome became a pressing social problem. The Roman proverb "The more slaves, the more enemies" was especially apropos for this period. Slaves dealt treacherously with their masters, revealed their secrets to the spies of the emperors, and facilitated the licentiousness of the emperors' wives, thereby ruining domestic harmony and the sense of personal security. Their tremendous number (about one-quarter of the population of Rome) alarmed their masters. When a rebellion broke out among the field slaves in Italy, "the inhabitants of Rome were seized by fear of the great masses of slaves who lived in the capital city."

Large numbers of these slaves were attracted to foreign religions. Some of them were Jews by birth, proselytes, or sympathizers, and Tacitus's remarks about the religions of slaves in general applied to them too. According to Tacitus, the question of the spread of alien cults among the Roman slaves was discussed at a special sitting of the Senate in the year 61. One senator, Cassius, described the gravity of the problem: "Now our households include foreigners with customs in conflict with our own, who subscribe to alien cults or who are entirely without religion; we will never coerce such a motley assortment of humanity except by terror." Tacitus, who undoubtedly was of the same mind as Cassius, considered the organization of slaves into religious communities according to their national origin a threefold danger to the social institutions of Rome: (1) foreign religions served the slave class as finely honed weapons against their masters; (2) religion was meant to strengthen their nationalistic sentiments; (3) religion and nationalism jointly united the slaves in groups that sought to sustain their intense hatred of their masters by employing methods customary in wars between nations. Tacitus judged foreign religions solely on the basis of their social character; his attitude toward them was determined by his anxiety for the endurance of a noble Roman society.

CONCLUSION

We have come to the end of our study on Tacitus and the Jews. Examination of his charges has shown that they were not made out of blind hatred, but with deliberate intent. They were not a hodgepodge of slanders and calumnies, but the expression of a unified conception by a son of Rome, who was predisposed to judge the laws of Israel from the standpoint of Roman tradition, which he regarded as quintessential to the existence of his country.

Following this analysis one must ask whether Tacitus's views were his alone, or were held in other Roman circles as well. Tacitus was undoubtedly one of the extremists among the upholders of national tradition in his day; it cannot be assumed that many of his social class agreed completely with his line of thought. On the other hand, it should not be forgotten that his conclusions were not based on principles he invented. The link that connects Cicero's views on the Jews to those of Tacitus was senatorial policy on alien religions; Tacitus's opinions on the Jews were the logical extension of Cicero's.

From a historical perspective, we must admit that Tacitus's reactions to the laws of Israel indicate how keen was his perception of the destructive forces at work on the foundations of the Roman state. His fears were not realized overnight, however; Trajan's and Hadrian's wars of annihilation shattered the momentum of the spread of the Jewish people. Ultimately, it was Christianity which conquered Roman society before it gained control of the state and completed its victory by uprooting the surviving remnants of Roman tradition. Tacitus's apprehensions were justified; he had correctly sensed the danger that foreign religions constituted for Roman customs.

Nonetheless, we must not ignore the fact that the true source of Tacitus's hatred of Israel was not the empirical results he feared; rather, that hatred developed from a philosophical bias. Tacitus deliberately exaggerated the differences between the Torah of Moses and the customs of Rome, describing the ensuing schism as a battle between two fundamental world views. The conflict he postulated between the idea of 'humanity' which had crystallized in the thinking of the Roman leadership in the period of the empire, and the Jews 'hatred of mankind', was really a clash between the faith of Rome and the faith of Israel in their struggle to realize the destinies of their respective nations. The idea of the election of Israel triggered Tacitus's intense aversion to Judaism. In the final analysis, the Jews' tenacious adherence to 'Thou hast chosen us' (*ata bahartanu*) was utterly incongruous to the spiritual mission of Rome itself, 'the chosen of the gods' (*numine deum electa*).

SUGGESTIONS FOR FURTHER READING

M. Stern, *Greek and Latin Authors on Jews and Judaism*, 3 vols. Jerusalem, Israel: Academy of Sciences and Humanities, 1974–1984. This was a project which Yochanan Lewy initiated but which he was unable to complete. See vol. 2, pp. 1–93, which cites texts, translations, and interpretations of Tacitus's writings on the Jews, together with a complete bibliography.

John G. Gager, *The Origins of Anti-Semitism: Attitudes Toward Judaism in Pagan and Christian Antiquity*. New York: Oxford University Press, 1985.

M. Stern, "The Jews in Greek and Latin Literature." In S. Safrai and M. Stern, eds. *The Jewish People in the First Century*, vol. 2. Assen/Amsterdam: Van Gorcum, 1976, pp. 1101–59.

H. Pucci, "A Note on Johanan Lewy (1901–1945)," *Athenaeum* 62 (1984):644–645.

B. Wardy, "Jewish Religion in Pagan Literature during the Late Republic and Early Empire," *Aufstieg und Niedergang der romischen Welt* II, 19/1, W. Haase, ed. Berlin/New York: 1979, pp. 592–644.

3

JOSEPH DAN

The Concept of History in Hekhalot and Merkabah Literature

The study of history cannot be confined to an attempt by modern scholars to understand historical developments; it must also include the attempt to understand the various conceptions of history which prevailed in the past. It is not enough that we know how we see our predecessors; it is necessary to know how they saw themselves. Usually, mystics pay little attention to the history of the world, which they wish to transcend in order to reach the celestial realm where they find their fulfillment. The following study is dedicated to an attempt to describe the complex attitude toward history by the ancient Jewish mystics of the third to sixth centuries, known as the mystics of the hekhalot *and* merkabah.

Joseph Dan is the Gershom Scholem Professor of Kabbalah at The Hebrew University of Jerusalem. He has written several books about the history of medieval Jewish mysticism and medieval Hebrew literature. His books in English include Jewish Mysticism and Jewish Ethics, The Early Kabbalah, *and* Gershom Scholem and the Mystical Dimension in Jewish History.

BACKGROUND

Scholars are divided regarding many enigmatic aspects of the Jewish mystical literature known as *hekhalot* and *merkabah* mysticism.[1] Opinions

This article first appeared in Hebrew in *BeOraḥ Mada'*, *Studies in Jewish Civilization in honor of Aaron Mirsky*, Lod: 1986. The translation/adaptation is by Dena Ordan.

The International Center for University Teaching of Jewish Civilization, Jerusalem, the author of the article, and the translator/adapter grant permission to photocopy this article for teaching purposes without further permission or fee.

regarding the date of composition and the chronological order of major treatises are not uniform,[2] nor is there consensus regarding their provenance, with some scholars ascribing these works to Palestine of the talmudic period, and others assigning a later Babylonian origin.[3] Furthermore, even the interpretation of basic motifs found in treatises like *Shiur Komah*,[4] *Hekhalot Rabbati*,[5] *Hekhalot Zutrati, Sar shel Torah, Sefer Hekhalot* (or *III Enoch*),[6] *Reuyyot Yeḥezkel*, and others, is open to question. Despite this lack of clarity (with further discoveries perhaps necessitating changes in our view of the matter to be treated here), examination of the concept of history in *hekhalot* and *merkabah* mysticism has intrinsic interest, due to the extraordinary phenomena associated with it. Perhaps directing attention to this unique aspect will provide a new perspective that will be helpful in resolving the riddles surrounding the initial appearance of Hebrew mystical literature in Jewish culture.

THE PROBLEM OF HISTORICITY

The central mystical experience in *hekhalot* literature is the 'descent to the chariot' (*yeridah la-merkabah*). The well-known account of the 'four scholars who entered *pardes*' (a garden, or paradise), found in the *Tosefta*, apparently refers to this type of mystical experience; however, the story appears without explanation.[7] The discussions of *ma'aseh merkabah* in rabbinic literature apparently did not involve actual mystical experiences, but rather refer to exegetical interpretations of the first chapter of Ezekiel with its vision of the Throne-Chariot.[8] The most important extant sources describing the mystical experience itself are *Hekhalot Zutrati* and *Hekhalot Rabbati* (Small and Great Book of the Celestial Palaces, respectively). *Hekhalot Zutrati* contains an account of R. Akiva's ascent to the upper realms, his progress from 'palace' to 'palace' until reaching the presence of the 'King in His glory' in the seventh one, while *Hekhalot Rabbati* recounts the 'descent to the chariot' by R. Ishmael ben Elisha High Priest, and his mentor, R. Neḥunya ben ha-Kanah. The treatise *Shiur Komah* does not present the mystical experience itself, but rather describes the 'appearance of the glory' of the Creator as revealed to one who achieves the descent. *Sefer Hekhalot* contains revelations concerning the biblical figure of Enoch and his transformation into the archangel Metraton, the 'Prince of the Presence' (*sar ha-panim*) in the uppermost palace.

In addition to the experiences of the 'descent to the chariot' and 'entering the chambers of the chariot' (*ḥadrei merkabah*), another outstanding element of this literature is a tradition of revealed divine esoteric knowledge which is applied in the lower, corporeal world. This knowledge has a purely magical aspect, endowing its possessor with supernatural abilities to influence terrestrial affairs. A further attribute of the mystic is perfect knowledge of the Torah, but it too is attained by supernatural revelation. The esoteric magical tradition, found in many treatises ranging from *Sefer ha-Razim* and *Harba de-Moshe* (essentially magic texts) to *Sar shel Torah*, is apparently of early appearance. *Hekhalot Zutrati* is the earliest source mentioning this tradition, as well as the experience of the 'descent to the chariot'; the book opens with the revelation of esoteric knowledge by R. Akiva, and then continues in a variety of directions.

However, none of the three major strata of *merkabah* mysticism—the early exegetical aspect, the mystical experience, and the esoteric knowledge—shows any direct connection to historical events. In fact, some compositions within this genre read as if completely divorced from any historical context. Although tannaitic narrators—R. Ishmael, for example—may be mentioned, they display no link to any particular historical reality. The use of names of tannaim, undoubtedly pseudepigraphical, cannot serve as a criterion for dating the work to a particular period. Nevertheless, some few works do contain historical references that are of so strange a nature that they hint at one of the most profound and interesting aspects of the *Weltanschauung* (world view) of these early Jewish mystics.

In light of the preceding comments, it is the treatise *Hekhalot Rabbati* that is of particular interest. Unlike R. Akiva's prototypical mystical journey to the celestial palaces, as described in *Hekhalot Zutrati*, R. Ishmael's 'descent to the chariot' in *Hekhalot Rabbati* occurs as the direct result of a request by his mentor, R. Neḥunya ben ha-Kanah, in response to the events surrounding the deaths of the 'Ten Martyrs'.

The story of the Ten Martyrs is extant in several prose versions, but is perhaps best known in the poetic version, *Eleh Ezkerah*, included in the Day of Atonement liturgy. Various serious attempts have been made to unravel the historical background of this martyrology,[9] which recounts the death under torture of ten prominent tannaim—among them R. Akiva, R. Simeon ben Gamaliel, and R. Ḥanina (Ḥananiah) ben Teradyon—by Roman imperial decree. The greater portion of these accounts is devoted to a description of the tortures endured by each of the sages; however, they all include variants of an opening story presenting the events leading up to the promulgation and execution of the imperial decree.

The significant common element in each story is the interpretation of the verse condemning to death one who sells his brother into slavery (see Exodus 21:16). The Roman emperor hears schoolchildren studying this verse in Rome, and makes an association between the verse and the unpunished sin of Joseph's brothers who sold him into slavery. He decides to execute ten prominent Jewish scholars as retribution for that sin. (Admittedly, this concept is difficult; medieval and Renaissance scholars questioned the historicity of the story, and its implied doctrine of the transmigration of souls.)

The story includes negotiations between Samael (Satan) and God regarding the death of the sages, and the apocalyptic element within it—God's redressing the martyrdom of the ten sages through a divine decree ordaining the complete and crushing destruction of Rome. With regard to the subject we are now considering, it must be stressed that close examination by historians establishes unequivocally that this legend cannot possibly have a historical basis. Scholars attempting to ground the legend in the Hadrianic persecutions following the Bar Kokhba revolt were forced to change the names of the sages (who were not all contemporaries), at times leaving only two names from the original ten, and adding others not mentioned in any other version of the story. Clearly, the legend of the Ten Martyrs cannot reflect a particular historical reality without distortion of the sources and creation of a new version not found in the extant texts.

It was the historian Solomon Zeitlin who deserves credit for having established that the legend of the Ten Martyrs has no actual historical basis or relevance,[10] and one must agree with him. However, he failed to explore the question of the literary-historical context of the legend. Not only does the story not reflect historical reality but, more significantly, it ignores the basic facts depicted in talmudic and midrashic historical narratives. The account of R. Ḥanina ben Teradyon's death, in the legend of the Ten Martyrs, bears no relationship to the detailed martyrology of this sage as recounted in the Talmud (Avodah Zarah 18a). It is not in the nature of early or medieval Hebrew literature to ignore literary precedents; certainly it is hard to imagine that a late scholar would omit completely the dramatic details of the talmudic legend with its description of R. Ḥanina wrapped in a Torah scroll, the parchment burning, and letters soaring on high. Thus, one may suggest that the historical 'discrepancies' in the list of the ten martyrs are almost certainly not the result of ignorance, but rather are deliberate.

Certain basic elements appearing in *Hekhalot Rabbati* run as a common thread through all the versions. The decree is promulgated by the emperor upon hearing the verse, "He who kidnaps a man—whether he has sold him or is still holding him—shall be put to death," with the concomitant connection to the sale of Joseph into slavery by his brothers. An agreement between God and Satan (here called Samael) appears—with Satan receiving permission to kill the ten sages and in return taking upon himself the future destruction of immoral Rome. The list of ten martyrs is historically impossible (the list differing only slightly from the names in the legend).[11]

The core of *Hekhalot Rabbati*—the descent of R. Ishmael to the chariot, his journey through the seven palaces, his encounters with angels and heavenly beings, the songs he hears, and the secrets revealed to him—is intrinsically interwoven with the legend of the Ten Martyrs. News of the Roman decree having reached the sages, the mystics among them, headed by R. Neḥunya ben ha-Kanah, are unable to determine whether this decree has divine sanction, in which case they must submit and accept it with love, or whether it is the result of an arbitrary impulse on the emperor's part, in which case the mystics, as possessors of marvelous magical powers, may be able to

I.3.4

nullify it. (Chapter 6 of *Hekhalot Rabbati* contains a detailed account of R. Hananiah ben Teradyon's successful escape, by magical means, from a death sentence, and his subsequent execution of his antagonist, the emperor Lupinus.)

R. Nehunya decides to send his youngest disciple, R. Ishmael ben Elisha 'High Priest', to the heavenly halls, to Suriya, 'the Prince of the Presence', to determine the meaning of the decree. By implication, the personal experience described in this key work of early Jewish mysticism is based upon an actual event, namely, the decree to kill the ten sages, and around that event the mystic web of *Hekhalot Rabbati* was woven. In that case, the problems of historicity raised in relation to the legend of the Ten Martyrs are equally applicable to *Hekhalot Rabbati*. However, the farfetched claim that the narrator of the legend was unlearned in Talmud and Midrash, hence his 'mistakes', cannot be made regarding the author of *Hekhalot Rabbati,* who demonstrates his talmudic erudition in several places.[12] It is thereby difficult to believe that the blatant distortion and disregard of talmudic and midrashic literary tradition, the confusion in the tannaitic genealogy, and the disregard of well-known talmudic martyrologies, can be anything but intentional. The relationship between the legend of the Ten Martyrs and *Hekhalot Rabbati* accentuates the problem of the concept of history in both compositions, eliminating the possibility of laying the blame for mistakes at the door of later storytellers.

THE INNER HISTORICAL LOGIC

This discussion opened with the problem of historicity in *Hekhalot Rabbati* because of the extensive scholarly attention and debate already devoted to this topic. However, this is by no means the only, and perhaps not even the major, question resulting from study of that work. Two other points deserve examination.

The High Priest

Why is R. Ishmael, who could not have held priestly office in the Temple (and who probably did not live during the Second Temple period) consistently referred to in *Hekhalot Rabbati* and other *hekhalot* literature as a High Priest son of a High Priest? It has been suggested that the title High Priest refers to R. Ishmael's father Elisha (later writers having introduced the confusion with R. Ishmael), but this is unacceptable because of an explicit talmudic reference to R. Ishmael's performance of priestly duties in the Temple (Berakhot 7a).[13] The talmudic account describes R. Ishmael's conversation with 'Akathriel Yah, the Lord of Hosts', upon entering the innermost sanctuary, in terms typical of similar visions found in *Hekhalot Rabbati* and other *hekhalot* literature. The conclusion is inescapable—the talmudic passage contains an authentic tradition from mystic literature, and R. Ishmael was indeed regarded by the early mystics as a genuine High Priest.

In addition to the chronological difficulty of the reference to R. Ishmael as High Priest, we are faced with the question of the importance ascribed to the priestly office. Was the position of the High Priest so highly regarded at the end of the Second Temple period as to warrant the ascription of this title to R. Ishmael by the creator of *Hekhalot Rabbati?* The historical situation depicted by Josephus and by rabbinic literature contradicts this assumption; the last High Priests were Sadducees, who were not distinguished by their piety. It appears that the esteemed figure of R. Ishmael, High Priest son of a High Priest, emerges in mystical writings independently of talmudic tradition, based on the writer's certainty of possessing a truth more profound than the plain meaning of rabbinic views. One might, of course, seek alternative explanations for these questions, were it not for the fact that the references to R. Ishmael as High Priest are fully consistent with the unique concept of history found in *Hekhalot Rabbati.*

The Temple

Hekhalot Rabbati meticulously describes the meeting place chosen by the mystics to discuss the Roman decree: R. Ishmael assembles the Great and the Small Sanhedrins in the third passageway in the Temple, addressing them while seated on a pure marble bench, a present from his father Elisha. (We are further told that the bench was originally part of R. Ishmael's mother's marriage portion.) The list of sages present exhibits the same chronological confusion that is found in the list of the ten martyrs. Nothing impeded the author of *Hekhalot Rabbati* from placing R. Ishmael and his colleagues, belonging mainly to the period of the Bar-Kokhba rebellion (132–135 C.E.), in the third passageway in the Temple (with his father's, the High Priest's, bench), as if the destruction had not occurred and the Sanhedrin continued to meet in the Temple itself!

THE RESEARCHER'S GOAL

Our goal is not simply to establish that legendary material often has no basis in historical reality, but rather to uncover its own inner historical logic. Legendary chronology, which may reflect literary rather than actual history, nonetheless embodies a well-defined concept of history. This is the case with midrashic legends. Although they do not always conform to archaeological and epigraphic finds, they possess their own internal literary truth. It is precisely the blatant and unexplained rebellion of *hekhalot* literature against talmudic and midrashic literary history that is so striking. Whereas the Talmud can describe R. Akiva as prophesying the rebuilding of the Temple at the site of its destruction (Makkot 24a–b), it is absolutely incapable of placing R. Akiva, along with R. Ishmael and R. Simeon b. Gamaliel, in the third passageway in the Temple which was destroyed sixty years earlier.

The four singular points characterizing *Hekhalot Rabbati*—(1) disregard of talmudic chronology, (2) disregard of talmudic martyrology, (3) the description of R. Ishmael as a High Priest, (4) the description of the assembly of the 'descenders to the chariot' in the Temple—prove that our author consciously rejected the familiar structure of talmudic and midrashic literary historiography, based on the absolute conviction that his words were grounded in a deeper, more complex stratum of the truth.

It may be suggested that the profound belief in a superior truth that contradicts universally recognized truths could be inspired only by mystical knowledge. The author of a mystic work is unconstrained by the need for historical accuracy, nor need he adapt himself to the limited knowledge and views of ordinary mortals. His vision penetrates the inner sanctum, and that reality is expressed in his writings regardless of the lack of conformity with traditions found in other sources. The mystic felt no compulsion to justify or explain how the Great and Small Sanhedrins met in the Temple entrance two generations after its destruction, or R. Ishmael's role as High Priest in this Temple, just as he felt no need to explain why angel A guards the fifth palace and angel B the sixth. The reality of this inner, superior mystical truth requires no justification or accommodation to knowledge acquired through limited human perceptions.

What is the basis of the mystic state of mind? What hidden symbols nourish the vision? Lacking clear-cut answers, I can only indicate a possible line of inquiry. Apparently the key in this case lies hidden in the manifold meanings of the concept 'Temple' (*mikdash* or *beit ha-Shem* in Hebrew). The abovementioned enigmas result from the identification of 'Temple' with the Second Temple constructed by Zerubbabel, restored by Herod, and destroyed by Titus. Perhaps, however, the mystic was referring to an entirely different Temple? Certainly many mysteries surround the Temple and its descriptions. Do we know with certainty which Temple was described in the concluding chapters of the Book of Ezekiel or in the *Temple Scroll* of the Dead Sea sect? Do both sources refer to the Second Temple built by Zerubbabel? Perhaps the Judean desert sectarians possessed an alternative image of the Temple that later found its way to the circles of 'descenders to the chariot'. Clearly the 'celestial Temple'[14] is not meant, since R. Ishmael describes a terrestrial Temple, located in Jerusalem, not in the celestial palaces. Perhaps the mystics had some concept of the 'true Temple' which could not be destroyed by Titus or by any other enemy, and in whose purviews they operated, isolated from the storms of history.

A METAHISTORICAL VIEWPOINT

Additional evidence confirming a unique mystical view of the Temple is found in *Sar shel Torah*, a later *hekhalot* treatise fortuitously appended to the

manuscript and printed editions of *Hekhalot Rabbati*. Although this composition is not the earliest or most important source for the tradition of the
revelation of secrets by *sar ha-Torah* (the Prince of Torah), but essentially an
adaptation of earlier traditions, it sheds further light on the mystics' concept
of history. The conjectured historical situation underlying the text concerns
the power struggle by a group of Palestinian Jews for spiritual and juris-
dictional supremacy during the talmudic or geonic period, when Babylonia
was the leading center of Jewry. Having failed to achieve this goal by tem-
poral means, they aspire to attain the desired status by means of secrets
revealed by *sar ha-Torah*. The petitioners are promised the unopposed authority to promulgate binding halakhic decisions, to intercalate the calendar,
and to appoint Patriarchs, Exilarchs, and judges. The text contains no revelations of hidden layers of Torah (or of the Oral Law),[15] but focuses on the
use of magical means to acquire the superior knowledge of Torah required
for the reestablishment of Palestinian hegemony over the Diaspora.

The mystical event depicted in the narrative is a collective experience of
the 'descent of the *Shekhinah*' (not an individual's 'descent to the chariot'
and a personal mystical vision) by a group of returned exiles from Babylonia
engaged in the rebuilding of the Temple under the leadership of Zerubbabel.
Hindered by the tribulations of the Exile from studying Torah, the returned
exiles, desirous of knowledge, circumvent the need for intensive prolonged
study, receiving instead direct revelation of the secrets of the Torah from
sar ha-Torah. The focal mystical experience, the descent of the *Shekhinah*,
occurs as the builders are gathered around the Throne of Glory in the
uncompleted Temple, receiving the revelations of *sar ha-Torah*. As in other
hekhalot works, the narrator is R. Ishmael, who here bases his teachings on
traditions ascribed to R. Akiva and R. Eliezer the Great. The impression
conveyed by the narrative is that the secrets revealed when the Second
Temple was being built had been transmitted by generations of scholars,
the author recording them according to a tradition ascribed to R. Ishmael.

Two distinctive features of this short treatise have direct bearing on our
main question. First, the author shows a clear preference for the Second
Temple over the First; he indicates that the generations of the First Commonwealth did not possess the secrets revealed by the *Shekhinah* to the
builders of the Second Temple. The Torah achieves its fullest revelation,
and the *Shekhinah* its unsurpassed glory, only in the latter Temple, the 'true
Temple'.[16]

This marked preference for the Second Temple—and the setting is unequivocally the rebuilding of the Temple by the returned exiles led by Zerubbabel—flies in the face of the relative status of the First and Second
Temples found in talmudic and midrashic literature. This is not the place
to go into detail; suffice it to say that rabbinic literature contains no similar
total denigration of the precepts of the spiritual leaders of the First Temple
period. (Moreover, the context does not permit the suggestion that the

reference is to the written versus the oral law.) The unavoidable conclusion is that the circle of mystics producing this treatise attributed far-reaching spiritual supremacy, holiness, and perfection to the Second Temple, in comparison to the First Temple.

In this respect, *Sar shel Torah* does not differ from *Hekhalot Rabbati* in its denial of talmudic and midrashic historiography. However, a second question now arises. What possible explanation can be given for the superior status ascribed to the Second Temple, centuries after its destruction? Praise heaped upon an existing Temple or one being rebuilt, as against a destroyed one, would be comprehensible. But what motivated this sharp preference for one destroyed Temple over another, in contradiction to the normative rabbinic view of history found in the Talmud and Midrash, the very same literature in which the returned exiles sought to achieve proficiency through the revelations of *sar ha-Torah?*

The explanation may lie in the possibility that the work refers not to the historical Temple of Zerubbabel as opposed to the historical Temple of Solomon, but rather to the building of a wonderful metahistorical Temple, a vision nurtured by Jewish mystics for generations, whose connection with the actual Temple eludes us.

Sar shel Torah contains yet another exceptional feature which, if it can be viewed in conjunction with the others (this being by no means certain), creates an unparalleled historical enigma. Although there are many traditions in early mystical literature concerning revelations by the Prince of Torah,[17] *Sar shel Torah* differs in one essential respect. In all those traditions, Moses and the Sinaitic revelation are the ultimate source of the secrets revealed by the Prince of Torah, which were then transmitted by the mystics from one generation to the next. *Sar shel Torah*, however, ascribes no central role to Moses, neither as the one who reveals *'raz'*, the most profound level of *hekhalot* mystic material, nor as the source of terrestrial magical formulas. Indeed, Moses is mentioned only once, and then in an offhand manner, in this text.

The revelations in *Sar shel Torah* are depicted as unique, the secrets having remained undisclosed until the descent of the *Shekhinah* to the builders of the Second Temple. The well-known story of the opposition of the angels to the giving of the Torah to the Children of Israel appears in the text; the reference however, is not to Moses but to the initial revelation of the secrets found in *Sar shel Torah*. The inference to be drawn is that this group of mystics, who lived in Palestine during the geonic period, evidently believed that their tradition was first revealed only during the Second Temple period, and was unknown to Moses, to the prophets, and to the First Temple scholars.

Thus, these mystics developed an idiosyncratic understanding of history, based on spiritual glorification of the latter Temple and ascription of superior mystical knowledge to the builders of the Second Temple (to the denigration of the prophets and scholars of the First Commonwealth). This remarkable attitude toward Moses, Solomon, and other prominent historical figures points to the existence of a *Weltanschauung* basically opposed to the accepted rabbinic view. Mystical truth, with the Temple at its nexus, blinds the members of this circle to talmudic and midrashic tradition, perhaps even to biblical tradition.

It is interesting to speculate on a possible connection between the mystics of the Sar shel Torah circle and the Temple Scroll sect of the Dead Sea. May we be so bold as to suggest that the *Temple Scroll,* that strange and wonderful version of Deuteronomy which makes no mention of Moses, is the Deuteronomy revealed by the *Shekhinah* to the builders of the Temple led by Zerubbabel? Lacking other confirmatory evidence regarding a connection between these two works that are separated by centuries, this suggestion must remain in the realm of hypothesis.

However, we can establish that the literary-historical content of talmudic and midrashic literature was not the sole source of inspiration for the Jewish mystics of the talmudic and geonic periods. An alternative metahistorical view, negating the validity of talmudic historiography as well as of historical reality, appears in a variety of *hekhalot* and *merkabah* works from different periods. This view may also be tied to material appearing in other types of Jewish literature from Second Temple and post-destruction times. The key to the strange inner world of Jewish mystics in antiquity lies in the exploration of their concept of history and their image of the Temple, as reflected in diverse mystical works.

NOTES

1. *Hekhalot* literature describes the ascent of the mystic through the celestial palaces, while *merkabah* mysticism centers on the mysteries of the divine throne-chariot. (See *Encyclopedia Judaica,* vol. 10, pp. 497ff.)

2. For a description of the major works included in this literature, with geographical and chronological placement, see: G. Scholem, *Major Trends in Jewish Mysticism* (New York: Schocken 1954), pp. 41–78; idem, *Jewish Gnosticism, Merkabah Mysticism, and Talmudic Tradition* (New York: J. T. S., 1960); and the more recent work of I. Gruenwald, *Apocalyptic and Merkabah Literature* (Leiden: Brill, 1980). Scholem's assumption that this literature antedates the geonic period is widely accepted (as opposed to the previously held view proposed by Graetz), but no consensus exists regarding the exact date and chronological order of the various treatises.

3. The later works are apparently the Aramaic magic texts, like *Harba de-Moshe,* which contain few Greek elements in comparison to earlier works. See M. Gaster, *The Sword of Moses* (New York: Samuel Weiser, 1973).

4. Regarding this treatise, see M. Gaster, *The Shiur Komah: Studies and Texts* (London: Maggs Bros., 1925–1928), vol. II, pp. 1330–1353; Scholem, *Jewish Gnosticism,* pp. 36–42; J. Dan, "The Concept of Knowledge and the Shiur Koma," *Studies*

in Jewish Religious and Intellectual History presented to Alexander Altmann (Alabama: University of Alabama, 1979), pp. 67–73.

5. See Gruenwald (Note 2), pp. 150–173; M. Smith, "Observations on Hechalot Rabbati," *Studies and Texts,* Alexander Altmann (ed.) (Cambridge: Harvard University Press, 1963), pp. 142–160.

6. H. Odeberg, *3rd Enoch or The Hebrew Book of Enoch* (Cambridge: Cambridge University Press, 1923). See J. Greenfield's "Prolegomenon" to the Ktav Publishing House reprint of Odeberg's book (New York, 1973); Gruenwald, *Apocalyptic and Merkabah Literature,* pp. 191–208; and P.S. Alexander, "The Historical Setting of the Hebrew Book Enoch," *Journal of Jewish Studies* 28–29 (1977–78): 156–180.

7. JT Hagigah II, I. For interpretations of this parable, see Scholem, *Major Trends,* pp. 52–54; idem, *Jewish Gnosticism,* pp. 9–14; and Gruenwald, *Apocalyptic and Merkabah Literature,* pp. 87–97.

8. See D. Halperin, *The Merkabah in Rabbinic Literature* (New Haven: American Oriental Society, 1980).

9. See L. Finkelstein, *Essays and Studies in Memory of Linda R. Miller* (New York: JTS, 1938), pp. 29–55.

10. S. Zeitlin, "The Legend of the Ten Martyrs and Its Apocalyptic Origin," *JQR* 36 (1945–46): 1–16.

11. Interestingly, the initial part of the text mentions four, rather than ten, martyrs. However, none of the extant versions provides clues as to whether the original number was four, equaling the number of sages who entered *pardes,* with the association with Joseph's ten brothers belonging to a later stratum.

12. For the halakhic elements in *Hekhalot Rabbati,* see Scholem, *Jewish Gnosticism,* pp. 9–13; S. Lieberman, *apud.;* Gruenwald, *Apocalyptic and Merkabah Literature,* pp. 241–244.

13. See Scholem, *Major Trends,* p. 356, Note 3, and sources cited there.

14. Aptowitzer, "The Celestial Temple as Viewed in the Aggadah," *BINAH: Studies in Jewish Thought,* Vol. 2 (New York: Praeger, 1989).

15. See Gruenwald, *Apocalyptic and Merkabah Literature,* p. 170.

16. "The Torah did not achieve its fullest glory until the building of the latter Temple, nor was its fullest greatness, glory, awesomeness, superiority, pride, brightness, strength, and dominion revealed until the descent of the *Shekhinah* to the latter Temple." (Free translation—the original contains many synonyms for strength and glory.)

17. The earliest works include *Ma'aseh Merkabah* (published by Scholem), *Ma'ayan ha-Hokhmah,* and the opening section of *Hekhalot Zutrati,* which is probably the earliest example.

4
YITZHAK F. BAER

The Origins of Jewish Communal Organization in the Middle Ages

How did the Jewish people survive nearly two millennia of life in exile, a minute minority within a hostile society? The answer to this central question of Jewish history can be found on many levels, in many areas—religious, cultural, philosophical, and historical—but there can be no doubt that the internal organization of the Jewish community contributed immensely to this unique phenomenon. The emergence of Jewish communal organization in the Middle Ages is described here by one of the greatest scholars of Jewish history, in an article that is regarded to this day as a classic study.

Yitzhak (Fritz) Baer (1888–1979) was born in Germany, and was appointed in 1930 a professor of history at The Hebrew University of Jerusalem. A founder of the Department of Jewish History, he was the great teacher of most of the historians in Israel. His most extensive studies were dedicated to the history of the Jews under Christian rule in the Iberian peninsula, and his two-volume History of the Jews in Christian Spain *is regarded as one of the finest examples of Jewish historiography. He was one of the founders and editors of the quarterly* Zion, *dedicated to research in Jewish history, in which most of his studies were published.*

BACKGROUND

Many of the social and political forces inherent in the long history of the Jewish people still await intensive scholarly research. The Jewish communal

---

This article first appeared in Hebrew in *Zion* 15 (1950). The translation/adaptation is by Zipporah Brody.

The International Center for University Teaching of Jewish Civilization, Jerusalem, the literary estate of the author of the article, and the translator/adapter grant permission to photocopy this article for teaching purposes without further permission or fee.

organization (*kehillah*) is one of the most significant of these forces. It has long been assumed that the kehillah was a product of the special circumstances of the Jews in the Middle Ages. This article, however, points to the corporate tendencies and doctrines that have existed in Jewish social history since the ancient period. It also considers the similarities and differences between Jewish and Western communal organization in the ancient period and in the Middle Ages, and the fruitful contact between the two civilizations in terms of their political development.

Historians have pointed to similarities between Jewish and Western culture in their striving for freedom, justice, and mutual responsibility; but from the very beginning, each developed in a different direction. The Greek city united its citizens in a single political body which included a religious component, but Greece, and its successor Rome, did not succeed in extending the parameters of this organism to encompass a nation unified by religious-political ideals. In Jewish history the opposite is the case. The nation began as a single body, united by its covenant with God and the tasks that covenant imposed on it in human history. These tasks are passed on to each city and local congregation centered around the synagogue, which accepts the responsibilities of the entire community.

After the disintegration of the national structure in the Land of Israel, the local kehillah remained—until the period of the Jewish enlightenment in the eighteenth century—as the only political expression of the invisible national community of Israel.

The foundations of the kehillah were laid primarily at the beginning of the Second Temple period within the general reorganization of the Jewish national polity. Certain laws of that period, for example, national administrative codes and laws concerning the government of Jewish towns, constitute evidence of this historical development and can be compared to similar laws enacted by other nations at parallel points in their history. A religious-democratic spirit permeates these laws. The same orientation which underlay the strict code of discipline of a sect like the Essenes, a code which has no parallel among the religious philosophical sects in the pagan West, gave rise to the kehillah, a communal organization representing the entire nation. This spirit is superbly expressed in the synagogue service in which—unlike pagan ritual limited to appointed priests—the community coalesces around the prayers. In no other culture of the ancient world do we find anything similar to the halakhot (laws) found in Mishnah Ta'anit (2, 1–2):

How did they order the matter on the [last seven] days of fasting? They used to bring out the Ark into the open space in the town and put wood-ashes on the Ark and on the heads of the President and the Father of the Court; and every one took [of the ashes] and put them on his head.. . .They stood in prayer and sent down before the Ark an old man, well-versed [in prayer], one that had children and whose house was empty [of sustenance], so that he might be whole-hearted in the prayer. . . .

This is a portrait of a vital society whose basic religious viewpoint is apparent in laws dealing with prayers, synagogues, alms, and charity, as well as with political and economic issues. One may consider the following baraitha (extramishnaic law), which was used by later halakhic authorities as the source for various communal enactments, as an early constitutional document:

The members of a city oblige one another to build a synagogue, to buy a Torah and Book of the Prophets; the members of a city can fix prices, weights, and wages, stipulate taxes.. . .(Tosefta Bava Metzia 11, 23).

This halakhah determines the minimal extent of the community's control over the individual. It deals with the synagogue, protection of private property against damage by another, price fixing, basic supervision of commerce, taxation for communal needs, prohibition of an individual's turning to outside authorities without the consent of the community, and the imposition of fines upon violators of the ordinances.

This baraitha provides no evidence of interference by a central authority, be it royal, priestly, or judicial; rather, an assembly of the local population determines religious, economic, and political issues. Reference to steps taken to avoid intervention by outside authorities may be evidence of its antiquity, dating it from the Greek period. Indeed, the prohibitions against turning to non-Jewish courts of law (regarded as a heresy in the Middle Ages) existed in antiquity even prior to the acceptance of such a halakhic norm. The Apostle Paul called upon his brothers, "the community of God in Corinth," to decide their cases in the courts of the "holy ones" and not in gentile courts (First Corinthians 6, 1–5). It is doubtful whether a parallel exists in Greek and Roman statutes.

The kehillah is, then, an immanent creation of Jewish history. Diaspora life did not create it, although its organizational structure is suited to all places and to all social and economic classes—farmers, artisans, and merchants—with the self-evident proviso that the structure of the community must be in harmony with the socioreligious ideals that created it, and must seek to concretize them, in contrast to the surrounding pagan world and the contemporary Greek cities.

Jewish literature of the Hellenistic period uses no special term to denote the unique sacred nature of the kehillah. Greco-Roman terminology was unable to fully express the nature of the Jewish community, whether considered as a miniature Greek city deprived of its rights or as one of the Greek religious confederations, or whether granted or denied legal identity according to Roman law. It is the religious perspective, which includes a

I.4.3

national component, that creates a unique organizational entity. The apparatus borrowed from other societies is of secondary importance.

The purpose of this article is to determine whether the structure of the early Diaspora communities and of the towns in Eretz Israel, both of which developed within the Greco-Roman cultural sphere and were influenced by certain of its organizational theories and concepts of political and corporate justice, display vestiges of a common Jewish origin which can still be discerned in the kehillah of the Middle Ages when a vital organizational entity emerged out of the ruins of external disaster and from behind the mask of imposed conventions. Because of differences in the nature of the sources and in the political conditions, this question must be explored separately with respect to the Land of Israel and the Western Diaspora.

Philo of Alexandria, the Jewish-Hellenist philosopher of the first century, whose attempt to place Jewish law and belief in a philosophic framework is seen as a precursor of Jewish rationalist philosophy, is an important source (despite the reservations of certain scholars) for the traditions of Alexandrian Jewry.[1] What little we know of that ancient Jewish community adheres to the general picture of the kehillah in Eretz Israel. The description of the synagogue which accommodated all social classes, and where members of each guild (goldsmiths, silversmiths, blacksmiths, weavers, etc.) sat together in order to be able to aid a newcomer seeking work, was a far cry from the style and spirit of the socioreligious confederation of Greece. The Alexandrian community's sense of unity with the entire Jewish people, not only in times of trouble but during the ordinary cycle of the Jewish year, is well known. The collection of taxes levied for support of the Temple, and a constant stream of letters and messengers from Eretz Israel, created a network which predated that of the Church. Yet the Alexandrian community was an independent and religiously vital community that developed its own tradition of interpretation of the Torah and commandments.

In the Land of Israel itself there were, no doubt, both prior to and after the destruction of the Temple, some Jewish towns in which the socioreligious spirit of Judaism mingled with the traditions and practices of Greco-Roman urban administration. However, certain problems arise when we attempt to describe such a community, and define it using Jewish sources. We must first ask the basic question: Does Jewish law recognize a community as a corporate body? Modern scholarship argues that talmudic law does not recognize organizations and institutions, nor even the town itself, as legal entities; rather, the residents of the town are considered as partners. Only during the Middle Ages do townspeople become an organic entity, a single, encompassing community. This view of modern jurists requires a certain amount of revision, for some elements in early halakhah are integral to the establishment of an organic communal unit. In some cases the town appears, for all practical purposes, as a legal unit; certain laws deal with the property of the community as a whole (not only of its members), for example, the public square, bathhouse, synagogue, and so on (Mishnah Nedarim 5, 5). In Tosefta Megillah 1, 5; 3, 4 the town appears as a specific administrative judicial unit, and each town uses the taxes it collects for its own purposes.

The town as a whole, as well as each synagogue, has officers and leaders, whether appointed by the community, the Nasi (the political head of the Jewish people after 70 c.e.), or the sages.[2] Aside from the levies imposed and centrally administered by the external authorities, taxes were collected for communal, not specifically religious, needs such as defense. Gedaliah Allon, a modern historian of that period, dealt with the existence of communal courts alongside those of the ordained sages, and concluded that town meetings served as judicial bodies in Israel as early as the third century c.e. The Babylonian sages recognized the legal validity of a transaction carried out during a town meeting, pointing to the existence of the concepts of public law and representatives of the people. The Babylonian Talmud even discusses the right of the townspeople to prohibit unauthorized commercial activities by strangers (Bava Batra 21–22). Clearly, long before the destruction of the Temple, features typical of the later kehillah existed in both the Land of Israel and in the Diaspora.

Despite the legal rights invested in the community in certain areas, however, the Talmud does not deal with the right of any public body to reach a decision by majority rule, despite the fact that this was an accepted principle in Jewish courts of law and in the Sanhedrin, and that Roman law so empowered all representative bodies. This omission in talmudic law created difficulties for later generations who, in their attempt to assert the natural authority of the community, found insufficient basis in Jewish law. There is no doubt that the Talmud deliberately downplayed the autonomous authority of the community and refused to recognize its corporate status, interpreting the terms 'town' (*ir*) and 'townspeople' (*bnei ha'ir*), first used to indicate a public body, as referring to the local population; other talmudic terms for 'town'—*karta, matia*—have no specific legal meaning.

Although one can derive from talmudic literature a complete picture of the community in Eretz Israel, as Adolph Büchler did in his description of the community of Sepphoris in Galilee, its political and social leaders, its various social strata, and the conflicts between its religious and 'secular' leaders,[3] we must note that in all of talmudic literature, both legal and nonlegal, there is no recognition of the concept of the kehillah as a legal concept or an organic, vital unit, nor is it granted any element of sanctity. The term 'holy community' (*kehillah kedoshah*) that has been in common Jewish usage since the Middle Ages, does not appear in the talmudic period. This is apparent in the story (Midrash on Song of Songs 2,5) concerning the rabbinic convention in Usha in the wake of persecution. It is clear that a communal framework existed which made arrangements for the accommodation of the rabbis, but the only term used throughout the midrash is "the people of Usha."

Nonetheless, the term *kehillah kedoshah* is not a medieval creation. It is also found in antiquity—but only in nonrabbinic literature. The Apostles address the communities to whom they write as the *ecclesia hagia* (holy community) of such and such a place, with the addition of various terms denoting sanctity, similar to those appearing in Jewish documents dating from the tenth and eleventh centuries. Moreover, archaeological evidence for the custom of describing local Jewish communities in sacred terms before the time of Paul is found in the remains of synagogues and cemeteries dating from shortly before the destruction of the Second Temple until the fall of the Roman Empire. (See, for example, the richly decorated Dura-Europos synagogue discovered in 1932 near the Euphrates River.) The inscription of the synagogue in Jericho—the most complete text to be found, although not the most ancient—first blesses "the masters and rabbis, the sacred congregation in Israel and Babylonia," then "this entire sacred congregation, great and small, children and women; may the Almighty bless you . . . " The inscription expresses the metaphysical dimension of the community which unites all the inhabitants and binds the local kehillah to the entire Jewish people. This tradition continues to find expression in the "Yekum Purkan" prayer in the synagogue service.

The lack of any ascriptions of a sacred nature in connection with the local communities, together with the use by the sages of the term 'the holy community in Jerusalem' to denote a small group of 'righteous men and men of good deeds', strengthens the impression that this omission in the Talmud is deliberate. This is typical of what was occurring in the relations between the sages and the people. Laws that grew out of existential reality before the destruction of the Temple assumed an independent significance and were interpreted and developed by the sages in their academies while, in the shadows, the life of the community continued—somewhat anonymously and suspect by the official religious authorities, yet preserving remnants of an ancient and legitimized tradition for future generations.

This blurring of the image of the kehillah in talmudic literature is surprising in view of the fact that the sages enlarged upon the concept of corporate responsibility. Although their comments were generally made in regard to 'Knesset Yisrael' (the overall community of Israel), or to a non-defined public body, the practical implications applied to every local community. The term 'Knesset Yisrael', expressing the tangible and at the same time transcendental unity of the Jewish people, which made its first appearance after the destruction of the Temple, probably predates the term 'ecclesia' used by Paul. One may assume that the germ of that significant corporate theory expressed by the Apostle was also contained in the Jewish concept. Under the changing conditions of the times and the influence of Greek philosophy, Jewish sages of the Second Temple period derived an old-new political theory from biblical tradition.

One of the most fundamental and popular concepts in Jewish tradition

I.4.6

is expressed in the talmudic dictum "Each Jew is responsible for his fellow Jew" (Shavuot 39; Sanhedrin 43b; etc.). Acceptance of the Law at Mount Sinai molded the Jewish people into a single body and a single soul, as the *Mekhilta of R. Yishmael* and other classical Jewish sources expound at length. Thus the Jewish people is one body; each limb is responsible for the sins of the other and of the community as a whole. This mutual responsibility carries implications in both the heavenly and the worldly spheres.

Such dicta point to the influence of Greek corporate theories, especially that of Plato (*Republic*, V, 462ff.), who sees unity as the highest good of the city. The ideal leadership of the city is one which feels itself part of one body, that feels the pain or rejoicing of each of the citizens as if it were its own. The *Mekhilta* cited above almost seems to be mocking the gentiles for not living according to their own doctrines, whereas Israel fulfills the Platonic ideal! In any event, the midrash provides the link between Platonic political theory and the theological doctrines of the Apostle Paul, who states that all Christian communities are the limbs of one body (the body of the Messiah). Just as each limb has its individual function, but feels the pain of the other limbs (First Corinthians XII, 4), so each member of the community has his own spiritual gift and duty, but is part of the body politic. The well-known German jurist, Otto von Gierke, defined the political significance of the Christian doctrine in these terms: "Christian theology defined the Ecclesia just as Greco-Roman philosophy understood the 'polis'— as a living organism, an independent and unified whole. In Christian theology this organic mode of thought took on a new religious-mystical dimension. . . . "[4] Without entering into the details of the differences between Christian and Jewish theology, we can state that these remarks are largely applicable to the doctrines developed within the Jewish tradition. Jewish thinkers loyal to their tradition revived this classical political doctrine and filled it with a religious spirit; Paul built his doctrine of the 'ecclesia' on religious foundations prepared by Judaism.

These ideas, both Christian and midrashic, shed light on rabbinic statements concerning Knesset Yisrael in its concretized form of the local community. Statements such as "the great suffer the small," and "the small suffer the great"; "when Israel heeds the great, they decree to the Lord and He fulfills," indicate their attitude. A 'great man' is one "who can say to the power of judgment—enough!"; God appoints him the community's leader. Talmudic literature views the hierarchy of the community as based on levels of spirituality. After the priest and Levite are called to the Torah, come "the scholars who are appointed officials of the community, and then the scholars worthy to be officials, followed by sons of the scholars who are appointed officials, then heads of the synagogues, and finally everyone else" (Gittin 59b–60a). In another version, the order is: "Scholars, distinguished personalities, heads of synagogues, collectors of charity, teachers of children, and lastly the common folk (*amei ha'aretz*)" (Pesaḥim 49b). Each person has his place in the living organism of Knesset Yisrael and of his local kehillah: scholars, people of good deeds, and those who are neither. All are bound together, as symbolized by the four species carried by Jews on the Feast of Tabernacles, and each atones for the other (*Pesikta de Rav Kahana*, Buber ed., 1868, p. 185).

The supreme representative of this hierarchy was the Nasi who, during the period of Roman rule, led the entire nation together with the scholars of his academy. But this was not the only paradigm for national unity. There are signs of an earlier type of leadership, similar to that of the early Christian Church, in which the central community sent missives to the communities of the Diaspora, as we find at the beginning of the Second Book of Maccabees (124 B.C.E.), concerning the date of the celebration of Hanukkah. It begins: "To our Jewish brethren in Egypt, your Jewish brothers in Jerusalem and the Land of Israel (send) warm greetings. . . . " A similar opening of a missive reads: "From Jerusalem the Holy City, to you, Alexandria, my sister: My husband dwells among you, and I remain in desolation" (Babylonian Talmud, Sotah 47; Jerusalem Talmud, Hagigah 2,2). Although the term 'kehillah' does not appear in these missives, it is apparent that the Jews of Alexandria are addressed as a vital entity equal to the Jews of Jerusalem. Neither missive mentions a supreme religious-national body residing in Jerusalem which sends communications abroad.

Only a few generations later, such missives were written as orders issued in the name of specific scholars: "From Simeon ben Gamaliel and Yoḥanan ben Zakkai to our brethren in the upper and lower south. . . . " However, they still must prove their authority: " . . . and we did not begin to write to you; rather our forefathers wrote to yours" (*Midrash Tannaim*, Hoffman ed., p. 176). From that time on, the Sanhedrin's authority to issue orders not only to the Jews in Israel, but to "our brethren in the Babylonian Diaspora" as well, is apparently established (Sanhedrin 11b). Thus, just as the kehillah provided a pattern for the Christian religious community, the Jews were also the first to construct a protoecumenical hierarchical organization, which the Church later developed systematically with episcopae, patriarchs, and pope, and which still later was to influence further Jewish organizational development.

The move away from the concept of the community as a representative body was approved by the Roman emperors. Whereas an imperial decree of Caracalla in 213 C.E. was sent to the *universitas Judaeorum* of Antioch as a legal entity, the decree of Constantine in 315 addressed "the Jews, their leaders and patriarchs," and ignored any official Jewish representation aside from the appointees of the Nasi. The bureaucratic tendencies of the Roman Empire which encouraged hierarchical rule led to the Greco-Roman city losing its autonomy; although it retained its administrative and social identity until the collapse of the Roman Empire, it was governed by centrally appointed officials.

I.4.8

The external destructive forces of the fourth through the seventh centuries added to the disintegration of the city, and by the eighth century it no longer existed in most of Europe in any political, economic, or administrative sense. The kehillah, in contrast, emerged from this period of chaos with its framework accorded recognition by its members, and its participatory government strengthened by its resistance to outside forces. In the end, the barrier between the hierarchical elements (the sages) and the populace had to come down. The very study of Torah required a community of students and was linked to national-organizational factors, while the legal process inherent in Jewish religious law necessitated a link between the leaders and the entire community. Although the interpreters of the law did not specifically mention the community in their teachings, it was to the community that they spoke.

A new element now appeared, uniting the sages and people; this was the liturgical poet (*payyetan*) who, while functioning within the talmudic tradition, was the spokesman for the community. Eleazar haKalir was the first to apply the terms 'communities of holy people' and 'holy communities' (*kehillot kedoshot*) to the congregation of worshippers who vie with the angels in proclaiming the kingship of the Lord. This terminology restored the traditional personal image of the community. The *payyetan* portrayed the spiritual leaders of the kehillah—who, like the 'righteous men and men of good deeds' of the mishnaic period, were not appointed by the community but by a higher authority—as those who "can turn aside the heavenly wrath," "are valiant to stand in the breach," "nullify the evil decrees," and so on.

In the social chaos that followed the breakdown of the city in the Roman Empire, the Jews did not follow the general pattern of agrarianization, but became a merchant class. Although this phenomenon did not emerge inherently from Jewish communal structure, it contributed to communal unity. It was a prototype of later commercial organization, and planted the seed for the reemergence of urban life in Europe in the tenth century.

Christian religious persecution also contributed to Jewish unity as a separate national minority which, in contrast to the barbaric hordes which destroyed the Roman Empire, was the bearer of an intellectually superior culture. The political chaos that severed the links between the Western Diaspora and its center in the East also forced the Western Jewish communities to stand on their own feet. We have evidence of organized kehillot dating from the period of the disintegration of the ancient world. Synagogues, and hostels to house indigent visitors, are mentioned in some of the letters of Pope Gregory concerning the Jews. Evidence of historical continuity undeterred by the general devastation is found in southern Italy (Venosa), Spain, France, and in Eretz Israel (Tiberias). The ninth century, when the authority of the Babylonian Talmud was accepted by all the Diaspora, marks the beginning of a new era in the history of the kehillah.

I.4.9

THE GEONIC PERIOD

The hierarchical system among the Jews reached its highest level of development during the geonic period (end of the sixth through mid-eleventh centuries). While many scholars have described this structure in detail, new light may be shed on it by a comparison with the episcopal and papal system of the Church, particularly in the West. A useful example is furnished by the question of the regularization of the calendar, which remained a burning issue in the Church for hundreds of years. Fixing the calendar became an issue in Judaism only in the tenth century when Saadia Gaon strengthened the position of the Babylonian geonate as against the Palestinian geonate by determining the new month on the basis of calculation, rather than on the Palestinian-centered system of visual reports of the new moon in Jerusalem.

The geonic system developed primarily in the area of the Baghdad Caliphate. Our interest is focused on the status of the local kehillot under its rule, of which Nathan ha-Bavli provides an eyewitness account.[5] The Exilarch (titular leader of Diaspora Jewry), and the heads of the academies who enjoyed separate administrative authority, appointed a judge for each community who, in turn, appointed two of the respected townspeople to sit in judgment with him; "and if he is just and honorable, the heads of the community write to the Exilarch and praise him, and if he is not, they write in complaint and he is replaced." This marks the extent of local authority during the geonic period; no mention is made of the community's role in taxation, and so on. The term 'kehillah' is not used with reference to a place; even in Baghdad there is no mention of a politically organized community. Nathan ha-Bavli's report uses terms like "the entire population," "public opinion," or "leaders of the people and the elders" to describe the influential members of the Baghdad community; no mention is made of a representative communal body as found in Europe in later generations. Nathan ha-Bavli uses the term "the communities (kehillot) of Israel" only in relation to donations and inquiries sent by western Diaspora communities to the major academies in Babylonia.

The geonim used their traditional religious-hierarchical terminology even when addressing the communities themselves. For example, Sherira Gaon's letter to the Fez community which, after its destruction, was forced to migrate to Ashir: "To all the rabbis, their students, householders, and public who dwell in Fez-Ashir, who left Fez: the good, excellent, chosen, enlightened, students of the Torah, learned in the Gemara. . .may God bless you." The Palestinian Gaon Aaron ben Meir writes to his followers in Babylonia in these terms: "To all the communities of our brethren Israel, who dwell in the Land of Shinar, the rabbis, elders, heads of synagogues and households, the leaders, administrators, teachers, cantors, and all the rest of our brethren Israel and our companions in the fear of the Lord. . . . " The ter-

I.4.10

minology recognizes the position of certain 'secular' strata, but only in relation to the value priorities established in the Talmud; there is almost no mention of the community in Babylonian writings.

Nevertheless, we can assume that even in Babylonia the hierarchical system failed to eradicate traces of communal autonomy. We know that the Karaites organized themselves in autonomous communities. Although there is no mention of this in official rabbinic documents, such organization was certainly derived from some Jewish source or accepted custom.

The clearest expression of the formal Babylonian hierarchy, in contrast to the autonomous communal leadership found in other places, appears in a responsum concerning the issue of 'stopping the prayer' on the Sabbath— a procedure whereby a Jew could demand justice against another Jew by publicly interrupting the prayers until his case was heard.[6] The Gaon responds in answer to a question sent to him:

In Iraq we do not know of this custom, since only the court, and not the public, is responsible for the administration of justice; and the public must obey the court's injunctions. Similarly, wherever there is a judge appointed to administer justice, the plaintiffs are required to address him and not the public.

We have previously noted that, from the ninth century on, the term 'kehillah' was common in the official terminology of the communities west of Babylonia. Its use in the epistles written in Eretz Israel and found in the Cairo Genizah is of particular interest since the term is accompanied by descriptive phrases which have no parallel elsewhere. The 'holy community' of Jerusalem is described as resplendent as the jewels in the garments of the High Priest in a letter sent to that community by Elhanan Rosh ha-Seder of Fustat in 1012. The heads of the Palestinian academies wrote in similar laudatory terms to communities outside of Palestine.[7]

The term used most frequently in these letters, *kehillah kedoshah* (holy community), was apparently handed down in an unbroken chain of tradition originating before the destruction of the Temple, and was preserved even within talmudic stylistic usage (although with changed significance) until it once again was accorded official recognition. Each sage is identified with his individual community. Even the sages of the Jerusalem academies do not issue decrees to other communities as their superiors, but address them respectfully as 'holy communities' according to the ancient custom of the early ecumenical organization of Judaism and Christianity. Jerusalem is the *primus inter pares*, but it is not qualitatively different from her sister 'holy communities'. Each and every community represents Knesset Yisrael and is addressed with the blessings bestowed upon it in the midrash and *piyyut* (liturgical poetry). Each kehillah is a miniature organism in which every individual—educated or simple—has his place; their conjunction makes the community an integral unit.

I.4.11

Thus, we may surmise that the democratic form of the kehillah was preserved and renewed in Eretz Israel during the geonic period, and that here were laid the organizational foundations of the medieval kehillot in Europe. A direct link between Eretz Israel and the Jewish communities of the Rhine area, via southern Italy, is evident in the traditions of liturgical poetry and in certain halakhic issues. The democratic custom of 'stopping the prayer' is found in particular in the kehillot of northern France and Germany. Undisputed evidence from Genizah documents shows that the custom of French Jewry concerning the return of the dowry under certain circumstances is a Palestinian custom based on generally accepted norms. One must recognize that the natural venue for creating and renewing autonomous communal organization was Eretz Israel with its long-established communities such as Tiberias, and its communities of priests that are mentioned in liturgical poetry. Indeed, from the ninth century on, Jerusalem was once again serving as the center for Jewish ideological sects which established separate organizational frameworks.

Against this, one can argue that, other than the mention of the 'clerk of the traders', who may be considered a representative of the merchant guild, it is difficult to find any material reference to an autonomous communal administration in the Genizah documents of the geonic period. Perhaps the traditional talmudic style of official terminology, which was later abandoned by the European Jewish communities, obscured the details of communal activity. Nonetheless, the ideal of communal behavior was well expressed by one of the leaders of the Palestinian kehillah:

For any community which does not have someone in authority to help it and attend to its needs, its needs remain unfulfilled; and when it has a member to stand up against opposition, and it stands with him, its needs are attended to properly, and it is respected.

This is an expression of the well-known talmudic ideal that the great take care of the needs of the small.

This was certainly the situation in Egypt. Fustat, for example, was a community of merchants; with its 'clerk of the traders' and its shops, it was, by the tenth century, reminiscent of contemporary European cities like Leon in Spain. A special tradition of commercial law already existed, and it is not accidental that the formulas of Jewish contracts multiplied in a fashion similar to the Byzantine and Latin documents of the same period. There is, however, no sign in political and judicial terms of the community as it existed in the Christian city and the Jewish kehillah in Europe. There is almost no mention, even in a large city like Fustat, of a communal assembly. It is not clear if a politically organized community existed, or whether there were only smaller congregations grouped around synagogues, as stated in one of the documents: " . . . we are two courts of law and three major com-

I.4.12

munities, the congregation of the Jerusalemite synagogue, the Babylonian synagogue, and the synagogue of the royal city called Al-Kahra." Similarly, we find in a letter to R. Hai Gaon: "We the communities praying in the Babylonian synagogue named after his academy."[8]

We must not be misled by the numerous descriptions of officials in the Fustat community. We have no exact knowledge of their functions or how they were appointed. One may surmise that they assumed leadership by virtue of their status, wealth, and proximity to the royal house. Legally, that is, according to the halakhic perspective which was the only one politically recognized by the Muslim rulers, the official leaders of the Fustat community were primarily the members of the academy of Fustat who were appointed by the geonate of Babylonia and Palestine. Other leaders were the Nesi'im ('Princes') of Davidic lineage which was also holy to the Muslims, and other worthies of the communities. When Maimonides lived in Fustat in the twelfth century, essentially nothing had changed, even though the academies had already declined in importance.

Apparently, however, one of the unique characteristics of Jewish history is that a hierarchical system cannot exist in its pure form over an extended period. The Babylonian geonate ruled only within the sphere of influence of the Baghdad Caliphate. Unlike the Church, 'Knesset Yisrael' was unable to divide itself into different patriarchates, and a central leadership of the Roman papal type did not develop in the western Diaspora. One may argue that the absence of hierarchical leadership reinforced the unity of the nation, which existed primarily in isolated democratic communities, those "scattered bones" of the body, "lacking a head and a heart," despite which the living God sustains them—in the words of Yehudah Halevi (*Kuzari* 1, 28–32). The remnants of democracy immanent in the organizational tradition of the Jewish community were to be renewed in those places which the geonate did not control.

Geonic responsa occasionally mention factors which gave rise to the autonomous leadership of the communities scattered throughout the Diaspora. There were communities without a permanent judge appointed by the academies, and the townspeople brought their cases before "the sages, the students and the city elders," that is, representatives of the local scholars and leaders. In some places the local community appointed its own judge. The geonim also supported the community's right to promulgate decrees binding upon the townspeople, by permitting the kehillah to issue a ban, formerly a prerogative of the sages alone. A geonic responsum of the mid-ninth century describes the process of issuing and abrogating a decree, but does not specify the nature of the *tzibbur* (public) which exercises this right. Is it a congregation attached to a specific synagogue, or is it comprised of all the Jews of that place? Does the 'public' function by gathering the entire population, or is it a representative body composed of learned men and other worthies? Most of the questions dealt with in the geonic responsa

I.4.13

concern the synagogue, prayer, and charity, with many references to public philanthropic institutions, a fact which points to the expanding framework of communal activity and perhaps to the continued existence of such institutions since antiquity.

It has also been suggested that differences of opinion regarding the text of the liturgy arose not only among the sages who followed the distinctive traditions of Eretz Israel and of Babylon, but also between the learned men and the simple people "who frequent the marketplace," thus creating a conflict between the house of study and the synagogue. The traders and merchants who constituted the commercial foundation of the community expressed their views primarily in issues of charity which were financial in nature. In addition, they began to establish regulations which related to the commercial interests of the local business community—and had political implications as well. The first such enactment we know of is mentioned in a geonic responsum sent in 872 to the community of Kairouan in North Africa. This important center of local commerce and international trade had legal, commercial, and philanthropic ties with nearby Jewish communities, and with kehillot in southern Italy, Spain, and later, Germany. The responsum deals with a question regarding an informer to non-Jewish traders; the Gaon had been asked about the amount of the fine to be paid by the informer. It appears from the question that it was the custom for the community to place a ban on the informer and impose a fine. The responsum deals with the steps to be taken with regard to the informer, who apparently was impudent as well, but it does not deal with the fine to be paid to the communal coffers, which seems to have been determined by the community, not by the courts appointed by the academies.

The extent to which the institutions like the communal ban were an established tradition may be seen in a responsum, apparently from the ninth century, concerning a wealthy Jew who had dealings with the local ruler. When the Jew died, the ruler appropriated his property and ordered the community to place a ban on anyone who attempted to repay a loan to the heirs, instead of the ruler. The question was whether such a ban had validity. The response was an emphatic 'no'. Evidently the ban was such an established instrument for commercial application that even the non-Jewish rulers knew of it and used it for their own purposes! (Enforcement of communal discipline by imposition of the ban, as well as by lashings, was an early development in the Jewish community; the New Testament and the Church Fathers testify to the use of such measures.)

Other responsa indicate that the geonim dealt with the community as a public institution whose decisions and needs were charged with halakhic validity. While the geonim almost never use the term 'kehillah', that entity existed and its democratic authority was at least partially recognized. In addition to dealing with religious and charitable activities, the community began to defend its common internal commercial interests and its relations to the authorities and to outside merchants. The limited information we have from the responsa provides evidence of a community prototypical of the later European kehillah, and of the mercantile guilds of the medieval Christian city.

Lyons of the early ninth century was an established Jewish community, with knowledge of the Babylonian Talmud and mystical literature. It was even familiar with the Karaite schism. It apparently had an organized communal structure which was new to the Frankish royal scribes who attempted to describe it in their legal documents. From southern Italy of that period we have literary and epigraphic sources which present a picture of a Jewish community on the medieval pattern. In Spain, the merging of the eastern rabbinic tradition with the aristocratic leadership of Jews close to the royal court gave rise to unique Spanish-Jewish public institutions. The responsa of R. Isaac Alfasi, the noted Spanish halakhist, and the *Book of Contracts* of Judah Barceloni, provide evidence of the transition from the geonic mode of hierarchical leadership to the democratic format which developed in medieval Europe.

THE KEHILLAH IN THE TENTH AND ELEVENTH CENTURIES

The decisive moment in the development of the medieval Jewish community occurred in Europe in the second half of the tenth and the beginning of the eleventh century—during the time of R. Gershom 'Light of the Exile', R. Kalonymus of Lucca and his son R. Meshullam, and R. Joseph Bonfil— at approximately the same time and in the same places where the earliest stirrings of the independent Christian city were felt. As in the classical period when the Jewish community encountered the Greco-Roman *polis*, a new era of parallel development in the Jewish community and Christian city now began. And, just as in ancient times, the question arises of the relationship between two public entities that are similar to each other in many ways, but essentially different in their world views.

There are three periods in the development of the kehillah. The first, which we have just dealt with (the ninth to tenth centuries), antecedes any sign of urban life in Europe. The second period, approximately the tenth to eleventh centuries, shows signs of preurban organization in Christian Europe. The third period begins in the twelfth century, when the Christian city had already achieved autonomous legal status in southern Europe, and the basis for such autonomy in northern Europe had been established by royal privileges.

The influence of the Christian city on the kehillah, its organizational structures, and perhaps even certain guiding principles, is clear from the twelfth century onward. As in the classical period, however, this external influence does not touch the foundations of Jewish organization, nor does it create anything new. The Jewish community takes from the Christian model only those elements which help it realize its immanent goals and consciously define them. During the tenth to eleventh centuries, when the Christian city was barely beginning to develop, it was the kehillah with its long cultural tradition that influenced the new organizational modes—not the reverse. Recognition of this relationship may lead to the reconsideration of a historical question that has troubled many generations of European historians, namely, the origins of the European city. A comparison of the development of the kehillah and the Christian city is a historically valid approach to understanding the common historical forces that are evident in both institutions.

Henry Pirenne, the noted economic historian, describes the commercial-social organization which appeared in several places in late tenth-century Europe as a revolutionary framework which ensured its existence by the use of draconian discipline and harsh punishment of transgressors. Pirenne's bold description is purely hypothetical and is based upon reconstruction of urban decrees and privileges of the twelfth century by and large.[9] From the Jewish responsa of the same period a picture emerges of a Jewish communal organization which performs certain functions found only later in the Christian city. Let us analyze this social entity in the context of internal Jewish history.

In the tenth century, the Jewish community appears as a vital organism which unites and gives equal recognition to all members of the kehillah in all areas of public life, both religious and 'secular', insofar as they can be differentiated. This 'holy community' (only now does this term come to be widely used by both scholars and the populace) is united in its defense and its 'martyrdom for the Holy Name' (*kiddush haShem*) during times of persecution. It is united in all personal and communal issues as well. The entire community participates in the joys and sorrows of the individual: It assembles at the sickbed to receive the dying person's last will and testament; inheritance and other personal issues are deliberated before the entire community. The individual can 'stop the prayer' and force the community to do justice. The kehillah enacts decrees in ritual, political, administrative, and commercial matters, and enforces communal discipline upon the individual by use of the ban and the imposition of fines. And since all activities of the kehillah had long been based upon the laws of the Babylonian Talmud, its leaders derived therefrom halakhic authority for their new decrees.

Thus, the community's authorization to enact statutes which impinge on the right of the individual is derived from the talmudic principle, "the court can expropriate property." Similarly, R. Gershom 'Light of the Exile' states that "even the least worthy who is appointed a public official is like the most noble of the nobility." From this talmudic principle, R. Meshullam ben Kalonymus derives the authority of the kehillah to impose penalties for damages (despite the accepted principle that damage suits are not judged outside the Land of Israel), enact decrees, and levy fines. R. Joseph Bonfil decrees: "We find that the sages empowered each kehillah to promulgate its own decrees, and no other kehillah can abrogate them. . . . "

While these scholars may not have been the first to derive the authority of the kehillah from talmudic law, one must assume that this method was initiated close to their time and is a sign of the turning point in the development of the Jewish community. The local community takes upon itself the rights of the courts and Sanhedrin, and enacts statutes by power of the ban and fines, for only through those means can one "subdue the evil men in our times." The power of the ban exercised by the kehillah was, somewhat later, further extended by the decree that the rabbi cannot excommunicate without the agreement of the community.[10]

It is clear that this revolutionary development was contrary to the inclinations of the talmudic sages and the Babylonian geonim—but it was a necessary development. The heads of the academies in Babylonia and Palestine could not lead the communities of northwestern Europe. It is true that in the eleventh century the scholars of those communities still turned to the major academies in the East with questions of practical and theoretical halakhah, but this exchange of correspondence did not touch on issues of communal leadership. Nor can one compare the relationship of the European communities and the academies with the personal and pragmatic links that existed between the geonim and the heads of the Jewish communities in Spain, all of whom were living within the Muslim world and were united culturally, if not politically. Neither did the kehillot of northern Europe have an opportunity to strengthen the authority of their rabbinic leadership via influential Jews at the royal court, which was the case in Spain.

There was no tradition of a hierarchical institution within the kehillot of Europe, and thus a new central institution of that type could not arise. R. Gershom 'Light of the Exile' was the only personality who was later considered to have the authority to issue statutes for following generations as well as his own.[11] However, aside from the prohibition of polygamy and other decrees in the realm of ethics, one may question whether he was indeed the source of most of the statutes attributed to him, which, in any event, did not relate to legal or community issues. Indeed, the tradition regarding the binding nature of the statutes of R. Gershom can be traced back only to the mid-twelfth century. Prior to that time, only one ban of R. Gershom is cited, in an important responsum of Rashi, regarding the prohibition against reminding forced converts (*anusim*), who returned to Judaism, of their sin. Even this ban was not known to all the communities of northern France, and Rashi, in his responsum, reached the conclusion that R. Gershom had not formulated his bans with the intention of making them binding upon future generations.

We also learn that, similar to the practice of the early Christian communities, the kehillot were linked to one another by mutual responsibilities and reciprocal supervision in case of a community's failing in its religious duties, although such supervision was a matter of conscience and was not legally codified. In the late ninth century, mention is made of courts established at the fairs to judge the cases brought by members of all the communities assembled there. However, in sharp constrast to the talmudic and geonic tradition, the constitutional center of Jewish life was the kehillah, and not a supreme religious organization from which it derived authority. This development was not intended to weaken talmudic principles or to rebel against the authority of the scholars, but expressed the justified assumption that the majority of the community were learned men; where reality did not match this ideal, it was understood that the "small obey the great." The long historic clash between the sages and the populace subsided for at least a few generations. During this period the community which had existed 'underground' for 1300 years emerged from its modest, almost suspect position, to assume official halakhic status.

Such a development would have been impossible without the new organizational forces which sprang into life within the communities. Responsa of the period reveal typical urban systems that were common in the kehillah at the end of the tenth and in the early eleventh centuries, several generations prior to their official formulation in the statutes of the Christian cities.

The first concern of a young kehillah was to enforce discipline and establish guidelines in cases of conflict between its members. From the responsa of R. Meshullam ben Kalonymus we learn that the communities of southern France had written regulations and schedules of fines for cases of assault. Such regulations, which constitute a halakhic innovation, mark the beginning of a public code of discipline and are to be found in most European kehillot from the twelfth century on.

The second priority of a new kehillah was to regularize its relationship with the non-Jewish rulers, institute a system for carrying out payments and other obligations to the ruler, and divide these burdens fairly among all members of the community. Interesting information concerning these arrangements can be found in the responsa of R. Joseph Bonfil dealing with the division of the tax burden among the community. By his time (mideleventh century, Anjou), the community already paid a lump sum to the ruler, instead of the arbitrary amounts demanded from individual Jews. This may be considered a step forward in the kehillah's struggle for autonomy vis-a-vis the authorities. The bourgeois Christian community did not achieve this degree of autonomy until a generation later.

On the other hand, unlike the Christian city, the Jewish community remained dependent upon the support of the secular ruler to enforce its authority, particularly in the early period when its jurisdiction over the individual was not yet fully established. From the responsa, we learn of a case where two members of a community fled to another community and asked it to lift the ban imposed on them by the first for nonpayment of taxes. The community to which they belonged was forced to ask the local ruler to enforce the taxation payment, since the community itself was unable to do so. The tone of the responsum already reflects the respectful fear for the community's existence with which the Jews of the Middle Ages approached public matters, including punctual payment of communal taxes. As stated in their statutes: "Let the heart of the public be as one to pay its taxes on time, out of reverence of God and fear of persecution." The details of payment were determined by all the members of the community, who enforced the decision by use of the ban. There is no mention of how voting was carried out. To prevent quarrels, an estimate of a person's wealth and his tax obligation was made by 'fideles'—respected members of the community whose decision would be accepted by all.

Another method of taxation is found in the responsa of R. Joseph Bonfil; each person was sworn to make an honest estimate of his wealth, and to pay a percentage that was designated by the community. Bonfil mentions this as an example of the higher level of public morality among Jews. This method of taxation was not introduced in Christian cities until the thirteenth century.

From other responsa (perhaps of Narbonne in southern France, or Catalonia in Spain), it seems that the tax was levied equally upon land and capital; in Bonfil's responsa one learns for the first time of a difference between the two. According to a decree attributed to Rashi, capital used for moneylending was the principal object of taxation in the kehillot of northern France. The kehillot of the Rhine also assumed responsibility for tax collection, as we learn from the tales of the persecutions of 1096.

The beginning of this practice can be dated to the early eleventh century. There is no basis for it in the Talmud, which is not surprising, for autonomous administration of taxation did not exist in the last centuries of the Roman Empire (nor in the lands ruled by the Muslims). These democratic methods of taxation developed in Europe, where the Jewish communities were the first to initiate the system, which the Christian communities adopted several generations later.

The relationship between the kehillah and the Christian city is slightly different in the area of commerce. As we have seen, the community of Kairouan promulgated decrees to protect the commercial interests of its members in the ninth century. In Europe, however, we have only one surviving reference to commerce in Jewish sources, again in a responsum of R. Meshullam ben Kalonymus. He mentions a decree forbidding a Jew to intercept traders along their routes and buy up their goods before they reach the town. R. Meshullam decides that this decree also obligates members of other communities who have come to the town to do business. This is a distinctly urban decree, similar to those in effect in the Christian cities of Europe. However, the responsum is of a late date, and the decree cited is the only one of its time. Once again, the Jewish organizational system

I.4.19

appears to precede those which developed in Europe, but it is difficult to argue that the Christians copied their systems from the Jews alone.

Other commercial arrangements of the early period of the kehillah have been stigmatized as 'ghettoized', and bearing no resemblance to the organizational structures which formed the foundation of the independent European city. Nonetheless, they also provide evidence for the corporative trend of the Jewish populace. The earliest Jewish source for commercial legislation is the responsa of R. Gershom which deal with the concept of *ma'arufia*.[12] This term is linguistically non-European in origin and was probably introduced into Europe by Jewish traders from the south, perhaps from Kairouan where we find a precedent for this relationship. This institution appears first in the Rhine valley and northern France from whence it spread to Germany and, later, Poland; there is no evidence of it in Spanish sources. During the period of R. Gershom there were places which, by use of the ban, forbade one Jew from encroaching on the 'ma'arufia' of a fellow Jew who held it either by inheritance or other means. R. Gershom attempts to find a talmudic precedent protecting the holder of a 'ma'arufia' by relating it to the special rights given the *talmid hakham* (learned man) in order to protect his business interests.

When we consider the more basic question of whether there is a historical continuity from talmudic times for such commercial legislation, the answer seems to be 'no'. There was no commercial organization in Babylonia similar to that which developed in medieval Europe. From the earlier period we know only of some communities defending their members' commercial interests by imposition of bans and fines, which were also invoked against informers who threatened commercial damage to the community.

In an area tangential to commercial legislation, we do find evidence of historical continuity. Another responsum of R. Gershom deals with returning lost or stolen property and provides clear evidence that the ancient talmudic tradition of announcing the finding of lost objects remained in force. Similar decrees are found later, in the statutes of the twelfth-century Christian cities where the community undertakes to help the individual recover his property.

THE KEHILLAH IN THE TWELFTH AND THIRTEENTH CENTURIES

The rich organizational history of the kehillah increases in clarity from the twelfth and thirteenth centuries onward. It is in Spain that the kehillah reached its apex of development and variety, resembling the Christian city in almost every aspect. In northern Europe, because the Jewish community was divested of rights, it could only borrow from its environment certain tools essential to its existence, and develop structures adapted to its special needs. Nonetheless, one who wishes to study the public law of that period must include the responsa and other legal writings of the rabbis of France and Ashkenaz. They and their communities almost single-handedly laid the foundation for the new system of public law in Judaism.

The rabbis of Spain, who had a much richer practical administrative tradition and knew both Roman law and the law of their country, still derived most of their knowledge of Jewish law from the Tosafists (the students of Rashi) and the scholars of Ashkenaz. Moreover, the rabbis of southern Europe continued the talmudic tradition of excluding outside considerations from halakhic discussions, whereas the rabbis of northern France and Ashkenaz lovingly nurtured every tradition linked to their 'holy communities', thus becoming the primary witnesses to the political developments in medieval Judaism. Since the halakhah was not directly helpful to such development, they resorted to novel interpretations of talmudic passages in order to deal with legal issues affecting the kehillah. Their innovations in public law were the result of a pragmatic approach to real problems, based on a true sense of the community's needs. Thereby they granted official sanction to the organizational forces which existed within the Jewish people throughout the generations.

The documents which best exemplify the development of communal activity in medieval Europe are the decrees promulgated by the kehillot under the leadership of Rabbenu Tam (the grandson of Rashi) and other scholars of France and the Rhineland, from the mid-twelfth to the thirteenth centuries. Their main purpose was to strengthen the authority of the community over the individual and to place the needs of the group above personal interests. The following issue, which constitutes one of the theoretical practical foundations of Jewish public law, provides an example of this trend.

Two paragraphs found in a collection of decrees from the late twelfth century determine the basic rights of the public vis-a-vis the individual. An individual who wishes to challenge the amount of taxation imposed upon him first must pay the amount determined, and only then may he bring his complaint to the court. As R. Meir of Rothenberg explains: "The community prefers to be a defendant and not a prosecutor." Furthermore, "If the townspeople issue a decree and the majority agree, the others may not disobey the decree and say 'we will take you to court', for this is not a matter for a court decision." It is clear that this represents a change to the system of majority rule, in contrast to the system of corporate justice then prevalent in Europe.

An interesting comparison can be found in the legal history of the Catholic Church. The Third Lateran Council of 1179 decreed that, if the cardinals do not reach a unanimous decision concerning the appointment of a pope, he can be legally elected by a two-thirds majority. The Fourth Lateran Council of 1215 extended this principle to the election of local bishops, who could be chosen by the majority, or by the worthier members of the electors. This was a break with earlier Church tradition in both the East and the West.

I.4.21

The Jewish decree precedes the Christian ones by several years; however, it does not deal with elections but with general public decisions.

In this case, we must conclude that the Tosafists learned their political concepts from their neighbors, the Christian jurists and canonists, for the principle of following the majority was not applied in talmudic law to urban and communal corporations (which were outside its frame of reference). Nor do we find any practical discussion of this matter in the geonic period. Nonetheless, the rabbis of northern Europe did precede the Christian scholars in defining the diffuse political concepts then in the air. From the twelfth century onward, the European community began to deal with these questions with great seriousness. The principle of majority rule in communal affairs was accepted generally in the thirteenth century, first in southern Europe, which was more open to the influence of Roman law, and later in northern Europe.

Two viewpoints concerning the power of the community to reach a binding decision were in confrontation at the time. According to the Germanic tradition then dominant in Europe, the decision of the community was authoritative only if it was reached unanimously; in case of conflict, the majority had to make the minority agree, either through negotiation or by use of force. This idea held sway until a new school of thought based on Roman law proclaimed that the majority vote could, via a legal fiction, be considered the will of the entire public body. They added, however, that the majority must be not only quantitative, but qualitative—*maior vel sanior pars* (the worthier members of the community).

These differences are explored theoretically in the writings of the rabbinic scholars. Rabbenu Tam opened the discussion of this issue. He is quoted as saying that the community can punish a transgressor and thereby enforce its rule upon the public. But under what circumstances? When those decrees have been accepted by all who must suffer their consequences—including the individual transgressor. This idea has no talmudic basis, but reflects the accepted concepts of the Middle Ages.

While Rabbenu Tam is still within the Germanic tradition of unanimous decision making, we witness the conflict between that system and the Roman law in a case discussed by the scholars of Ashkenaz in the thirteenth century. The case deals with the method of determining the amount of taxation—by the individual who is sworn on pain of the ban to give an honest estimate, or by the appointment of officials to determine each member's share. The question, posed by the scholars of Worms to the scholars of Mainz, was whether a community could change its decree against the wishes of some of its members. The scholars of Mainz reflected the Germanic school of thought, holding that the majority cannot force the minority to pay taxes against its wishes. However, R. Eleazar Joel Halevi (of Mainz) stated that the majority can enforce its decision upon the minority, basing himself on the principle that the majority is like the entire community.

Although this basic principle came from Roman law, R. Eleazer, like other medieval rabbis, sought to authenticate his opinion by basing it on the Talmud, through a reinterpretation of the plain meaning of certain passages. His interpretation was accepted even by the RaSHBa, the great Spanish rabbinic scholar.

Another thirteenth-century rabbi, R. Simha of Speyer, in an opinion concerning the status of the community with respect to taxation, stated that all members of a kehillah are partners, therefore cannot exclude themselves from the public at large, and must pay their part of the levied taxes. He based his decision on the legal code dealing with a caravan traveling in the desert. It is attacked, and one man drives off the attackers; but the property he recovers is considered the property of the entire caravan and not his alone. R. Simha was the first in a long line of rabbis to make use of this halakhah. Perhaps its value lies not only in its legal content, but in its symbolic value for the Jewish community surrounded by enemies.

At the end of the responsum, R. Simha tells the story of his uncle R. Kalonymus who would use his influence with the king to reduce the taxes of the community, and then ask the king for a personal reduction in return for various services rendered. He would then share this further reduction with the community. R. Simha concludes with these words which should be remembered for generations to come:

I used to believe that this act [of R. Kalonymus] was a measure of his kindness and saintliness; but I now see that it was a measure of justice, for all Israel is responsible for one another in bearing the burden of the Exile, and will thereby be privileged to share together the consolation and redemption.

It emerges then that the affairs of the kehillah should not be considered in terms of a partnership. In Jewish law, the kehillah is treated as a living body which is judged for its action in both the upper and the lower world. This view of the community as a living body, with a shared responsibility for the execution of justice, sustained the Jew throughout his long history and exile.

NOTES

1. For a detailed study of Philo's thought and his place in the history of Jewish philosophy, see H. A. Wolfson, *Philo: Foundations of Religious Philosophy in Judaism, Christianity and Islam*, 2 vols., Cambridge: Harvard University Press, 1962.

2. In the course of time, the Greek administrative titles 'archonite' and 'boloite' appeared with increasing frequency, reflecting the Greek influence on Jewish towns.

3. A. Büchler, "The Political and the Social Leaders of the Jewish Community of Sepphoris in the Second and Third Centuries," *Jews' College Publications*, no. 1, London: 1909.

4. The significance of this development in early Christianity, for political thought as well as theology, was closely analyzed by Otto von Gierke, a political historian of the last century, in his three-volume *Das deutsche Genossenschaftsrecht*, Berlin: Weidman, 1881. A shorter presentation of his 'Genossenschaft' theory can be found in his *Political Theories of the Middle Ages*, Translated by F. W. Maitland, Cambridge: Cambridge University Press, 1927.

5. A parallel account of Jewish autonomy in Babylon is provided by Benjamin of Tudela; see M. N. Adler, *The Itinerary of Benjamin of Tudela*, London: Frowde, 1901, pp. 39–42. For a detailed study of the local Jewish communal organization in the geonic period and beyond, see S. D. Goitein, "The Local Jewish Community in the Light of the Cairo Geniza Records," *Journal of Jewish Studies* 12 (1961); also S. D. Goitein, *Mediterranean Society*, Berkeley: University of California, 1967–1983, vol. 2, B, The Community, pp. 40–68.

6. A discussion of the origin of the custom of interrupting the prayers can be found in L. Finkelstein, *Jewish Self-Government in the Middle Ages*, New York: JTS, 1964, pp. 382ff.

7. J. Mann, *The Jews in Egypt and Palestine under the Fatimid Caliphs*, New York: Ktav, 1970.

8. J. Mann, "Responsa of the Babylonian Geonim as a Source of Jewish History," *Jewish Quarterly Review* 7 (n.s.) (1916/17): 477, 478, n. 22.

9. H. Pirenne, *Medieval Cities; their Origins and the Revival of Trade*, Princeton: Princeton University, 1939. See also, H. Pirenne, *Economic and Social History of Medieval Europe*, New York: Harcourt, Brace and World, 1937.

10. Finkelstein, *Jewish Self-Government in the Middle Ages*, pp. 228, §13, 242, n. 4.

11. The texts of the so-called decrees of R. Gershom, as well as the various communal decrees and ordinances promulgated by Rashi and Rabbenu Tam (discussed later in this article) have been collected and translated by Louis Finkelstein, op. cit.

12. The *ma'arufia* (client) was the Christian feudal lord, layman, or cleric, whose affairs the Jew managed, serving as his purchasing agent and monetary broker. Such a relationship was considered a monopoly enjoyed by the individual Jew, and was protected by the community.

SUGGESTION FOR FURTHER READING

S. W. Baron, *The Jewish Community*, 3 vols. Philadelphia: JPS, 1942.

5

H. H. BEN-SASSON

The Generation of the Spanish
Exiles Considers Its Fate

The expulsion of the Jews from Spain in 1492 was not only a physical blow to the Jewish communities in Europe, whose most ancient and prosperous center was thus destroyed, but also a spiritual event which brought about a period of reflection and self-examination on the part of the exiled Jews who sought to understand the significance of their fate. The following study is the classical description of the various, often conflicting, reactions of Jewish thinkers and historians to this cataclysmic event in Jewish history.

Professor Haim Hillel Ben-Sasson was one of the leading historians in the Department of Jewish History at The Hebrew University of Jerusalem. A specialist in medieval Jewish history, he was the editor of the three-volume History of the Jewish People, *in which he wrote the second volume dedicated to the Middle Ages. He published other important studies dealing with the history of the Ashkenazi Hasidic movement, and the relationship of the early Protestant groups to Jews and Judaism.*

BACKGROUND

This study examines the views of the generation of Jews exiled from Spain: their perception of the great Jewish community which was destroyed; their attitudes toward the Spanish Catholics; and their feelings regarding their brethren who had chosen to convert to Catholicism (the Marranos) in order

This article is an amalgam of two articles which appeared in Hebrew in the *Yitzhak F. Baer Jubilee Volume*, Jerusalem, 1960, and in *Zion* 26 (1961). The translation/ adaptation is by Dr. Carol Bosworth Kutscher.

to remain in Spain after the 1492 Edict of Expulsion. We also gain an understanding of the unique organization and strength of the exiled Spanish communities and perceive the roots of social and apologetic trends which emerged in later generations of this exiled Jewry.

THE VISION OF A VANISHED GLORY

Even in exile, Spanish Jews maintained an unshakable pride in their lofty ancestry and glorious past. Many stories told among the exiles or to Jews in other lands clearly idealized their past in Spain, especially on the eve of the Expulsion. These traditions maintained that the eminence and tranquility enjoyed by the Jews in Spain were the greatest in the Jewish world up to the very eve of the Expulsion. According to Isaac Abravanel (1437–1508), statesman, biblical commentator, inspiring proponent of the messianic salvation of the Jews, they enjoyed boundless wealth and every divine blessing in absolute peace. They were God-fearing, upright, generous; the community was famous for its great poets and orators, biblical and talmudic scholars, students of secular sciences, and influential counselors to kings. Then, suddenly, they were violently uprooted from this perfect existence.

Other exiles, however, present a diametrically opposed picture of a constantly deteriorating Spanish Jewish community. The kabbalist Abraham ben Eliezer Halevi, for example, calculating the coming of the Redeemer in his commentary on *Nevuat HaYeled*, reports that Spanish Jewry's troubles steadily intensified from 1485 when Queen Isabella occupied the throne, and that increasingly onerous taxes were imposed on the Jews until the Expulsion. Halevi's brother-in-law, the chronicler Abraham Zacutto, dates the beginning of the Jews' suffering to 1482, when the Christians won the final battles of the Reconquista and expelled the Muslim Moors from the Iberian Peninsula. That date marked the start of the Inquisition's actions against the Marranos (or *conversos*), and the segregation of Jews in separate neighborhoods. Solomon ibn Virga, the great Spanish historiographer of Jewish persecution, who was himself expelled from Spain and then forcibly converted in Lisbon, goes even further. He maintains that, from 1381 onward, Spanish Jewry's distress steadily intensified, and that most Spaniards wanted to annihilate the Jews.

Rabbi Elijah Capsali (ca. 1483–1555), author of an excellent history of Spain and the Expulsion, merges these two views, explaining that Spanish Jewry enjoyed peace and prestige until the Reconquista, when the Christians forced the Jews living in the formerly Muslim regions to convert on pain of death, and enforced several local expulsions before the comprehensive expulsion of all the Jews in 1492. Capsali nonetheless claimed that the high-ranking ministers of the Spanish court "all loved the Jews like the apple of their eye." Unfortunately, King Ferdinand was so powerful and revered as the great warrior who had routed the Moors from Granada after 409 years of occupation, that these nobles were not able to oppose his Edict of Expulsion.

The glaring contradictions in these accounts of pre-Expulsion Jewry may be explained by each author's emphasis on a different aspect of Spanish Jewish life. It is evident that, until the Expulsion, upper-class Spanish Jews possessed immense wealth and enjoyed a luxurious life-style. The sense of being deeply rooted in Spain was real, and not merely the product of post-Expulsion idealization. Evidence of this deep sense of belonging, even on the very eve of the 1492 Edict, appears in testimony before a Muslim court in Fez. The witness reported that the expelled kabbalist Judah Hayyat, while still in Spain, had told his followers to make effigies of the Muslim prophets (sic!) and drag it (sic!) through the streets and marketplaces of Granada to celebrate the city's conquest by the Catholics in 1492—this, after the Edict of Expulsion had already been signed by King Ferdinand. While life in Spain may have been idealized, there was much objective and emotional truth in the exiles' perception of their past spiritual, social, intellectual, and economic greatness, and their aristocratic lineage and privilege.

Indeed, in the eyes of those who were expelled, the willingness to be exiled for their faith was testimony to the courage, honor, and merit of Spanish Jewry. The humiliating Expulsion, they claimed, was their "setting out . . . to seek the word of the Lord." They were proud to be Jews. Solomon ibn Virga, in *Shevet Yehudah*, quotes the words of an exile who lost his entire family in the course of his wanderings: "Lord of the world, You have done much to make me abandon my religion . . . You must know that . . . I am a Jew and shall remain a Jew no matter what You have wrought or will wreak upon me."

Every community of the Diaspora has had its tradition of Jewish service and influence in royal courts. But in Spain, courtiership was a central feature of Jewish life. This relationship began during the period of Moorish rule, but Jewish court officials reached the greatest heights of wealth, splendor, and influence in the Christian courts of the twelfth and thirteenth centuries. In Spain, the Jewish communities were not governed by their religious leaders, but by the Jewish officials of the Christian kings.

A comprehensive doctrine detailing the role of the Jewish courtier and community leader, and providing a justification for his way of life, was elaborated in Spain. In the latter half of the fourteenth century, the kabbalist Don Joseph ben Shoshan set down guidelines for the Jewish court official of a gentile king. In his commentary on the tractate Avot, ben Shoshan wrote that the Jewish official "must view himself as an emissary of God who gave him grace in the eyes of the king so that the king would hearken to his counsel." In his role as divine emissary, the Jewish court official also ruled the Jewish community with an iron hand, crushing all heresy and glorifying the synagogue.

The great Rabbi Joseph Caro even worked out a solution to the difficulties

I.5.3

of Jewish religious observance in the midst of court life. He cited the Talmud which permitted a Jew who is close to kings to follow "the customs of the gentiles" because his position gives him the power to save the Jews through his influence upon the ruler.

We find no criticism among the exiles of Jewish courtiership, despite the fact that this institution was instrumental in bringing Jews into contact with non-Jews and with Christian culture, leading them to abandon the Jewish religion. Indeed, the exiles continued to feel tremendous pride in those who once occupied themselves with court service and community leadership, as reflected in numerous tales told to R. Elijah Capsali and recorded in his *Likutim Shonim*.

RELATIONS BETWEEN JEWS AND MARRANOS

A century before the Expulsion, Spanish Jewry was already divided into those who remained Jews even in the face of the persecutions which began in 1391, and the Marranos who yielded under duress and converted to Christianity, at least outwardly. Spanish Jewry excluded from the community those apostates who had become Christians of their own free will and then engaged in anti-Jewish activities. The plight of the forced converts, however, cut to the very heart of the conceptions of nationhood, race, and faith and exercised both the faithful and the Marranos.

How did the faithful view the Marranos, and what was the relationship between the two groups? The first and most decisive formulation was attempted by Profiat Duran following the persecutions of 1391. In his *Ma'aseh Efod* he held that, as in other times and places of Jewish dispersion, the Lord did not exclude from the seed of Abraham those who had worshipped other gods. So, too, in the Spanish Diaspora "if part of the people fails . . . because of the fear of persecutions . . . He, may He be blessed, knows what is in the depths of their hearts." These unhappy Marranos belong inseparably to the Jewish race and this ensures their continued ties with the Jewish people, faith, and God, despite the fact that they have "intermingled with the gentiles."

Some of the Spanish rabbis maintained this indestructible unity of the Jewish people until the very eve of the Expulsion. R. Isaac ibn 'Arama (ca. 1420–1494), the renowned preacher and defender of the Jewish faith against Christian conversionist sermons, told of a talk with a Christian scholar who asked him why a Jewish man who converts to Christianity is immediately required to grant his wife a bill of divorce. After all, when a man leaves his religion he should be considered as if he no longer existed, and his wife therefore, as if she were a widow. The reply was, "He did not change his religion on his own; it was only a circumstantial change, as for example a change of name or address; he cannot change his essence, because he is a Jew." But in the case of the gentile wishing to convert to Judaism, his essence *can* be changed by his sincere wish to join the Jewish religion and perform its commandments. Once an individual is a Jew for several generations, however, there is no way for him to leave the Jewish people. For this reason, in his *Akedat Yitzhak*, ibn 'Arama expressed his compassion for the anguish of the Marranos who, "although completely intermingled with those gentiles, they have found no rest among them . . . because they always despise them, and they are always suspected of Judaizing [practicing Judaism in secret]. . . . "

The kabbalist Abraham ben Eliezer Halevi expressed an extremely lenient attitude even to those Jews who left with the Expulsion, only to return to Spain and convert because they could not endure the hardships of exile. Even such as these, said Halevi, were part of the Jewish people who would enjoy the restoration to the Holy Land.

Gradually the attitude toward the Marranos changed, particularly toward those who elected to live as Christians in Spain rather than be expelled. Some, like Rabbi Joel ibn Sho'eb, an influential anticonversionist preacher before and after the Expulsion, could not forgive the Marranos for rejecting their membership in the Jewish people.

. . . They thought they could escape the flames by separating themselves from the people, but the Lord separated them for evil from the rest of the Tribes of Israel . . . may they fall into that from which they thought to be saved and may they melt in the fire in utter destruction in this world and the next.

In his commentary on Psalms, *Norah Tehillot,* ibn Sho'eb warned the Marranos that, "Even though you would forget your God, you will know no peace because the enemy wants only to annihilate you in any case. . . . From the sufferings of apostasy there is no escape nor aid, neither earthly nor divine." Yet hostile as he is to the Marranos, ibn Sho'eb still relates to them as Jews.

With time, the element of compulsion dwindled among the Marranos and, increasingly, they espoused Christianity of their own free will, although they continued to extol their secret faithfulness to Judaism. We must also bear in mind that the post-Expulsion Marrano community was by no means homogeneous. Joseph Jabez, the great preacher and comforter of the exiles, distinguishes among the different kinds of Marranos: (1) those who willingly converted; (2) those who converted under duress but afterward assimilated of their own free will, showing that they were "never the Lord's and the Lord takes no delight in them"; (3) those who later fled the Iberian peninsula, repented, and returned to Judaism. It is only this third group of Marranos which Jabez is willing to pardon. As a result of this heterogeneity, exiled Jews were not of one mind regarding the converts who remained behind in Spain.

Isaac Abravanel expressed ambivalence toward the Marranos. Although

I.5.5

he considered them 'criminals,' he was aware of the horror of their fate, namely, the contradiction between their wealth and high status and the constant inner fear with which they lived.

The nations will always be their enemies and a sword will always be hanging over their heads. . . . No matter how hard [the Marranos] and their descendants try to be good Christians . . . the Spaniards will always call them Jews . . . and will falsely accuse them of Judaizing. And they will burn them at the stake. (Commentary on the Pentateuch, Deuteronomy)

But Abravanel is optimistic about the ultimate fate of the Marranos. He is sure the persecutions in Spain will continue until "at the End of Days, the Lord will illuminate the hearts of the Marranos or their descendants so that they will return to the Lord and observe some of the commandments secretly." And then they will flee Spain for their lives.

On the other hand, Rabbi Isaac Caro, head of the Toledo yeshiva before fleeing to Turkey in 1497, adopted a hard line regarding the Marranos, maintaining that conversion under duress is "a great sin" because "we are obligated to die a martyr's death" (*Toldot Yitzhak*). Marranos should not be accepted back into Judaism even if they repent, since they want to repent only because they were not accepted into Christian society as they had hoped to be. The gentiles will say, "They did not change their religion because they believe in our faith, but in order not to be killed. And they do not observe either our religion or their own."

Other rabbis refused to read the Marranos out of the Jewish people, going so far as to counsel them on how to observe the minimal commandments in secret. In Joseph ben Don Meir Gerson's first sermon after his arrival in Salonica in 1500, he expressed his grief for his brethren who stayed in Spain and continue to live in apostasy

although they want to worship the Lord. But they do not permit them to leave, so they worship other gods *against their will* [Ben-Sasson's emphasis]. Which God-fearing man can be happy so long as our brethren and relatives are still living in apostasy?

The passionate desire to help the Marranos preserve the essence of Judaism moved the kabbalist Abraham Saba, who fled Portugal after enduring great suffering for his religion. His prime concern was the first generation of forced converts in Portugal, particularly the young children. He stated that the brief prayer "Hear, O Israel" was all that was left them of Judaism, yet it was enough; for it included the teachings of monotheism and religious martyrdom. The only religious commandment that remained to preserve their Judaism in apostasy was that of circumcision.

The traditions of the expelled Jews preserved the memory of the Marranos' secret religious observance and devotion; these practices were worth their lives if informers revealed them to the Inquisition. Well might the exiles ponder whether it had been right for the community, on the eve of the Expulsion, to demand on pain of excommunication that Jews reveal the identity of Marranos to the Inquisition, thereby causing the death of many *conversos*. This shameful and appalling chapter in Spanish Jewish history later gave rise to grave self-accusations which may have salved the conscience of the Jewish informers when they bewailed the 'sword of excommunication' which hung over their heads wherever they went.

The split in Spanish Jewry into the faithful, forced converts, and willing apostates raised difficulties regarding the interrelation between faith and the soul, and the degree of blame or justification attaching to the surrender to pressure and intimidation. The Marrano question was bound up with the problem of the unity of race, nation, and faith. Even those who most vehemently rejected the Marranos could not dissociate themselves from the concept of Jewish unity from birth, as an inseparable part of the Jewish soul. There is no contemporaneous evidence for the assertion of modern scholars that practicing Jews were completely alienated from the Marranos before the Expulsion. The faithful did express rage against the converts, but it was an anger against fellow Jews who had tried to cut themselves off from their common Jewish fate.

THE RELIGIOUS SIGNIFICANCE OF FORCED CONVERSION

The coercion exerted to make Jews convert to Christianity raised questions regarding divine justice in the hearts of loyal Jews as well as among the converts themselves. Sometimes the tragic attempts of Marranos to preserve their Judaism only widened the gulf between them and those who had remained openly faithful. Yet the complex tie between these communities, which endured even after the Expulsion, made the faithful aware of the relevance of religious coercion for themselves as well.

Isaac ibn 'Arama viewed forced conversion as an aspect of the fate of the Jewish people. Moses had warned the Israelites that, if they would not obey God's commandments in the Promised Land, "the Lord will scatter you among all the peoples... and there you shall serve other gods... which neither you nor your ancestors have experienced" (Deuteronomy 28:64). The meaning of this verse greatly exercised the generation of the Expulsion, for how was it conceivable that God could *want* His people to worship other gods against their will? What kind of God hardens His heart against the lamentations of His children and does not remove the coercion and torture? Joseph Gerson explained that if God did not answer persecuted Spanish Jews when they cried out to Him, it was because "it was destined according to Moses: 'And I will surely hide My face in that day,' " on account of all the evil which they have done, because they have turned to other gods.

I.5.7

Torture and conversion under duress were a divine decree, according to Gerson, part of God's administration of the world. This conception saved Gerson and his generation from yielding to utter despair and heresy. It was a generation united in tragedy and grief, accepting the severity of the divine decree while attempting to escape that decree, either by fleeing Spain or remaining there as Marranos.

Joseph Caro (1486–1575), the kabbalist, was less sympathetic to those who converted. He assessed their reasons for converting with harshness: The convert believes that these "Christian fetishes" have the magical power to make their worshippers rich. "Then, once he is rich, he will go back to worshipping the Lord." Apparently some Marranos intended to amass wealth as Christians and then emigrate from Spain and settle in comfort someplace where they could worship as Jews once again. But Caro does not believe in the good intentions of the Marranos; their sole motivation is "material desire," and the rest is merely a means to evade divine punishment.

The inability to endure the tortures inflicted by the Spaniards was another reason impelling Marranos to go through the outer motions of Catholic worship while continuing to be believing, faithful Jews inwardly. Some Jews, like Joseph Caro, felt that this was merely a selfish attempt to have the best of both worlds—Catholic prosperity, and the peace of mind that comes of knowing that the Lord pardons him because he is a Jew in his heart.

Some Marranos took this dualist view very seriously indeed, even evolving a Catholic doctrine of sorts, to explain how they could continue to be Jews. They believed that intention and principle are the essence of Judaism; one's sinful actions in this world are pardonable if one has the proper faith. This may have been the dogma of second- and third-generation *conversos* who were influenced by Christian beliefs, even as they rebelled against them. They performed few Jewish religious commandments; their Judaism consisted of preserving its pure monotheism in their hearts.

THE IMAGE OF CHRISTIANITY

The Jewish exiles had a highly ambivalent attitude toward their persecutors and the religion they espoused. Interestingly, the vicious religious hatred they experienced did not detract from their basic appreciation of the Christian way of life. Perhaps the exiles' rosy picture of Catholic Spain was intended to emphasize their own resoluteness in leaving that desirable country for the sake of the pure faith. In fact, for some of the exiles, the viciousness of the Spaniards was expressed in the sophisticated torment meted out by skilled debaters and jurists, as compared to the brute physical violence suffered at the hands of the Muslims in the lands of refuge after the Expulsion. The convincing, seductive, articulate religious preaching of the Christians, and the polemics centered around the Bible and religious philosophy, tormented the Jews and undermined their faith in the Torah.

Rabbi Joseph Jabez, an exile who preached about the significance of the Expulsion, even recognized certain virtues and achievements in the Spanish religion and culture. For example, he claimed that, ethically, the Spanish upper classes were superior to the Jews because the officials among them performed charitable works among the poor for their own sake and for the love of God. Moreover, their scholars were pleasant to each other, which could not be said of the Jewish sages. And if a Christian priest preached in Spain, even if he spoke against the king and his officials, no one would utter a word or express scorn, as the Jews did when anyone chastened and criticized the behavior of their own community. So attractive, in fact, was Spanish Christian preaching, that Jews attended public sermons to enjoy their philosophical content and elegant, polished rhetoric, even though the ideas themselves were vain and idle. Some of the exiles even borrowed images and ideas from these Christian preachers, for example, the Jews bearing the curse of Cain. It required great inner strength for a Jew not to be attracted to this glittering life of spiritual and worldly success.

Joel ibn Sho'eb injected a healthy note of criticism of the Christian life which was so attractive to some Jews. He said that the Christians try to appear righteous and pious when in fact their faith is for appearance's sake, and they are overly concerned with asceticism. The Jews' best defense against Christian belief and asceticism is the well-known moderation and rationality of the Jewish faith and way of life.

On the eve of the Expulsion, the battle for Jewish souls intensified. The generation of the Expulsion felt the full force and venom of Christian claims of spiritual and religious superiority over Judaism. Ibn Sho'eb described the religious pressure on the Jews to convert as a form of torment which increases "as it adheres to the soul."

THE UNIFIED CATHOLIC KINGDOM IN THE EYES OF THE EXILES

The Jews were well aware that Christian hatred of them was partly due to their constituting an obstacle to the religious and political unification of the Iberian peninsula. However, the Jews also clearly appreciated that this hostile attitude of the Christians stemmed partly from political and religious views which were intrinsically valid. Abraham Shalom, the Spanish translator of Greek philosophical works (died 1492), puts into the mouth of an anti-Semite eight reasons for destroying the Jews in Spain. One argument is that the Jews cannot be permitted to exist in a kingdom united by Christianity, since a king rules on the basis of a consensus which is challenged if some subjects are of a different religion. Furthermore, the Jews constitute an exclusive foreign body, which sets a bad example of evil customs and laws that may spread throughout the Christian kingdom (*Neveh Shalom*). The Jews wholeheartedly agree that religion is vital to the orderly existence of the nation; thus, if they stubbornly refuse to adopt the religion of the land they must be destroyed. In ancient Israel itself, kingship and religion were mutually supporting and the king was empowered "to force the people to practice the religion of the state" and "to cleanse the wicked from the world."

When the Spanish kings began to impose the religion of the land on their subjects, they also granted Jewish leaders the authority to impose Jewish religious laws on their community, and to punish offenders. According to the aristocratic kabbalist Joseph Shoshan, the Jews considered the granting of religious autonomy a divine miracle, and many Jewish writers approved the trend toward a state religion. Later, this religious separatism was to weigh heavily against the Jews as a threat to the unification of the kingdom.

The extant Hebrew documents dealing with the Edict of Expulsion emphasize the religious motivation of the decree even more than does the edict itself. All the Jewish sources agree that the piety of the Catholic monarchs and their gratitude to God for the conquest of Granada and the unification of Spain were the main motives for the expulsion of the Jews. Abravanel explains that the Catholics thought they could demonstrate their gratitude to God by forcing the "wayward daughter" Israel to come "under His wings" and by expelling all those who refused to do so. For the Jews, he added, the Edict of Expulsion marked the end of the "spiritual miracle," the period of the "unnatural toleration" which had hitherto prevailed in Spain.

Interestingly, questions of religious persecution, forced conversion, and the expulsion of the Jews have continued to trouble the conscience of Christian Spaniards even in the present century. A scholarly book, *The Structure of Spanish History* by A. Castro, blames the Jews and the spirit of Judaism for the persecutions and expulsion.[1]

THE ROLE OF RATIONALISM AND MYSTICISM IN CONVERSION

All the exiled scholars, even those such as Isaac ibn 'Arama and Isaac Abravanel, who were familiar with and utilized rational philosophical methods in their exegesis and preaching, explicitly state that rationalism and the nonobservant way of life of the Jewish court officials and their circles sapped the inner spiritual and communal strength of Spanish Jewry long before the Expulsion. This made conversion easier than resistance and flight. These scholars laid the blame for the submission and conversion of Spanish Jews on the 'Greek spirit' of the so-called 'Averroists'.[2] However, the situation was far more complex than this one-sided explanation. For when we come to Jewish charges of 'Averroism' among the Jewish courtiers, and complaints of the wicked intellectual trends and way of life of the Jewish 'philosophers', we find *only* the accusations of the faithful! There is no literature by these 'philosophers' or any Jewish or gentile judicial verdicts involving them which could prove that an 'Averroist' trend or way of life existed. In fact, the purest philosophical Jewish works of the time, those of Joseph Albo and Abraham Shalom, are permeated with strict orthodox religiosity and recognition of the kabbalah (Jewish mystic teachings). Furthermore, it was precisely these writers who were in the forefront of the polemical war with the Christians. No other Jewish philosophical literature from this period is extant. Ironically, the literature condemning Jewish 'philosophy' is itself permeated by the philosophical, rationalist spirit!

To be sure, there are judicial verdicts and contemporaneous writings which attest to the frivolous life led by some Jewish court officials. Yet no rabbi claims that this was a reason for Jews not to serve in the royal courts. Their unavoidable way of life was held responsible for their religious laxity, not their 'Averroist' views. It would seem that both Christian and Jewish antirationalist spirit was increasing throughout Spain, causing leaders of both religions to see and condemn Averroism everywhere. Furthermore, the mass of Jewish converts did not receive any personal guidance from nonobservant Jewish court officials who might have recommended that they, too, free themselves from religious observance. Could this tiny handful of courtiers, even if they did preach religious nihilism in their palaces, have had the power to corrupt so many Spanish Jews?

Rather, there seems to have been an inner crisis of faith within Spanish Jewry, a crisis of despair of a mystical and ascetic tendency, which corresponded to the dominant trend in the larger Christian society. The entire history of Jewish polemics in Spain, from Nachmanides's disputation in Barcelona in 1263 until the Expulsion, shows the dual tensions between the Jews' rationalist religious position vis-a-vis the 'absurdities' of Christian faith, and the mystical religious (kabbalist) position within Spanish Judaism. In other words, vis-a-vis Christian society, *all* Jews were 'Averroists' so to speak, whereas within Judaism the kabbalists were espousing increasingly extreme mystical ideas. For this reason, it was precisely Jews tending toward mystical doctrines who were subjected to the tremendous inner tension between the arguments they used to reject religious Christianity and those they used to buttress their own faith. Sometimes this tension was resolved by conversion to Christianity. The most notorious apostates who, with their descendants, became fanatical enemies of Judaism, all came to conversion through their own mystical-ascetic tendencies. There was certainly nothing 'Averroist' in these Jews before their apostasy.

The twelfth and thirteenth centuries were the only period in which the Averroists openly expressed their views in Spain. But how can there have been any direct links between them and the alleged religious cynicism of fifteenth-century courtier *conversos* tried by the Inquisition? It seems more

I.5.11

plausible to assume that such cynicism and nihilism were the result of the torments of forced conversion which destroyed faith in the God of Israel without creating any true loyalty to Jesus. These *conversos* were proud persons, accustomed to rule and to be treated with respect; now they had to act in one way outwardly, while feeling entirely different in their hearts. Could not this situation cause such persons to become cynics with no religion or ideals?

Generally speaking, then, no specific philosophical movement or social group can be blamed for the spiritual crisis in Spanish Jewry. As the situation deteriorated, the mystical-ascetic trend became the most dynamic force throughout all of Spanish life and culture; Spanish Jewish mystics, like their Christian counterparts, vehemently attacked those who interfered with the unification of their society through faith. Rationalism was but a faint voice within Spanish Jewry, even though the Jews invoked it so insistently in self-defense against Christian doctrines.

COMBATING DESPAIR

When the Jews of Spain were expelled in May 1492, the exiled rabbis attempted to give meaning to the catastrophe that had overtaken them. Some employed the symbol of Cain to describe their fate of endless exile and accursedness, borrowing this image from the Church, which had been the first to apply it to the Jews. However, according to Isaac Caro, the Expulsion was more onerous than Cain's fate, since there were no kingdoms in Cain's time and hence he was not expelled from his own kingdom but merely wandered from place to place "and would come back to his first place." Joseph Hayyun, the last rabbi of Lisbon before the Expulsion (died in 1497 in Constantinople), saw something positive in the curse of Spanish Jewry—their fate would be a perpetual warning to the rest of the Jews to be virtuous. The loss of their fabulous wealth and high status was a punishment 'worse than death' for Spanish Jews.

Rabbi Isaac Aboab (1433–1493), author of an enduringly popular work of religious inspiration and an advocate of secular studies, consoles his fellow exiles with a parable. A father and son are walking along a road. The son is tired and weak and keeps asking his father if they are far from the city which is their destination. The father tells him, "When you see the cemetery, you will be near the city. . . ." Aboab adds that when we see that troubles are close it is a sign of the coming of Messiah. Aboab also compares his people to a woman in labor whose relatives comfort her in her pangs by saying, "He who saved your mother from this pain . . . will answer you . . . and will raise us up. Amen" (*Nahar Pishon*, a commentary on Genesis).

Some of the exiles, however, gave way to the frankest expressions of despair over their tragedy. The Expulsion seemed to be the confirmation of the Christians' claim that conversion was the only way to redeem the Jews.

But must we assimilate with the Christians in order to survive, asked these exiles? Abraham Saba feared that, if the persecution of the Jews continued, by the time of the Redemption there would be no more Jews left to redeem! Isaac Abravanel, in *Zevach Pesach,* his commentary on the Passover Haggadah (written in 1496), asked, as the Israelites had asked in ancient times, "Would it not be better to be slaves in Egypt than to die in the wilderness" of the peoples? What had the Jews in the Diaspora gained from their forefathers' Exodus from Egypt? Maybe they would now be living in peace and plenty in Egypt! In his description of the End-of-Days, Abravanel writes that he will tell

how I used to say, "Men are all a vain hope" [Psalm 116:11], that is, all the prophets who prophesied my redemption . . . were false . . . Isaiah lied with his consolations. . . . Let the nation remember all the despairing words that were uttered at the time of the Exile [the Expulsion].

Joseph ibn Yahya (1494–1534), a second-generation exile born in Italy, felt compelled to ask Job's question regarding the suffering of the just and the prosperity of the wicked. He noted that many of the 'ignorant' Jews felt that the Expulsion was unjust and that they had no Redeemer. It took all the exiles' strength to overcome their doubts and despair.

Ironically, as noted above, some Christian ideas were used by the great Isaac Caro to comfort his fellow exiles. He expressed himself in a parable in his commentary *Toldot Yitzhak.*

A sage and his student saw by the road a golden image and a dry bone from the body of a wise man. The student took the image and the sage took the dry bone, kissed it, wrapped it in a fine garment, and buried it. . . . So it is with us and the gentiles. We are the lifeless dry bone . . . but you admit that from us came our holy patriarchs and priests . . . we have hopes of returning to . . . splendor . . . and holiness.

In other words, desiccated ancient Judaism had to compete with the glittering, attractive golden idol of Christianity. The terrible pressure exerted by the Spanish Church's claims is reflected in Joseph Jabez's lament in his commentary on Psalms, that Israel may be compared to "a man against whom false witnesses have come . . . and he cannot refute the witnesses; he can only weep."

RELATIONS WITH THE NEW ENVIRONMENT

The great majority of the Spanish exiles went to Muslim countries within the Turkish Empire. There they suffered the psychological hardships of an utterly foreign culture and language as well as the Muslims' physical beatings and verbal insults. Abraham Saba, a Spanish kabbalist and preacher who settled in Morocco after the Expulsion, maintained that the Spaniards were more wicked than the Muslims, because "in their *wisdom* they did everything evil to the Jews, but they did not kill and beat [the Jews] . . . the way the Ishmaelites do."

Although the exiled Spanish Jews continued to serve as court officials and to maintain forceful and centralized control within their communities, they also encountered the inevitable friction between newcomers and the settled Jewish communities in their lands of refuge. According to Isaac Abravanel's *She'elot laHakham Shaul HaKohen*, those Spanish exiles who settled in Germany and France mocked the Ashkenazi Jews for their inferior learning, and disparaged the Hebrew style of their rabbis whose ordination, they claimed, was not taken seriously even by the Ashkenazim themselves. In turn, the Ashkenazim accused the Spanish exiles of having taken their books from the gentiles, since most of the greatest Spanish Jewish writers spent "all their time in the courts of gentile kings and ministers."

Undoubtedly this friction was aggravated by Spanish pride in personal superiority, lofty lineage, glorious history, and past positions of authority in the Christian and Jewish worlds. On the other hand, this pride and sense of being the bearers of a superior culture helped maintain morale, and gave the exiles personal and social status even under the most trying and difficult conditions.

The exiles felt the need to explain to themselves and perhaps also to their Spanish persecutors why they refused to embrace Christianity and preferred exile. They stressed the uniqueness of the Jewish people, and its heritage, which were the secret of its survival and creativity even under the most brutal conditions of the long Jewish dispersion. It is their loyalty to their forefathers, to the Jewish people, and to their Torah and its kabbalah, which enables the Jews to withstand the temptations of Christianity. Joseph Hayyun and others went so far as to view it as "God's blessing" that "the tormented people scattered in exile for several years" (after the Expulsion) continue to preserve the Torah, the Talmud, and other commentaries, even adding to them continuously, and obey the commandments. For Jacob ibn Haviv, the fifteenth-century Hebrew poet, grammarian, and moralist from southern Italy, the very existence of the Diaspora reveals the hand of God, since it is a miracle that the Jews continue to exist, scattered, with all their differences, among seventy nations. It is a miracle as great as the parting of the Red Sea. Ibn Haviv is perhaps the only one of his generation to note that "neither our forefathers nor we have tried hard to live in the Holy Land" and that this is a sin. The only compensation for this misfortune is the high quality of religious life and the aspiration to "personal salvation" in the Diaspora.

Looking back, some of the exiles countered their longing for Spain, their shock and hurt, and the sense that they were "like merchandise whose owner abhors it," by reminding themselves of Isaac Abravanel's explanation that the Spaniards "all curse you because you are not of their faith." They argued further that the expulsion of the Jews from Spain was actually proof of the superiority of Judaism, since the kings had instigated the autos-da-fé because they feared that they themselves would lose their religion if they did not rid the country of the Jews.

Joseph ibn Yahya examined the reasons for the Expulsion, and asked why the Jews did not resist. He gave the very realistic answer that it was because the Jews lived in tiny, powerless groups scattered all over Spain, and exercised no vital military or economic function.

In addition to looking back, the exiles also discussed the Muslim lands which had given them refuge, and emphasized how much Turkey had gained from its Jewish refugees. Sultan Bayazid was rewarded by God for his kindness to the Spanish Jews; they taught the Turks all the most advanced European arts of warfare, especially the use of firearms, thanks to which the Turks went on to defeat many nations. It was a source of satisfaction to the exiles to hear that the son of Marco Barberigo, the Doge of Venice in 1485, mocked King Ferdinand of Spain for his stupidity in expelling the Jews and driving them into the arms of his enemies.

HOPES OF REDEMPTION

In the first years after the Expulsion, some exiles entertained hopes of revenge upon the Spanish monarchy. Isaac Abravanel, for example, expressed the messianic hope for a Christian crusade against the Muslims which would end in the downfall of the Christians. Probably he is thinking of Spain. Abraham ben Eliezer Halevi hopefully suggested that the Turkish conquest of Constantinople marked the beginning of God's revenge against Spain, which would be accomplished through the Turks and their conquests in Europe, especially in Italy.

A prophecy arose among the Spanish exiles that the Redemption of the Jews would come about in their own generation, because of their dispersion and suffering. The prophecy was based on Obadiah, v. 20, as Abraham ben Eliezer Halevi tells us in *Ma'amar Mishra' Katrin be Sefer Daniel:*

The exiles in Halah who are of the people of Israel shall possess Phoenicia as far as Zarephath [the term for France in medieval Hebrew literature]; and the exiles of Jerusalem who are in Sepharad [the term for Spain in medieval Hebrew literature] shall possess the cities of the Negeb." For there will be no Jews in Zarephath in their time. And although there were many Jews in France after the Expulsion, they are not French since they were not born in France. But the Jews who are in Sepharad are the Spanish Jews who left Spain, and hence the salvation of the Jews will come through the Spanish Jews, "the exiles of Jerusalem who are in Sepharad.

I.5.15

Abraham Halevi prophesies the Redemption no later than 1530, since after
that date the generation of "the exiles of Jerusalem who are in Sepharad"
would have died out.

Elijah Capsali also viewed the Expulsion as the basis for the redemption
of all the Jews. He justified the then-current prophecy that the Redeemer
of the Jews would come in 1492. Although clearly the Redeemer had not
come, but only the Expulsion, the prophecy had not been false. For the
Expulsion was the beginning of the Ingathering of the Exiles into one place
(the Turkish Empire) which would herald the coming of the Redeemer.

Even more than Capsali, Isaac Abravanel stressed the significance of the
expulsion of the Jews from western Europe and their coming to the Turkish
Empire 'opposite the Holy Land'. The *conversos* fleeing the Inquisition were
also moving closer to the Holy Land. Abravanel explained the expulsions
from England and Portugal as further expressions of the will of Providence.
Even Italy, where some of the exiles settled, was considered to be 'opposite
the Holy Land.'

In this way the Spanish exiles derived comfort from the belief that their
sufferings signaled the end of the Jewish dispersion and the restoration of
the Jews to their holy land. God would reward His faithful for their stead-
fastness in the face of the sufferings of the Expulsion. The Spanish exiles
proudly considered themselves the generation of the Messiah, 'a few people'
willing to go forth into 'the wilderness of the peoples' despite their enormous
fears and doubts.

NOTES

1. A. Castro, *The Structure of Spanish History*, Princeton: Princeton University
Press, 1954, especially Chapter 13.

2. 'Averroism' was a term originally applied to followers of the great Islamic
philosopher and physician Averroes (1126–1198). His commentaries on Aristotle
did much to spread the spirit of rational philosophical examination of religious
belief among Jews and Christians in twelfth- and thirteenth-century Spain. However, from the 1350s to the 1400s, the term came to imply corrosive religious
nihilism and, as such, was an epithet freely applied to the opposing side in religious
and social conflicts within the Spanish Jewish community.

SUGGESTIONS FOR FURTHER READING

Y. Baer. *History of the Jews in Christian Spain*. New York: JTS, 1961, 1966.
Encyclopedia Judaica; see the various entries.
A. Marx. *The Expulsion of the Jews from Spain; Studies in Jewish History and Booklore*.
        New York: JTS, 1944.
B. Netanyahu. *Don Isaac Abrabanel*. Philadelphia: JPS, 1968.
C. Roth. *History of the Marranos*. Philadelphia: JPS, 1932.
G. Scholem. *Major Trends in Jewish Mysticism*. New York: Schocken, 1954.

6

JOSEPH KAPLAN

From Apostasy to Return to Judaism: The Portuguese Jews in Amsterdam

The expulsion of the Jews from Spain and Portugal in 1492–1497 brought to an end the history of the organized Jewish community in the Iberian peninsula. However, the Spanish and Portuguese Jews, both those who converted to Christianity and those who went into exile, continued to express their Jewish identity in various ways. Communities of converted Jews who succeeded in escaping from Spain and Portugal and wished to return to Judaism were established in several countries. The following article studies one of the most important centers of these Jews—Amsterdam, in which a unique Jewish cultural center was established in the seventeenth century.

Joseph Kaplan is a professor of Medieval Jewish History at The Hebrew University of Jerusalem. Most of his articles, as well as a major book, deal with the history of the 'Sephardi Diaspora', the history of the Iberian Jews after their expulsion, and the characteristics of their historical activity and cultural achievements.

BACKGROUND

Most members of the Portuguese Jewish community in seventeenth-century Amsterdam were former crypto-Jews or children of *conversos* who had openly returned to Judaism and committed themselves to observing God's commandments. The experience of their ancestors, who had undergone

---

This article first appeared in Hebrew in *The Jewish Heritage of Spain and the Eastern Mediterranean Lands*, Jerusalem, 1982. The translation/adaptation is by Natan Ginsbury.

The International Center for University Teaching of Jewish Civilization, Jerusalem, the author of the article, and the translator/adapter grant permission to photocopy this article for teaching purposes without further permission or fee.

forced conversion in the Iberian peninsula, and had been compelled to deny their religion and people and accept, outwardly, the beliefs and mores of Christianity, continued to trouble them. After joining the Jewish community in Amsterdam they continued to ponder the experience of forced conversion, its implications, and its religious and historical significance. A sizable number of *conversos* remained in Spain and Portugal throughout the seventeenth century; among them were relatives of crypto-Jews who had emigrated and openly returned to their faith. There was, however, a continual migration of *conversos* from the Iberian peninsula; they returned to Judaism and were integrated within Sephardi Jewish communities in the Diaspora. Thus the painful issue of the crypto-Jews was concrete and immediate.

TYPES OF *CONVERSOS*

Not all *conversos* were of the same ilk. Immediately after the persecutions of 1391, Rabbi Moshe ben Sheshet Barefet (*Rivash*) distinguished between two types. There were *conversos* whose initial apostasy might have been the result of coercion, but who subsequently abandoned all vestiges of Jewish life willingly, followed the gentile laws, and transgressed the precepts of the Torah. They even persecuted the unfortunate Jews among them and denounced them, in order to destroy them as a people so that no vestige would remain of the name of Israel. They also reported to the authorities those *conversos* who secretly remained faithful to Judaism. Other *conversos*, said the Rivash, would willingly and wholeheartedly have given up their apostasy but were unable to do so because they could not afford the expenses involved in getting themselves, their wives, and their children out of the country.[1] This distinction is evidently also true with respect to later generations, even after the Expulsion from Spain in 1492, and the 1497 decree of forced conversion in Portugal, when the problem became even more acute.

Scores of responsa on halakhic issues concerning the crypto-Jews of the Iberian peninsula were written by the rabbis of Spain and of the subsequent Sephardic Diaspora. The historian finds therein much material about the problems of the crypto-Jews, and the attitude of normative Judaism to them. But this literature, rich as it is, cannot fully encompass the attitudes of the rabbis, and it certainly cannot reflect the reactions of the Sephardim to the *converso* issue. In their responsa, the rabbis intended only to define the halakhic position of the crypto-Jews, in order to resolve painful human problems. There were, for example, widows, and wives who had returned to the Jewish community but whose husbands remained within the Christian fold; they had to be freed of any obligation toward their remaining relatives in the Iberian peninsula, so that they could be rehabilitated and enabled to open a new page in their lives.[2] Seventeenth-century responsa mention "crypto-Jews who have forgotten and abandoned the Lord," alongside others "whose spirit the Lord has awakened" and who continue to observe "some precepts" and even "reveal some of the precepts to their children."

Rabbi Saul Levi Morteira (1596–1660) distinguished between two main types of *conversos:* (1) those who live in kingdoms in which they are not only prevented from keeping the Torah, but in which "the gates are locked before them" and they are unable to leave, and (2) those who live in kingdoms which they can leave without delay, to go wherever they wish. Rabbi Morteira also added a third category, namely, those who, although born into the Jewish people, are truly believing Christians. Nonetheless they admit to being Jewish (although they are not), because they fear torture and death at the hands of the Inquisitors, despite the fact that the latter are clearly aware that many people, under duress, make false declarations against their consciences. And therefore the blood of many innocent people has been shed.[3]

Fear of the Inquisition lay heavy on many who had already cut their ties to Judaism. Nonetheless, a systematic perusal of the many items of evidence preserved in the Inquisition's files from Spain and Portugal, and study of the emigration of thousands of crypto-Jews in the sixteenth and seventeenth centuries and their return to Judaism, leaves no doubt that a vast number of *conversos* secretly maintained their connection with Judaism, despite the grave dangers this entailed.

Further material on the departure of crypto-Jews from the Iberian peninsula and their return to Judaism is found in the literature of the Portuguese community in Amsterdam, particularly that written in Spanish and Portuguese. In view of the limitations that have been noted regarding rabbinical responsa literature, the personal and intimate revelations preserved in the writings of members of the Sephardi Diaspora have great historical import. From these writings we learn of the writers' ideological attitude regarding the *converso* issue in all its complexity, and of the deep spiritual conflicts created by that phenomenon.

In his *Carta Apologética* written to Juan de Prado, Isaac Orobio de Castro describes openly and forthrightly his past life as a crypto-Jew.

In Spain I pretended to be a Christian because life is dear; but I never did it well and it was discovered that I was none other than a Jew. And if there, facing the danger [of losing] freedom, honor, property and even life, I was in reality a Jew, and a Christian [only] in outward appearances, is it not right that in a place where Divine Providence has given me a life of freedom I should be a real Jew.

In another work, de Castro refers to his past and that of the crypto-Jews of his circle in Spain, and adds, "We concealed our faith and, although there is no forgiveness for one who conceals the truth or denies it, none of us knew that it was our duty to acknowledge it. . . . "

I.6.3

For many crypto-Jews, the return to Judaism was accompanied by expressions of regret over their Christian past and the way of life that forced conversion had imposed upon them. An emotional expression of the feelings of the returnees to Judaism at that time is found in a sonnet called "De un pecado arrepentido" (From a sinner making repentance), written by Daniel Levi di Barrios:

Not with tears [Lord] will I wipe out the stain / That hides Your holy light from my soul / For my iniquity, my grievous stupidity / I shall feel more if I put not an end to my tears. / I am humble, obedient to You and praise You / And seeking the path to salvation; / In my blindness, I gave myself over to the cruel fate / Of the perversion that enslaved me / . . . . Mercy [Lord], for from myself I flee / And in Your loving-kindness I shall try not to be myself / So as to merit praise and to be Yours.[4]

Feelings of regret over their Christian past did not prevent these Jews from relating to the *conversos* who still remained in the Iberian peninsula as Jews who shared fully in the history, hopes, and aspirations of the nation. In many of their writings the *conversos* are termed 'hijos de Israel' (Children of Israel), 'Israelitas', and 'Judíos', and are clearly considered an integral part of the Jewish people. A question that Isaac Orobio addressed to Rabbi Moses Raphael d'Aguilar reflects his concern for the fate of the crypto-Jew, whom he defines as "a Jew born and educated among the gentiles," in the next world. D'Aguilar states in his reply that the gate of salvation is open to the crypto-Jew, since the sin of those who do not believe in the Torah, but pretend to be believers and keep its precepts, is greater than the sin of those who believe in the Torah but are prevented through their weakness from observing it. Such a one may "deserve the anger of the Lord, but the mercy of the Lord is not denied him." Moreover, d'Aguilar sees the highest level of the love of God expressed by the victims of the Inquisition, the Jews of Spain and Portugal who are burned at the stake solely for their desire to glorify God's Name and prove their love of Him. D'Aguilar defines their death as martyrdom (*kiddush haShem*), and his attitude was shared by the members of his community in Amsterdam. In *Contra la verdad no ay fuerça* (No force can withstand the truth), a drama by Daniel Levi de Barrios (printed in Amsterdam, date unknown), Truth declares, referring to the crypto-Jews of Spain: "Take an example from those who live permanently with God, who died for their love of Me." Jacob Abudiente repeats the same concept in a sermon delivered in memory of Abraham Nuñéz Bernal and Ishac de Almeida, who were burned alive at Inquisition stakes in Cordoba in 1655:

They proved that they were imbued with perfect love of God, as they granted Him the greatest gift that men can give, offering their lives as a sacrifice in honor of His holy Name, thus glorifying God, making known their lineage, and multiplying the merits of the Chosen People.

This deep spiritual attachment to the fate of the crypto-Jews, and the willingness to view them as an inseparable part of the Jewish people, did not mean that the gravity of their daily deeds, when out of necessity they bowed down to 'gods of wood and stone' and pretended to be Christians, was ignored. An anonymous work written in memory of Abraham Nuñéz Bernal states:

But let not an idol-worshipping Jew / Draw from here empty hope / [And think] that he may expect the blessing of God. / If he does not always meticulously maintain / His loyalty to God as you did / He draws away from [the mercies of] Heaven and from his own good. / He who seeks salvation in idols / Denies the commands of wisdom / For he does not abandon vulgar custom.

Isaac Orobio himself, although viewing the crypto-Jews as part of the Jewish people, did not ignore the fact that they were mired in idolatry, the like of which Israel had never known.

Much more stringent is the attitude of Abraham Israel Pereyra (Amsterdam, 1671) who refused to distinguish between the hidden intentions of the crypto-Jews and their overt actions: "As for the erroneous assumption of those who think that it is enough to have good intentions, this is none other than the work of Satan. . . . " With this determination, he comes out against the view of many crypto-Jews that he whose inner feelings are not reflected in outer appearance and who hides his deeds within, out of fear of the gentiles, is exempt from the judgment of Heaven.

The rabbis of seventeenth-century Amsterdam were divided over the punishment in the next world awaiting those crypto-Jews who died without renouncing Christianity and without returning openly to their ancestral faith. One view was expressed by Rabbi Isaac Aboab da Fonseca (1605–1693), a pupil of the kabbalist Rabbi Abraham Cohen de Herrera, who claimed that all Israel is one body and their soul is hewn from the place of God's unity, regarding which it has been said: "All Jews are responsible for each other."[5] Aboab da Fonseca determined that when the sages said that "A Jew who sins remains a Jew" (Babylonian Talmud, Sanhedrin 44a),[6] they meant that even a Jew who sins will not be cut off forever from the tree of the Jewish people, but will remain a Jew; "even if he opts for the new gods instead of the Lord, he will be called a Jew again, through transmigrations and punishments, and everything is according to the righteous law, as we have clarified."

In counterdistinction to Rabbi Aboab da Fonseca, who held that crypto-Jews who did not return to the Torah of the Lord are nonetheless assured a place in the next world after their souls are purified by transmigrations and punishments, Rabbi Saul Levi Morteira claimed that it was "heresy to believe that these thoroughly wicked persons will not receive eternal punishment." He added that "they falsely trust in their salvation, saying, absolute evil will not come to us as we are of the Children of Israel." Morteira argued that the attitude of Rabbi Aboab not only runs counter to the opinion of the early sages and of contemporary scholars, but could also lead the crypto-Jews astray, for they

rest on their laurels in their enemies' lands and daily "float like a cloud, like doves to their cotes" (Isaiah 60:8); for, were they to hear such a thing, none of them would leave, and such has indeed happened, and woe to him who brought this upon them. . . .

Daniel Levi de Barrios, in his poem "Epístola a un mal encaminado" (Letter to one taking crooked paths), without doubt directed at a crypto-Jew who had not yet returned to Judaism, described that group's detachment from both Jewish and Christian society: "In the eyes of one people you are not liked / Because you have distanced yourself from it; / The other does not consider you loyal / Because it has seen you as an imposter." The poet has, therefore, just one piece of advice: "From [this] world you will go victorious if, before the repose of death, you return to the sacred shores. . . . ; Leave the splendid illusions / And then you will surely merit the light of truth / In Jewish heavens. . . . ; Return to the House of God / And with a loving heart. . . . " (The poem was published in Amsterdam in 1683.)

Unceasing efforts to bring the *conversos* back to Judaism were made by Portuguese Jews. In testifying before the Inquisition in Madrid, on May 15, 1635, Esteban de Arias de Fonseca described in detail the ways in which Jews had tried to bring him back to the Jewish religion:

[In Pamplona] he met Miguel Fernández de Fonseca, a Portuguese, then a resident of Bordeaux (who, he had heard, was now living in the kingdom of Spain in the city of Cádiz). They went together to the town of Bordeaux. On the way, and after they had reached the said town, he [Miguel] persuaded him [the witness, Esteban] to abandon the religion of Our Lord Jesus Christ and turn to the religion of Moses, which is the true religion and the one in which he will be saved. In this way and with persuasive words, the above mentioned Fernández de Fonseca, the late Dr. Duarte Henriques, his brother Miguel Gomes Bravo, *licenciado* Diego Barbosa, Miguel Gomes Vitoria, and Manuel de Sira brother of Fernando de Montesinos—all of Bordeaux—persuaded him to be a Jew. When he was about to return to Spain, he asked them to help him on the way but they refused to do so, saying that he should first go to Amsterdam in Holland, where he had relatives who would help him. Then he would be able to go to Spain and he could go as he saw best. They attempted to persuade and convince him to be circumcised before he set out, for should he die while at sea he would not merit salvation unless he were a Jew, and it was good to bear the mark of God. So he went on board ship and reached Amsterdam, nine or ten years ago, and there found some relatives of his. ... They welcomed him with great joy and told him that these were the wonders of God that, in unimaginable ways, bring to Judaism those living in the blindness of the Christian religion. They immediately began to deal with him in order to make him a Jew and circumcise him because [they said] he was the son of a mother of Israelite extraction. When he saw this, he did not want to be circumcised and did not want to be Jewish, and they brought him to a certain rabbi, called Morteira, an expounder of the Mosaic Law, who sought to persuade him to uphold [that religion]. When he had spent over six months with him and they realized they were unable to persuade him, they imposed a ban on him in the synagogues that no Jew should come into contact with him nor talk with him. Having been so for 15 or 16 days, without anyone talking to him or helping him, he went [to them] and agreed that they circumcise him, and when they did so, they gave him the name of David. The person who performed the circumcision was Ishak Farque, a ritual circumciser whose other name is Antonio de Aguiar, whom the witness had seen eight days previously in Madrid. He had only come here to perform circumcisions, as in other places in Spain, because he was the best expert for circumcision, and made much money in this occupation for which he was well paid. . . .[7]

It is dubious whether we can rely on all the details of the above testimony, as this *converso* was speaking after he had willingly returned to Spain and wished to purify himself and present his Judaization in Amsterdam as an act forced upon him contrary to his wishes. But there is no doubt that we can learn from his testimony about the collective efforts to bring errants back to the Mosaic law, made by the Portuguese community in Amsterdam and even by *converso* congregations in southern France who had not yet returned openly to Judaism. It is evident that the Portuguese Jewish community attributed great importance to the circumcision of *conversos*, viewing it on the one hand as a sign of the honesty of the individual's intention to return to the Jewish religion and, on the other hand, as a means for preventing his return to the 'lands of idolatry' where discovery of his circumcision could endanger his life. It is also evident that circumcizers were sent to Spain itself to bring *conversos* into the covenant of Abraham, despite the dangers involved.

THE 'NEW CHRISTIANS'

A considerable portion of the literary works of Amsterdam Jews was designed to serve the community effort to bring 'New Christians' back to the Jewish Law. Various works of apologetica, allegedly intended to counter the claims of Christianity against Judaism, were directed at the New Christian community, in particular those who had left Spain but preferred to continue living as Catholics in southern France or in Antwerp, far from the threat of the Inquisition. Rabbi Moses Raphael d'Aguilar addressed the New

Christians of Bayonne emotionally: "Flee, flee in haste from this Babylon and come, find a remedy for your salvation, for it depends only upon you and you are able to do it."

Isaac Orobio had, as noted, claimed that "he had pretended to be a Christian because life is dear"; Abraham Israel Pereyra, on the other hand, refused to justify crypto-Jews remaining in the Iberian peninsula for reasons of economic and social convenience:

Let us not be so cruel and, because of some small matter of property that is not of permanent value, or out of fear for its loss, jeopardize what is essential. A man must give everything that he has for [the salvation of] his soul, as the king of Sodom, although an idolater, said: "Give me the persons and take the possessions for yourself" (Genesis 14:21). We tend to turn things round and say to our enemies: Take the persons and give us the goods. The reason why some remain in those places does not, we know, derive from any absence of true good will, but from an inability to understand [the gravity of] the obligation imposed upon them. . . .

Pereyra was grieved by those of his congregation who left the haven of refuge after they had already returned to the Jewish community and been educated in Judaism, and had gone "to search for a better life in idolatry." This phenomenon, which at certain times reached considerable proportions, concerned the leaders of the Portuguese congregation. In 1644 a regulation was passed that required all members of the congregation who came back to Amsterdam after having left for the 'lands of idolatry' to stand before the Ark in the synagogue and ask forgiveness *coram populo,* and forbade them from serving in any public office in the congregation for the first four years after their return.[8]

The attitude of Portuguese Jews in Amsterdam to the *conversos* was, without doubt, ambivalent. On the one hand, they had no doubt that they were part and parcel of the Jewish people, and even accorded those burned at the Inquisition stake a place alongside the martyrs of Israel of all generations. On the other hand, they were not prepared to make peace with the fact that crypto-Jews remained in the Iberian peninsula or in other places where they could not openly return to Judaism; and they refused to find any justification for those who lived in the 'lands of idolatry' and persisted in idolatrous Christian worship.

Not even the escapees from the Iberian peninsula who joined the Jewish community could erase the stain of their past with a wave of the hand; only through "profound repentance," wrote Abraham Israel Pereyra, "will I escape from the falsehoods into which I sank."

But woe is me! They are so impressed on my being . . . that I can with difficulty free myself of the distorted opinions in which I was instructed. . . . Make use of wisdom and will-power, and if you have already managed to flee from the danger of the Inquisition and have come to worship the Lord, shake yourself free of weakness [of the mind], for it will sentence you not to a prison term of four years, but to hundreds of years of punishments and tortures, the harshest of which will be the Lord's concealing His face from you.

Repentance annuls the evil decree. It is incumbent upon the *converso* who returns to the bosom of Torah to make full repentance and to view this as the purpose of his life. It is reasonable to assume that the great repentance movement that swept the Amsterdam Portuguese community in 1665, at the time of the Sabbatean ferment, had its roots in the efforts of former crypto-Jews to atone for their sins dating from the time when they had lived as Christians.

The literary works of these Jews also express a particular understanding of the place and mission of the crypto-Jews in Jewish history. Isaac Orobio, in refuting the Christians' claims that God had rejected the Jewish people because of their refusal to accept the gospel of Jesus, raises a counter-argument:

It is possibly because such a large number of members of this people have broken the covenant they made with God and have accepted Papal Christianity, that they [the Jews] suffer this lengthy exile. For innumerable Jewish families have joined the Papal Church over the generations, and one cannot find a monastery in Spain without descendants of Jews among the priesthood. Even the inquisitors themselves all originate from or are associated with this people, and so it is with most of the families in Portugal, many in France, and innumerable families in Italy. . . . As long as so many sons of the Jewish people continue with this idolatry, the people will suffer the exigencies of exile. And since, to this very day, there are so many Jews who worship the vile and impure abominations of Christian idolatry and keep its loathsome customs, who would dare to claim that this people is not deserving of all the suffering that weighs upon it or is not totally responsible for this continuing sin?

Orobio's words were, without doubt, directed primarily at the *conversos* of the Iberian peninsula who served as a symbol of the continued existence of idolatry on the part of Jews. Nor was Orobio the only one to hold this view. It can be found in the writings of a number of members of his congregation who, like Orobio, viewed the existence of *conversos* as fulfillment of the curse "... and you shall serve other gods, of wood and stone" (Deuteronomy 28:36). In commenting on this verse, Rabbi Isaac Aboab da Fonseca wrote:

"The Lord will drive you and the king you have set over you, to a nation unknown to you or your fathers ..." (Deuteronomy 28:36); this is what happened at the time of the First Temple. " ... and you shall serve other gods, of wood and stone"; this is what experience teaches in the lands of Spain and elsewhere.

I.6.9

Rabbi Isaac Naar also referred to this prophecy in his commentary on Isaiah 53:

...many of the seed of Israel can today be found under the rule of tyrannical princes; they worship idols in a way that is worthy only for God; and in them is the prophecy fulfilled: "And the Lord will scatter you among all peoples, from one end of the earth to the other, and there you shall serve other gods, wood and stone, whom neither you nor your ancestors have experienced" (Deuteronomy 28:64).

On the connection between this malediction and the existence of crypto-Jews, de Barrios is even more explicit:

The book of Deuteronomy describes the atrocities that will befall Israel at the ends of the Spanish world, from which they were expelled to many parts of the world at different times, from the days of King Pyrrhus who brought them in captivity to the border of the land, to the city and district of Asta, today called Jerez, which was then at the border of the land; "And the Lord will scatter you amongst the peoples, etc." And even though outwardly they [the crypto-Jews] worship idols, they live in constant fear and trepidation of the cruel Inquisition....[9]

In another essay, de Barrios added:

Those who have acknowledged that they have moved towards the Lord are the ones who regret their idolatry, proclaim the unity of God, and die as martyrs. In Deuteronomy 28:65–67 the atrocities, fears, terrors and disappointments that befell those who turned to Judaism in the terrible autos-da-fé in Castile and Portugal are prophesied: "And even among those nations you shall find no peace, nor shall your foot find a place to rest. . . . In the morning, you shall say: If only it were evening! And in the evening, you shall say: If only it were morning!—because of things which your heart shall dread but your eyes shall see." There, among the *familiares* [of the Inquisition], the terrified sons of Moses bend the knee in mock ceremonies before the idols, and with deep pain search for the true God who justly punishes them with forced idolatry in a strange land, because they willingly worshipped idols in their land . . . "wood and stone" refers to the cross. "They sacrificed to demons, no-gods, gods they had never known, new ones who came but lately, and stirred not your fathers' fears" (Deuteronomy 32:17). The demons are none other than the *familiares*, for this name was given to the demons who stab the souls of Jews with olive leaf and sword [the symbol of the Inquisition], and those who are taken to the terrible prisons confess and betray others so that they, too, will fall, as it is said in the fourth (sic!) Book of the Torah: " . . . the sound of a driven leaf shall put them to flight. Fleeing as though from the sword they shall fall though none pursues. With no one pursuing, they shall stumble over one another as before the sword, when none pursues. You shall not be able to stand your ground before your enemies, but shall perish among the nations; and the land of your enemies shall consume you" (Leviticus 26: 36–38).

I.6.10

The lost ones [from the Hebrew root: *a-b-d*] are none other than those who pretend to follow the law of the Church, for in the Holy Tongue that is the meaning of 'Abad' (Spanish for Abbot). And 'Abads' are the priests and the Land of Spain that devours the Jews, for anyone there who turns to Judaism is called a criminal, and those of the sons of Moses who have remained in Portugal are termed 'New Christians'. They are tortured until they admit their sins and those of their fathers; but this is only lip service, for in their hearts they continue to be loyal to Judaism. And thus the Holy King warned them: "Those of you who survive shall be heartsick over their iniquity in the land of your enemies; more, they shall be heartsick over the iniquities of their fathers; and they shall confess their iniquity, and the iniquity of their fathers, in that they trespassed against Me, yea, were hostile to Me" (Leviticus 26:39–40). "... then at last shall their obdurate heart humble itself" (Leviticus 26:41). And in the lands whence they go from Portugal they manage to keep the Law of Moses openly, which the cruel inquisitors term an iniquity. But this is the iniquity that the Children of Israel most desire, as prophesied in the Book of Leviticus: "And then they shall desire their iniquity."

Confirmation of the view that the prophets of Israel in antiquity had spoken about the existence and persecution of the *conversos* was found in Isaiah. On the verse: "He was maltreated, yet he was submissive; he did not open his mouth...." (Isaiah 53:7), Rabbi Isaac Naar expounded: "... no one who is familiar with the sorry condition of our people who can say no word against its oppressors, particularly those who are under the hand of the Inquisition, could find any difficulty with our interpretation." And about the verse "And his grave was set among the wicked" (53:9), Rabbi Moses Raphael d'Aguilar said:

The grave of the wicked refers only to the grave of those who were slaughtered over many generations by the courts of the Inquisition for, after their bodies turned to ashes, they are proclaimed contemptibles, lacking all titles, rights and honors, and are sentenced by public proclamations as heretics and sectarians before a large crowd that gathers to hear it.

Abraham Michael Cardoso held that the Messiah will be forced against his will to abandon the Torah and, by this punishment, will atone for the sins of all Israel. Gershom Scholem has pointed out that underlying this determination was Cardoso's desire to give life under coercion a religious and messianic significance. A similar intention can also be discerned in the commentaries and sermons of the Amsterdam scholars. However, contrary to Cardoso, who held that "the principal secret is that we are all bidden by the Torah to be crypto-Jews before we can leave the Exile," they viewed the *conversos* of the Iberian peninsula as experiencing the prophecy of reproof, with the words of the verse "and you shall serve other gods, of wood and stone" (Deuteronomy 28:36) being realized on their persons. Against their will, the *conversos* become emissaries on behalf of the entire Jewish people, carrying out 'a religious act achieved through a wrongful deed', without which the Redemption cannot come to pass. Their return to Judaism was interpreted as an omen and sign of the beginning of the redemption process. The words of the prophet: "... but do not profane My holy name any more with your idolatrous gifts" (Ezekiel 20:39) came to pass in the form of the crypto-Jews who left Spain and joined the Jewish community. R. Isaac Naar commented on this verse: "Until the prophecy of Ezekiel is realized, not through our merit but through the merit of the Name of God that is profaned in the sight of the nations; the time He has chosen in His holy legislation will come—and then we shall leave the long exile."

ATTITUDES OF THE RETURNEES TO JUDAISM

In 1698, Mosseh Zurreño delivered a sermon in the Rotterdam synagogue, before leaving for Palestine. In it he thanked Divine Providence for having saved him from the idolatry into which he had sunk in the Iberian peninsula, "and for having set me among the pious and the righteous." He solemnly declared, "... I have not missed my parents, for every Jew has been a father to me." Zurreño, a crypto-Jew who had been welcomed into the Portuguese Jewish community in Holland, viewed the act of return as a complete break with his Christian past. Similarly, the poet Daniel Levi de Barrios declared in an emotional confession that since returning to Judaism he felt himself a different person (*estoy en otro convertido*).

We have learned some interesting details regarding the way in which Abraham Israel Pereyra returned to Judaism. Rabbi Moses Raphael d'Aguilar wrote about him:

The esteemed gentleman arrived from Spain with only such simple and hazy information about the veracity of our holy Torah that those lands make obtainable. He came here, where [Torah] can be upheld and taught in adequate freedom, but [he came] at an adult age, when the study of the holy tongue was difficult and wearying for him. Nonetheless, since piety is part of his inner nature, he began first of all to participate consistently in academies of learning, to listen attentively to the words of Torah spoken there, and to learn from the books of faith; and so he accumulated a priceless treasure of holy wisdom.... But this kindly man did not make do with acquiring knowledge himself, and tried to involve others in his devout learning, because 'it is not good for man to be alone', to which end he abandoned the affairs of this world, gave up worthless conversation, and devoted himself to the inner life and a life of reflection.

In his essays, Pereyra proposed the path that he felt a crypto-Jew returning to Judaism should take:

When you leave the synagogue and come to your house, you must take a copy of the Bible and read it ... and, when studying, give it all your attention, not

I.6.12

reading without it. . . . Note every difficulty and ask about it, fixing for yourself a specific time at one of the academies of learning, for this is the true remedy and through it will you learn, by presenting your doubts . . . and listening to the learned answers. Thus, at the set time, you will heal your soul . . . and in this way you will benefit from the constancy and attention that you devote to study of the Torah and to the reading of other books. . . . It was in this way that I myself studied at the Torat Or Yeshivah at the feet of our faithful shepherd, the noble gentleman, the scholar, Rabbi Isaac Aboab, and enjoyed his teachings and the sweet company of the other gentlemen and colleagues. . . .

Not all those who returned to Judaism were able to detach themselves easily from the burden of the past, nor did all of them burn their bridges to the Spanish Catholic world on which they had turned their backs. In reality, matters were much more complicated than appears from the words of the above authors. The break with the past involved supreme efforts, and demanded many sacrifices that not all were prepared to make. Quite a few stumbled on the path of their return to their ancestral faith, and there were some who collapsed under the burden of the precepts that they found difficult to bear. Uriel da Costa complained about the 'fences' that the sages had placed around the Torah. He held that they were "certainly not good, as they could easily mislead people regarding intention, which is the principal element in guilt." In da Costa's estimation, the restrictions had become a law in their own right, more stringent than the Torah of Moses "and almost impossible to keep."[10]

Isaac Orobio, a philosopher and physician, viewed the crypto-Jews "who leave idolatry and move to districts where Judaism is granted freedom," as "sick with ignorance," an illness which only contact with Judaism, the "sacred medicine," could cure. Abraham Israel Pereyra frankly described the mental crises he had gone through since moving to Amsterdam and openly embracing the Torah of Moses:

Only with difficulty could I shake free of the distorted opinions I had been taught, for it is hard to be cut off from the roots . . . since I was well-versed in secular writings, I considered myself (what ignorance!) wiser than the scholars of the Torah . . . and when I used to talk about them, I undervalued them. Since my desire then inclined to the pleasures of life I purposely presented arguments intended to confuse sincerity.

The crypto-Jews who fled from the Iberian peninsula lacked a basic Jewish education. What information they had was drawn mainly from secondary and often hostile sources, such as the anti-Jewish literature that was rather widespread throughout the area in the sixteenth and seventeenth centuries. The returnees' absorption into Jewish society was made even more difficult because of the cultural baggage they brought with them from Spain and Portugal, and the Catholic concepts that many had internalized as part as their education in the most orthodox and zealous church institutions of the Catholic world.[11]

Isaac Orobio considered the university education acquired by some of the *conversos* who returned to Judaism to be the main obstacle preventing their acceptance of the yoke of the Torah and its precepts. Abraham Michael Cardoso, a *converso* who returned to Judaism, also came out bitterly against those whose philosophical and scientific education led them to reject the authority of the sages and doubt the truth of the Torah. This generalization expressed by Orobio and Cardozo was, however, exaggerated and inaccurate. Not all of the returnees who had received a university education in Spain and Portugal rejected the discipline of the halakhah or tried to undermine the authority of rabbinic leadership.

The case of Isaac Orobio, a student at the School of Theology at Alcalá de Henares University, provided proof positive that education at a Catholic university did not inevitably prevent identification with the world of Jewish ideas and beliefs or acceptance of the precepts of the Torah. On the other hand, there is no doubt that Orobio discerned the dangers latent in the intellectual and value content of the education received by the crypto-Jews in their countries of origin. He realized that part of Juan de Prado's reservations about Judaism and the rabbinic tradition had their roots in his friend's educational background. He even sensed that seeds of the same heresy could be latent in him, and that he had to make great efforts not to fail as had his former friend. His writings, such as a letter to Prado, reveal the doubts that visited him after his meeting with the world of Judaism in Amsterdam: "The truth is that many customs, responsa, and rulings that do not themselves touch on the Torah of the Lord, do not sit well with my intelligence which rejects them." He also knew of customs generally followed in different Jewish communities, that had never been approved by Jewish scholars nor accepted by most Jewish communities. Orobio never concealed his perplexity in the face of the world of the precepts that was revealed to him in all its stringency; he found the solution to his difficulties among the 'believing agnostics' whose theoretical concepts he had internalized during the days spent within the portals of the universities of Alcalá and Toulouse. If, in matters of belief, only the divine decree is the determinant, for human reason is restricted by its very nature, then there is no value to questions that the intelligence raises with respect to the religious tradition. Orobio writes in his *Carta Apologética:*

What, then, does it matter that this or that restriction appears not to fit in with our understanding? What does it matter that we do not understand the prohibition against eating milk foods with poultry?.... Should we [because of our lack of understanding] profane the Sabbath? Or eat our fill on the Day of Atonement? Or eat blood?.... Whoever loves [the Torah], believes in it and fears God, will not look for excuses to abandon it.

I.6.14

The Torah does not have commandments that run counter to natural law: It does not command "the eating of children, or murder and theft, but imposes the doing of holy and essential things, or others that have no special significance (*indiferentes*)." But the Torah does encourage discipline and humility. According to Orobio, that which is incomprehensible in the Torah cannot lead him to break its precepts, and "it is not wise to disturb the quiet of others with these doubts and encourage them to have thoughts" that could lead to a profanation of the Torah's holiness. Human intelligence cannot determine matters of faith; thus there is a vital need to find some factor having the ability and authority to lead the believing public. Orobio accepts the authority of Jewish scholars of all generations: "It is necessary that at all times the law be taught to the people by scholars who have gone into its meaning in depth, as did the priests, judges, and prophets of old, for no one is familiar with the law from birth." Whoever holds that the scholars, whom Divine Providence has delegated to instruct the people in the laws, deceive and mislead the people, casts doubts on God Himself, since "God has not in the course of hundreds of years used another means for expounding His Torah, and the people accept their teaching as the words of truth."

When refuting Christian charges against the Talmud, Orobio noted in his *Epístola Invectiva* that, in addition to "sublime doctrines and sacred counsel," the Talmud also contains opinions that are not worth accepting and that "were never accepted by the entire Jewish people." The worth of the Talmud is not hurt thereby; the Talmud is neither the Torah of the Lord, nor a creation of God. It is the work of mortal man and, although it contains no errors with respect to the holy precepts and the "oral tradition that the sages received from their forefathers at the time of Moses," it does contain errors in interpretations and in personal opinions. The sages of the Talmud were able to err,

just as Plato, Aristotle and other great philosophers of those centuries erred; Seneca expressed many falsehoods, as did Pliny and other great scholars. Why, then, should the talmudic scholars not have made erroneous judgments on those matters that were basically conceptual, philosophical, or theological, rather than legal?

Orobio did not have to agree with this or that opinion quoted in the Talmud or in the name of any one of the sages; all of this belonged to the world of opinion and in no way prejudiced the sanctity of the Torah and performance of its precepts: "Why should it matter if Ramban and fifty sons of Uziel mouthed more nonsense than the number of hours in the days of the year?" Isaac Orobio put these deliberations and thoughts into writing during his first years in Amsterdam; these were also the first years in which he lived an openly Jewish life in a Jewish context.

It is instructive to compare Orobio's stance with the reservations of Uriel da Costa, formulated in 1616, as that author took his first steps in the Jewish community. In *Reservations on the Jewish Tradition*, da Costa referred to opinions prevalent among Jews that were "unworthy of acceptance by those who are called Israel, and were fit for the nations of the world and then not for all of them but only the foolish among them."[12] Like Orobio, who considered the Greek philosophers to be a reference group from whom it was legitimate to argue by analogy about the sages of the Talmud, da Costa utilized "the books of the peoples" and "the laws of the nations" to draw conclusions about the world of the sages. But while Orobio distinguished between Jewish precepts and laws, and opinions and hypotheses within Judaism, and considered the former to be binding and unchallengeable by the flaws in the latter, da Costa found flaws and distortions in the precepts and laws of Judaism that were rooted in the misinterpretations bequeathed by the rabbinic sages, and "that are also contradictory to higher ethics."

While da Costa denied the authority of the rabbinic leadership and demanded changes in the religious way of life and the fashion in which the precepts were observed, Orobio openly identified with the oral law and rabbinic rulings. He defended the restrictions, holding that they were intended only to enable more complete performance of the precepts, and were not drawn up—as da Costa argued—solely to make the laws more stringent. Other peoples also had restrictions of this sort, and their whole purpose was to prevent unethical conduct on the part of man. As to the claim that some of the restrictions were not connected with the precepts of the Torah but had been added in the wake of historical events, such as the laws of certain festivals and fast days, Orobio replied that "these are not restrictions but sacred customs and praiseworthy mores, to honor and glorify the Creator."

Yehudah Aryeh (Leone) Modena (1571–1648), in his replies to da Costa's criticism, insisted that "an important basis of the divine purpose of the Torah is that we should all observe every part of its minutiae in the same fashion, and not one this bit and another that bit, for otherwise Israel would not be one people." In 1663, Orobio, who had just joined the Jewish community, expressed identical arguments. In his opinion, the *republic* must ensure that the festivals and days of mourning shared by the whole nation not be observed differently and separately by its sons. Uniformity in observance of religious precepts not only teaches the supremacy of Judaism over segmented and divided Christianity, but points to God's care for His people. Anyone who rejects a law, restriction, or regulation laid down by the sages casts doubt on God who, in His wisdom, inspired them to bequeath the Torah to Israel and to safeguard its observance in a uniform manner in all the countries of the dispersion.

It is patently clear that Orobio unreservedly accepted the authority of the law and of rabbinic leadership. Nonetheless one reads between the lines his perplexity in the face of those beliefs and opinions of Judaism which did not harmonize with the philosophical and theological concepts that remained part of his inner world even after he had joined the Jewish community. We are unable to learn from Orobio's writings which "erroneous statements" of the talmudic sages aroused his opposition.

It may be assumed that his attitude did not provoke any objection or resentment on the part of the rabbinic leadership, which viewed his criticisms in the spirit of Yehudah Aryeh Modena. The latter, in the first quarter of the seventeenth century, came to the defense of the physician David Farar, a crypto-Jew who had returned to Judaism in Amsterdam where he was suspected of sectarianism: "And what if he interprets one of the sayings of the sages that is unacceptable in its literal sense, or interprets the Scriptures in a way that differs from that of Rashi and the early commentators of blessed memory; is that not the way of every casual reader and preacher?" It appears that similar criticisms were common among some members of the educated class of the Portuguese community in Amsterdam, such as the physicians David Farar at the beginning of the century and Isaac Orobio in its latter part. The rabbinic leadership was not stringent with them and ignored their critique as long as they did not express reservations about performance of the precepts. David Farar aroused the admiration of Rabbi Yehuda Aryeh Modena[13] who noted that he

has laid phylacteries and fringes almost the whole day and has not imbibed wine and strong drink of theirs [non-Jews] since he came under the shelter of the Lord, and he is stricter with himself over rabbinic injunctions than many of those who were circumcised on the eighth day [i.e., born Jews]; and Torah teachers in our provinces have been lenient with them.

It may be assumed that Orobio's way of life did not differ from that of Farar in this sense. At various opportunities, Orobio repeatedly emphasized the importance of deed, that is, performing the precepts of Judaism,

for to expound the Torah skillfully, to compare moral issues with vigor, to term the precepts not once but many times 'holy matters', without keeping them, without fulfilling them, without upholding them literally, is to act explicitly against the desire of the Lawmaker who did not command that we expound them but that we learn them in order to keep them.

In fact Orobio held that Judaism's roots in Torah and in the practical commandments made it superior to Christianity, which he described as a religion of dogmas and doctrines.

CONCLUSION

In summation, it is clear that the Spanish Catholic cultural background of some of the *conversos* who fled from the Iberian peninsula did form an obstacle of sorts to their joining Jewry. In addition, quite a few of them recoiled from the world of halakhah, which they perceived as "almost impossible to observe." At the same time, however, it may be said that the educational and value concepts brought by one group of crypto-Jews from the Iberian world helped them accept the authority of the halakhah and of Jewish spiritual leadership. The 'believing scepticism' with which they had been acquainted from their life in Catholic countries prepared some of them to respond positively to congregational discipline and rabbinic leadership. For these *conversos*, a Jewish way of life with its practical precepts constituted a way to achieve religious certainty in a world subject to a crisis of faith that undermined values.

NOTES

1. B. Netanyahu, *The Marranos of Spain from the Late Fourteenth to the Early Sixteenth Century*, New York: American Academy for Jewish Research, 1966, pp. 29ff.

2. Y. H. Yerushalmi takes issue with Netanyahu (above n.1). See *From Spanish Court to Italian Ghetto. Isaac Cardoso, A Study in Seventeenth-Century Marranism and Jewish Apologetics*, New York: Columbia University Press, 1971, pp. 24–31. Also A. A. Sicroff, "The Marranos—Forced Converts or Apostates," *Midstream*, October 1966, pp. 71–75.

3. According to Rabbi Morteira only the first of the three categories of Marranos would merit salvation, since they are unable to leave 'the lands of idolatry'. This is so only thanks to the mercy of God who makes allowances for man's weakness, since He knows that their souls are willing to worship Him. The second category is doomed to eternal disgrace, not because they have abandoned Judaism but because they remain in their country despite the fact that no one prevents their departure.

4. The poem first appeared in Brussels, in 1665.

5. See the critical version of *Sefer Nishmat Haim*, published by A. Altmann, "Eternality Of Punishment: A Theological Controversy within the Amsterdam Rabbinate in the Thirties of the Seventeenth Century," *PAAJR* 40 (1972): 1–88.

6. For the changing halakhic meaning of this statement, see J. Katz, "A Jew although he sins remains a Jew," *Tarbiz* 27 (1958): 203–217 [Hebrew].

7. This testimony appears in the file of the trial of Francisco Mendes Britto, the son of Jorge Rodrigues de Acosta, Canciller de la Santa Cruzada, inhabitant of Madrid; National Historical Archives, Madrid, Inquisition file Toledo 142 No. 6, fol. 39r–42v. The trial was held between the years 1653 and 1657. Mendes Britto was tortured and sentenced to burning at the stake. The quotation is taken from a Hebrew translation prepared by H. Beinart.

8. *Livros dos Acordos*, *1*, of the Talmud Torah Congregation, in the Amsterdam Municipal Archives, PA 334, No. 19, p. 172.

9. Salomon Ibn Verga mentions this legend regarding the antiquity of Jewish settlement in Spain, in *Shevet Yehuda*: "And Pyrrhus took ships and transported all his captives to old Spain, that is Andalucia, and to the city of Toledo, from

where they dispersed, for they were many in number and the land could not support them, and some of the royal offspring went to Sevilla and from there to Granada." What he says is based on the words of Isaac Abravanel at the end of his commentary to the biblical Book of Kings. The town of Asta was established by the Romans (*Diccionario Geográfico de España*, V. Madrid: 1958, p. 577). However, Spanish chronicles describing the beginnings of Jewish settlement do not mention a Jewish community there.

10. See Uriel da Costa, "Reservations on the Jewish Tradition," in C. Gebhardt, *Die Schriften des Uriel da Costa*, Heidelberg: C. Winter, 1922, p. 9.

11. For information about the Jewish education of crypto-Jews in the Iberian peninsula in the seventeenth century, see H. Beinart, "The Converso Community in 16th and 17th Century Spain," in R.D. Barnett, (ed.), *The Sephardi Heritage*, 1. London: Vallentine Mitchell, 1971, pp. 465ff. Also Y.H. Yerushalmi, "Marranos who return to Judaism in the 17th Century: Their Jewish Education and Spiritual Preparation, *Proceedings of the Fifth World Conference of Jewish Studies*, B. Jerusalem: 1962, pp. 201–209 [Hebrew].

12. See note 10, above.

13. It has been suggested that Farar and da Costa belonged to the same circle, and had come to Venice to debate matters of faith there with R. Emanuel Aboab; see I. Sonne, "Da Costa Studies," *JQR* 22 (1932): 247ff; and idem, "Leon Modena and the da Costa Circle in Amsterdam," *HUCA* 21 (1948): 1–28. This assumption seems unlikely to the author. Rabbi Yehudah Aryeh Modena knew Farar and da Costa at first hand and, while he related to the former with open esteem, finding no fault in his loyalty to Judaism, he termed the latter "a sectarian and complete unbeliever, impudently speaking against the words of our sages of blessed memory."

7

JACOB KATZ

The Dispute between Jacob Berab and Levi ben Habib over Renewing Ordination

One of the most unusual groups of Jewish scholars and thinkers, whose mark is evident on Jewish culture to this day, emerged in the sixteenth century in the small town of Safed in the Upper Galilee. The most important halakhic work of modern Judaism, the Shulhan Arukh, *was written there by Rabbi Joseph Caro, and Jewish mysticism was revolutionized by Isaac Luria in the same town and the same period. But prior to these achievements, an unusual phenomenon occurred which was to color the atmosphere in Safed in the decades to come and have a mark on its culture: an attempt to resurrect the traditional rabbinic ordination,* semikhah, *which, it was believed, would be renewed in messianic times. The following article, which is still regarded as a classic nearly forty years after its first publication, presents the first comprehensive historical study of this significant event.*

Joseph Katz is professor emeritus of Jewish History and Sociology at The Hebrew University of Jerusalem. He is one of the leading historians of modern and medieval Jewish history, and has served as a Rector of the Hebrew University. Many of his books have appeared in English, including studies of the relationship between Jews and non-Jews in the Middle Ages and modern times.

This article was first published in Hebrew in *Zion* 16 (1951), and appeared in a revised version in Katz's collection of historical studies, *Between Halakhah and Kabbalah*, Jerusalem: 1985 (Hebrew). The translation/adaptation is by Roberta Bell-Kligler.

The International Center for University Teaching of Jewish Civilization, Jerusalem, the author of the article, and the translator/adapter grant permission to photocopy this article for teaching purposes without further permission or fee.

STATUS OF RESEARCH

The most complete description of Jacob Berab's attempt in the sixteenth century to revive the institution of rabbinic ordination (*semikhah*) and the ensuing dispute with Levi ben Habib was provided by the Jewish historian Heinrich Graetz (1817–1891). His prodigious *History of the Jews* (1887, published originally in German) was the first comprehensive attempt to record their history as a living people from a Jewish point of view. It is a monumental work, and Graetz's description of this particular episode epitomizes all the elements—both good and bad—of his scholarship. Graetz's treatment of the controversy over rabbinic ordination appears in the sixth volume of the English version of his work (1949). The events are viewed against the general background of the period, and the details are meticulously collected and incorporated into a flowing, suspenseful story. However, there is, as well, excessive emphasis on personality-related causes, criticism and praise meted out according to preconceived biases, and, worst of all, a judgment that ignores the motivations of the two disputants.

Graetz discerns messianic tendencies in this attempt to revive the institution of rabbinic ordination, and shows the connection between this particular incident and the various contemporaneous messianic movements. He also touches on the desire of the Spanish exiles to find absolution through punishment by an 'ordained court' (*bet din shel smukhim*) whose authority would be like that of the ancient Sanhedrin, namely, to mete out corporal punishment. Graetz attributes the actual eruption of the controversy, however, to personal motives: Jacob Berab's quest for status and ben Habib's sense of insult. Graetz's intense personal opinions almost led him astray in his attempt to appraise the incident and the involved parties.

On its own, Berab's tendency toward messianism would have incurred Graetz's censure, for the historian was unequivocally antimystical, viewing such trends in Judaism as malignant growths. However, he considers the benefits that might have been derived from a central institution for the dispersed Jews as a result of the renewal of rabbinic ordination; thus he looks positively on the attempt and upon its initiator, and chastises ben Habib for not rising above his humiliation for the sake of the positive results of renewed ordination. This consideration, however, did not even surface during the actual debate. Graetz states that ben Habib's detailed and adamant halakhic rationalizations against ordination were mere verbal cover-up for his own personal leanings, for in actuality the rabbinic and talmudic literature with which he supported his argument contains "such a mix of opinions that one could argue that it supports both the pro and con of any given issue."

Scholars who have dealt with this dispute after Graetz have added almost nothing new to its consideration. A not unfair analysis of Simon Dubnow's (1860–1941) treatment of the issue is that he dismissed every aspect of

Graetz's description that was based on sources, and upheld the factor that was a figment of his predecessor's imagination, namely, the realistic goal of establishing a central institution for Judaism. Other historians emphasized a variety of factors that Graetz had considered, without adding substantially to our understanding of the dispute.

The issue of renewing ordination again came to the fore during the era of Jewish national reawakening in the early part of the twentieth century. Halakhists and writers suggested it as a way to establish for the Jews in Palestine a central authority bearing the title and status of the Sanhedrin. These deliberations were, in a sense, a continuation of the dispute between Berab and ben Habib. While the historical material served as the basis for these modern discussions, the facts were subsumed within categories of halakhic thought; they were even given a tendentious interpretation and reworked to fit the necessary halakhic goals. This process is not unknown in other areas of Jewish historical research; halakhic debate and historical study are conducted on separate planes, and those involved in the undertaking do not understand each other or contribute to the other's understanding. The truth of the matter is that public differences of opinion regarding halakhah will not be understood unless we succeed in forging an integrated outlook, incorporating both halakhic and historical approaches.

Before discussing the extant sources that shed light on this intriguing chapter in sixteenth-century Jewish history, we must briefly review the background against which they were produced, and provide a few sentences of introduction to the personalities who wrote them.

The Land of Israel in the sixteenth century was a mixture of poverty and wealth, anticipation and despair. Jews arrived in the aftermath of the infamous Spanish Expulsion (1492) with fresh and painful memories of inquisitions, forced conversions, and torture. Among them were many scholars who kept Jewish learning and religion alive. A major trend that concerned many of them at this time was mysticism with its intensely messianic fervor—a phenomenon that was despised by Graetz.

Jacob Berab (ca. 1474–1546) was born in Spain, but following the Expulsion he traveled extensively, teaching Judaism and engaging in business. From age 18, when he was appointed rabbi of Fez, he was considered very knowledgeable; he was well respected, although his domineering personality and superiority complex led to many conflicts. Berab settled in Safed about 1524 and became involved in its messianic fervor. In 1538 he took the initiative of renewing the institution of rabbinic ordination which had not existed for hundreds of years, and convinced other Safed rabbis of stature to support his effort. Berab became the first ordainee (*samukh*), with the intention of ordaining others.

Levi ben Habib (1483–1543), known as the *RaLBaH*, also settled in Israel, via Salonika, after being expelled from Spain and Portugal. He was famous as a talmudist and served as rabbi in Jerusalem. He vehemently opposed

I.7.3

Berab's ordination attempt and protested vigorously when he heard of it via a messenger sent from Safed. Ben Habib's written objections and account of the episode comprise most of the extant primary sources.

THE SOURCES

Later scholars possessed only one contemporaneous source that Graetz did not: a summary of a responsum (in a commentary on Maimonides's *Code* [Sanhedrin 4:11]) by David ben Solomon ibn Abi Zimra (1479–1573), the Jewish Egyptian talmudic scholar, halakhic authority, and mystic known as the *RaDBaZ*. In 1881, two documents concerning the fate of ordination in the period subsequent to the controversy were published, and one apparently refers to Berab.

The bulk of the material dealing with this episode, therefore, remains the collection of documents published by ben Habib in order to bring the controversy to the attention of the rabbinic public. It is known as the 'Ordination Treatise,' dubbed 'Ordination of the Elders' by its author; it was appended to his Responsa, *Teshuvot RaLBaH*, published in Venice in 1565. (In the list of sources below, and in the body of this article, any unspecified references to primary literary sources relate to this collection.) We shall study these documents most carefully, to uncover or clarify details that have not previously received sufficient attention. Scholars, in fact, have ignored modifications in the positions of each side during the controversy, failing to make proper chronological distinctions.

Since 1951, when I published the first version of this article (*Zion* 16, pp. 23–45), two additional documents have been brought to light by my colleague Chaim Zalman Dimitrovsky ("Two New Documents Regarding the Ordination Controversy in Safed" [Hebrew], *Sefunot* 10 (1966): 112–192). One of them (item 3 in the following list) was referred to by the leading figures in the drama back in the sixteenth century. The second one (item 8 below) was unknown until its recent discovery. These documents fill gaps in our knowledge concerning the course of events, and help confirm or invalidate earlier speculations.

The sources below are arranged in the order of their appearance, including those documents that are no longer extant (noted with an asterisk), but that were mentioned by those involved in the controversy. Whenever possible, the place and date of publication is noted in parentheses.

1. Declaration by the scholars of Safed on the revival of ordination, and the ordination of Jacob Berab as the first ordainee; p. 277c–d.

2. Berab's Certificate of Ordination to ben Habib; p. 310c.

3. Moses de Castro's responsum annulling the ordination; *Sefunot*, pp. 146–192.

4.* Letter of encouragement to Safed from Jerusalem scholars.

5.* Letter from ben Habib to the scholars of Egypt.

6.* Two court decisions of anonymous scholars of Safed, one approving and one invalidating ordination.

7.* Protest of the court decision by the scholars of Safed, signed by Joseph Caro, countering the opposition of the scholars of Jerusalem.

8. Berab's comments on de Castro's criticism; *Sefunot,* pp. 146–192.

9. Berab's Ordination Epistle substantiating ordination; pp. 285b–289a.

10. Ben Habib's first treatise annulling the ordination; pp. 278a–285b.

11.* Letter from ben Habib to Joseph Caro (response to 7).

12. Ben Habib's second treatise (response to 9); pp. 289a–298a.

13. Berab's second treatise (response to 10); pp. 298a–303b.

14. Ben Habib's third treatise (response to 13); pp. 303b–328d.

15.* Query from the scholars of Safed to the scholars of Egypt.

16. Ibn Abi Zimra's responsum regarding the revocation of the ordination (response to 15).

SEQUENCE OF EVENTS

The general issue of renewing ordination was first discussed by various scholars in the years preceding the events precipitated by Jacob Berab in Safed in 1538. In his writings, Berab states that he called to bear witness "heaven and earth, that all the scholars that I saw, especially after I came to Egypt, desired to come to the Land of Israel and perform it [ordination]." This is not, however, evidence that the scholars agreed with him on the actual implementation. It appears that Jacob Berab discussed the subject with his friends while still in Egypt and met a noncommittal yearning. It is probable that Berab was not the only one—and perhaps not even the first— to raise the idea of renewing the institution of ordination. In fact, ben Habib admitted that at first he "also yearned for it." He mentioned a "Spanish scholar" who had died in Jerusalem and who, according to rumor, also subscribed to the idea of renewing ordination. This may be a reference to Berab himself, though the rumor may have originated in the wake of Berab's propaganda.

The halakhic aspect was discussed only in 1538, when Berab succeeded in prevailing upon the scholars of Safed to renew ordination and to make him the first ordainee with the authority to ordain others in accordance with the opinion of Maimonides in his *Commentary on the Mishnah* (Sanhedrin 1:1):

I deem it appropriate that when all the scholars and students in the Land of Israel agree to put forward one person as their head . . . this person can convene the

I.7.5

assembly, and he will be ordained himself and qualified to ordain whomever he desires afterwards.

This proclamation provided halakhic support for those who wished to renew ordination, and became the source that figured the most prominently in the debate over the validity of such an undertaking.

Graetz's description of the rich and mighty Berab merely dropping a hint and the scholars of Safed hurrying to do his will is erroneous. The agreement of the Safed rabbis was unquestionably preceded by sharp discussion during which the claims voiced later by those seeking revocation of the ordination would have been articulated. The intense messianic anticipation, together with Berab's powers of persuasion and ordination, temporarily put the doubts to rest.

The news of Berab's actions was brought to Jerusalem by Solomon Hazzan, a messenger from Safed. The messianic element, which was central to the course of events in Safed, was certainly felt in Jerusalem and perhaps grew as rumors of the revival of ordination spread. In Jerusalem, the messenger from Safed was shown "an ancient book relating that a certain wise and righteous man once attempted ordination in Israel, but his plans went awry." Some scholars apparently even offered Berab encouragement; a certain Yehiel, a scholar from Jerusalem, gave his signature to the Safed declaration. Even the opposition of ben Habib was not spontaneous or immediate. After some time he adjured the messenger from Safed to testify that "all my efforts were to request place and proof in order to perform ordination." And certainly when ben Habib, following discussions with the messenger from Safed, with his friend de Castro, and perhaps even with the rest of the scholars, reached a negative rabbinic judgment—for reasons we shall discuss below—it was a disappointment to many in Jerusalem and, to a certain extent, even to ben Habib himself. The first result of the judgment was that the declaration's signatories in Jerusalem annulled their own signatures.

The mere two weeks during which Hazzan was in Jerusalem was the zenith of the short-lived ordination renewal and of Berab's power as the first ordainee. Berab presumably succeeded in acquiring for himself, in a secret meeting of all or some of the renewers of ordination, the title of 'Nasi (prince), Head of the next Sanhedrin'. There is no doubt that he was thus designated; Berab himself admitted it somewhat shamefacedly in his response to ben Habib. We can imagine that Berab hastened to ensure for himself the primary position in the future hierarchy, but was reticent to do so openly when the scholars of Jerusalem had not yet agreed to the renewal of ordination. In any event, this must have happened before the return of their messenger from Jerusalem, when the unanimity was shattered even in Safed. The few days that the messenger was outside of Safed were a time of exultation for the Jews in the city. That same Sabbath, Berab gave a sermon before the city's entire population (divided among several synagogues). The populace flocked to these events to hear the greatest sage, appearing in the glory of his new title. Berab explained the halakhic foundations of the monumental decision and certainly expounded upon the related messianic hopes.

The return of the messenger from Jerusalem undoubtedly dampened the exultant atmosphere in Safed. Instead of the hoped-for agreement, Hazzan carried ben Habib's outright refusal to accept the ordination, as well as his and Moses de Castro's protestations of its validity. The scholars of Safed then renewed their deliberations. Those who had previously been uncertain about the decision now had their doubts confirmed. The Jerusalem scholars' objection in itself constituted sufficient grounds to invalidate the ordination, for Maimonides's condition that "all the scholars . . . in the Land of Israel" must agree, had not been met. Although Berab himself had considered whether unanimous agreement was necessary, or whether a majority assent was enough, he rejected the objection.

Aspersions were cast on Berab's ordination from every front. Seeking support, he reassembled the scholars of Safed and called upon them to reaffirm his ordination even in the face of objections from the Jerusalem scholars. This reconvening of the rabbis was apparently not for the purpose of repeating the act of ordination which, on the basis of the first assembly's agreement, he held to be valid. Their approval regarding a *bet din* was intended to confirm that they did not rescind their first decision.

The composition of the new assembly, however, was not identical to the first. Now only the "major scholars here in Safed" participated. This ambiguous expression was used by Berab himself to obscure the fact that his support had decreased. Actually, it was already clear to him that his grand vision of a Sanhedrin would not come to pass at that time. He was satisfied to settle for less: ordination of two colleagues in order to create a *bet din* with greater authority than the regular *batei din* and from which, when the time was right, the Sanhedrin would emerge.

Even this revised plan did not succeed. One of the two nominees who was to be ordained by Berab refused to receive the ordination in this way. Although formally Berab was now the only one (in conjunction with his two unordained colleagues) authorized to ordain others, this scholar requested that his ordination be comparable to that of Berab, that is, granted by the entire body of Safed scholars. Few of the assembly's members supported this position and, needless to say, the egotistical Berab had good reason to oppose it.

It is difficult to find the halakhic justification for the demand of that scholar and his supporters; Maimonides is clear that ordination renewal is a one-time act. Once a scholar is ordained, based on the decision of his contemporaries, only he is to ordain others. The halakhic sources on which the procedure is based give no support to performing the act of ordination renewal twice. There is, however, no doubt from Berab's testimony that this is what occurred; he complained that "due to our sins in this generation, there are several trouble-makers who say that one of two people we wished to ordain should receive ordination only from all the scholars, as I did."

The assembly ended with a most diplomatic decision. It refrained from ordaining anyone at that time, and determined "not to ordain anyone today or henceforth until such time as the law is clarified, and someone comes to the meeting who is well-learned and pure of mind; then we shall ordain him." As if in all of the intellectual wealth of sixteenth-century Safed there were no suitable candidates! The scholars involved, though, were acutely conscious of the fact that changing candidates would only intensify the controversy. They were satisfied, therefore, to establish guidelines to legitimize ordination in the future, hinting that future candidates would, in fact, need unanimous approval. Thus, Jacob Berab's ordination remained intact, and he gained the time to realize his right to ordain others in the future.

Ben Habib also mentions this controversy, referring to two separate court decisions. One relates that "two very important elders" approved the ordination; the second states that those two and three more canceled it. Ben Habib had seen one of these documents beforehand; the other he only knew of secondhand. Thus he was unable to ascertain which of them—the one that permitted the ordination or the one that voided it—preceded the other. In any event it was clear to him, as it was to Berab, that the issue of ordination, begun in such a spirit of exultation, was turning into a struggle for power and honor. The note of satisfaction heard in ben Habib's words is not surprising.

Who these very important elders were we shall never know, but their actions indicate that they were quite independent, and not accountable to Berab; he, on his part, was unable to ignore them. Berab did not lack for young supporters of stature. Joseph Caro (1488–1575), the brilliant legalist and mystic, headed the supporters, and one may surmise that the three other eminent scholars later ordained by Berab were also among them; ben Habib also acknowledged their stature and claimed only that there were other scholars who were older. Joseph Caro and others sent a 'court decision' to the Jerusalem scholars, expressing approval of the ordination, and protesting the opposition of the scholars of Jerusalem. Ben Habib's response defended the honor of the Jerusalem scholars, impugned by the sharp tone of the verdict's wording.

The scholars of Jerusalem did not stop with mere protests. Both de Castro and ben Habib, each in his own style, recorded the reasons for their opposition to renewing ordination, with the clear intention of diverting the dispute to halakhic grounds. Ben Habib even consulted one of the scholars of Egypt, perhaps ibn Abi Zimra. Neither de Castro nor ben Habib, though, published his opinions at this stage. De Castro was a student of Berab, and though he felt obliged to send his criticism to his teacher and rabbi, he was reluctant to show the treatise to others, "in order not to appear boastful in differing from his teacher," as stated by ben Habib. And ben Habib, who was a long-standing opponent of Berab on many issues, feared a head-on collision with him, and therefore addressed his writings in general terms to 'the rabbis of Safed'.

Berab came across ben Habib's letter only several months later, in Damascus, where he had gone following the decisive step of ordaining four colleagues who had not previously been mentioned as candidates. We shall never know how ben Habib kept the existence of his treatise from Berab while bringing it to the knowledge of the Safed rabbis; perhaps he gave it only to those rabbis who kept the secret. For Berab, learning the contents of the treatise had no importance, as the majority of its claims appeared in Moses de Castro's letter.

As soon as Berab received de Castro's letter, he did two things. He answered de Castro point by point, and at the same time he began writing his Ordination Epistle, intending to bring the issue of ordination renewal to the rabbinic public at large. Berab peppered this message to his former student with insults and rebukes for daring to disagree with his teacher. If ben Habib's estimation of de Castro—as surpassing the stature of his former teacher Berab—was extreme, it is nonetheless clear that de Castro was indeed a brilliant scholar, as is evident from the extant version of his charges. Berab's derision of de Castro was not actually meant for publication; it was written at a time of rage and frustration, with the opposition blocking his ambitions on all sides. The frustration increased Berab's wrath at his student, but did not cause him to abort his plan.

Berab continued writing his Ordination Epistle, which included halakhic claims favoring the renewal of ordination and omitted polemics against his adversaries. Only once did the teacher hint about an 'errant student', and he did not intend that everyone know to whom he referred. These words were stated in the tranquil tone befitting a proclamation to anyone interested, announcing the innovation undertaken by the assembly of Safed rabbis. The text of Berab's Ordination Epistle was written at the same time as his polemic comments to de Castro. The closing in which Berab announces the ordination of his four colleagues was added only *ex post facto*, however, because he was forced to leave Eretz Israel. The answer to de Castro contains no mention of the ordination of the four.

The reason for Berab's leaving Eretz Israel is disputed by historians, and it is worthwhile to note the literary source at the root of the problem. Berab wrote:

And I, the youngest of the multitudes of Jacob, was ordained. After about two or three months had passed, what happened to the late Judah b. Baba, would, Heaven forfend, have happened to me. [The story of Judah b. Baba is related in the

I.7.9

Babylonian Talmud, Sanhedrin 14a.] Two slanderers arose against me with no wrongdoing on my part—God will punish them for their evildoing—and I was compelled to leave Eretz Israel.

Ben Habib was incensed that Berab dare compare himself to Judah b. Baba, who sacrificed his life because of ordination. He claimed that Berab fled Safed not because of the ordination, but because of a dispute over money. Some historians accepted ben Habib's word, while others read the analogy with Judah b. Baba as alluding to a political situation, and connected Berab's flight to interference on the part of the Turkish government, which did not view the establishment of an independent Jewish authority with favor. Actually, nothing in Berab's words supports the premise that the government interfered with the ordination. On the contrary, the linguistic usage of "with no wrongdoing on my part" points to the presence of an informer, due to a financial dispute. The facts also support this hypothesis. Had Berab fled for political reasons, it is unlikely that he would have gone to Damascus to be saved. In addition, it is not logical that Berab would have run for his life, endangering the four colleagues whom he had ordained and who remained in Safed; for had the government opposed ordination and intervened, all would have been in mortal danger. Berab apparently sought to assume for himself some of Judah b. Baba's righteous fame, without comparing the circumstances of his flight to the political persecution suffered by the ancient rabbi.

Probably there is no causal relationship between the two clauses "two slanderers arose against me" and "I was compelled to leave Eretz Israel," as indicated from analyzing a passage in Berab's second treatise that has generally been ignored:

The time became troubled, and I swear before heaven and earth that on the day that I ordained four of my colleagues, at the very same time, a danger similar to what happened to Judah b. Baba faced me; I escaped from my home, and afterward God agreed that I had ordained them.

Here the flight occurs while undertaking the ordination. He merely fled the house, which resulted in a short delay in carrying out the ordination. Leaving Israel is not even mentioned. It is, however, known that Berab regularly traveled to Damascus for business.

A correct understanding of the passages, then, produces the following picture. After the failure of the ordination of the first two candidates, Berab waited for things to settle down. He then sought to disregard the selection procedure of ordination that had been decided upon, for it was likely to reawaken the controversy and delay the process. His decision was motivated by his upcoming trip abroad; if he did not return, ordination would forever be discontinued. He therefore chose four of his intimates, and in the course of ordination the slander incident transpired in connection with a dispute he had about financial matters. Ben Habib had made such a charge, which no one contradicted.

In any event, Berab succeeded in completing the ordination before he left the country, which he states occurred about two or three months after he himself was ordained by his colleagues. The Ordination Epistle had long been written, but there was no point in publicizing it until he was able to end it with the report of the new ordinations. Berab completed the document either before he left or, more likely, after he returned from Damascus. He presented his rivals in Safed with a *fait accompli* and demonstrated his adherence to his position—even in the face of the opposition of the Jerusalem scholars.

In short, while Berab's flight was not a result of the ordination, it was still a turning point in its story. Until that time, each protagonist expressed disagreement with the other, with give-and-take on both sides; the dispute was not yet a polemic.

Berab's comments on de Castro's remarks were indeed insulting, but they were not meant for publication. As a result, Joseph Caro's court decision with its offensive style, and ben Habib's reply, remained a private dispute between them. The Ordination Epistle was written in an impersonal tone, and its conclusion that Berab's departure from Safed led him to ordain four of his colleagues was written by way of self-justification, in order to avoid reproach. It is possible that Berab only sought to placate his colleagues in Safed for having ignored their mutual decision to select candidates jointly. To ben Habib, however, the Ordination Epistle appeared to ignore the protest of the Jerusalem scholars. Ben Habib himself described this turning point: "I thought that the thing had quieted down, was past and finished, until I heard that the rabbi whom they sought to ordain . . . is still holding on to his ordination and continuing, in his way, to ordain others."

At this point ben Habib decided to publish his treatise, which until then had been seen by only a few. This treatise was moderate in tone. Its conclusion was conciliatory and suggested, in his name and in the name of the Jerusalem scholars, "that we gather in one place . . . to negotiate impartially." Even as the treatise was published, though, ben Habib had already despaired of dealing peaceably with Berab. The ordination of four scholars in Safed had turned a dispute into a polemic, and had fanned the negotiations into a conflagration of controversy.

From this point on, a contentious tone prevails in the writings of the two sides. Soon after the first treatise was dispatched from Jerusalem, Berab's Ordination Epistle arrived there. Ben Habib immediately countered with a long and argumentative response in which he saw fit to protest the injury done to de Castro's honor by Berab's criticism of his former student. By the time this answer reached Berab, he had already published his answer to ben Habib's first treatise. The response included not only relevant halakhic

I.7.11

material, but also innuendoes and attacks—mostly of a personal nature. These included the infamous hint regarding ben Habib's past, that is, that he had in his youth been a secret Jew—one of the Portuguese *conversos* who had not been willing to sacrifice their lives to sanctify God's name, but instead underwent baptism, hoping to maintain their Jewish identity in secret. Ben Habib's bitter and harsh answer completes this episode, as much as we can garner from the sources.

The entire controversy did not last more than a single year. Scholars outside of Israel did not get involved. Ben Habib apparently did not receive an answer from ibn Abi Zimra in Egypt; if he had, he certainly would have referred to it in his later writings. Some time thereafter, the Safed scholars turned to ibn Abi Zimra and his Egyptian colleagues, who now pronounced that ben Habib definitely had the halakhah on his side. Even now, however, the scholars of Safed did not admit failure. Berab himself died eight years after the ordination episode, a fact that was used to give additional force to his decision, for "one does not talk back to the lion after his death."

The ordainees held on to their titles, and even exercised their right to ordain others. It is known that Joseph Caro ordained Moses Alsheikh who, in turn, ordained Hayyim Vital. The title was also passed from other teachers to students, and there is evidence of its use by various scholars in Eretz Israel through the first half of the seventeenth century, for example, Rabbi Hayyim Abulafia the Elder and Rabbi Josiah Pinto. There is also a letter of agreement from Rabbi Jacob Berab the Second, the grandson of Jacob Berab the First, to seven students whom he ordained, including Moses Galanti and Yaakov Abulafia. Recently an attempt was made to deduce, from the continuing usage of the title of ordination, that the objection of the opposition had subsided. Ben Habib died soon after the episode; ibn Abi Zimra, though, lived many more years, and spent time in Jerusalem and in Safed, even serving together with R. Joseph Caro in a *bet din*—something that would have been impossible, it is argued, had he continued to oppose Caro's ordination.

There are logical grounds to assume the fading of the dissent over ordination. Those who supported a revival of ordination did not seek to undertake new judicial responsibilities based upon their new status. At issue was the source of their authority on matters already in effect, such as imposing fines and dispensing lashes for those who came to receive punishment as religious penitents. The title holders even abstained from using their ordination as a source of authority for these purposes. The *bet din* of Moses di Trani, who claimed to have been ordained by Berab, continued to mete out penalties based on geonic rulings; it did not invoke the authority of an ordained *bet din*.

Joseph Caro, though he supported the renewing of ordination and even hoped to ordain others, did not consider himself ordained by the earlier ceremony. Sixteen years after the renewal of ordination, Caro defended the superior authority of the Safed *bet din*, claiming for it the status of 'great *bet din*' in accordance with Maimonides's definition (*Commentary on the Mishnah*, Sanhedrin 6:9), because "Nowadays the *bet din* in this city is recognized by the public and is great in wisdom and numbers. We have heard from all over the world that their questions were answered and afterwards they were satisfied." However, its status as an ordained *bet din* is nowhere listed among its qualities. Caro's opinion in the *Shulhan Arukh* and in *Beit Yosef* that "we do not have ordained judges, and in our time none are ordained," is tantamount to an assertion of the fact that the *bet din* did not function based on the authority of the ordainees.

After ibn Abi Zimra's decision, the ordainees themselves ceased to accord their ordination total halakhic sanction. It is not that they backed down because of halakhic considerations, as contended by those who oppose ordination in our day, but rather that they refrained from claiming for themselves any authority not universally recognized as legitimate. Among themselves they continued to retain the title of ordination, and even saw themselves as authorized to ordain those who came after them. However, as ordination carried no real authority, it became an honorific title that scholars gave to their outstanding students. Berab had already sought to stop use of the title from spreading, limiting the right to be ordained to those possessing exceptional knowledge. His grandson, R. Jacob Berab the Second, ordained his students with the understanding that they would not ordain others without his approval. Nonetheless, even in its attenuated form, ordination remained attractive as a mark of the great and special scholar.

The formal aspect, then, was not the main motivation for transmitting ordination to coming generations. We can assume that sixteenth-century messianic expectations also entered the picture, based upon Maimonides's assertion (*Code*, Sanhedrin 1:3) that the establishment of a great *bet din* will precede the Messiah's arrival. For if Berab's ordination was a true *semikhah*, the messianic destiny could be fulfilled at any moment. There were always those who looked toward an imminent 'End-of-Days'—even after the calculations of the earlier dates for messianic fulfillment had proved to be false.

MOTIVES FOR THE CONTROVERSY

Now that the actual events are clear, we shall attempt to shed light on the factors that led to the eruption of the controversy over ordination. The most simplistic explanation is based upon the angry accusations of the participants in the dispute. Ben Habib berated Berab for seeking personal status, and Berab accused ben Habib of jealousy and animosity toward his rival. The controversy over ordination had indeed been preceded by arguments and friction between the two over a period of some fourteen years. However, this explanation provides only the psychological background of the controversy, which intensified the bitterness once the new dispute had erupted. Ben Habib himself indicated that, aside from this embroilment, the two had not been involved in any argument outside the realm of the usual intellectual exchanges. As was the custom of the time, these discussions were conducted in sharp tones, but without acrimony. In any event, the latent bitterness was initially well hidden, and at the outset of the controversy each participant tried to be respectful of his opponent. Thus the personal psychological explanation has no validity regarding the outbreak of the controversy.

Graetz's proposal of an intercity competition between Jerusalem and Safed is no more productive as an explanation for the controversy, although it is subscribed to by some contemporary scholars. This competition did, in fact, exist. For a full generation Safed had been undergoing a process of development, and with the great influx of refugees from Spain—many of them renowned rabbis and scholars—material prosperity (in 1495 the Jews of Safed were reported to be actively trading in spices, cheese, oil, vegetables, and fruits) began to be matched by intellectual wealth. During the sixteenth century, Safed became the vibrant center of Jewish mysticism, and also produced some of the most authoritative legalistic works of Judaism.

Jerusalem presented a completely different picture. Because of government pressure and lack of sources of income, the Jerusalem community had to fight for its existence, so that even some of those who truly yearned to shelter themselves in the city's holy shadow were frightened away. The Jews of Jerusalem had nothing save their pride in the city's supreme holiness, a dignity preserved by the faithful even in their poverty and distress.

The rivalry between Jerusalem and Safed was mirrored in the competition between the two scholars to procure donations for their respective communities. Yet this is merely one additional detail in the background to the ordination controversy. There is neither evidence nor even a hint of the assumption that Berab wished to expropriate Jerusalem's holiness by affording Safed special privilege; ben Habib acknowledged that, in sending him the first ordination, the scholars of Safed had intended to pay honor to the holiness of Jerusalem. While the intercity rivalry did add to the controversy's virulence as time went on—Berab criticized ben Habib's custom of calling himself 'the man of Jerusalem', and ben Habib pointed to the devotion of the Jerusalem community which remained steadfast despite extreme material suffering—the basis for the eruption of the controversy cannot be found here.

The reason for the embroilment must be sought in the renewal of ordination itself, about which the two scholars adopted diametrically opposed stands. Berab's basic motive for his action was messianic; it was based on Maimonides's formulation that, even if the chain of ordination (i.e., the appointment of ordained judges by other ordained judges) had been broken, the process could be renewed by the agreement of all the scholars of the Land of Israel to "put forward one person . . . to be ordained himself and [who will] be qualified to ordain whomever he desires afterward."

Maimonides had no halakhic source for his determination, but described his thought process. As is common procedure, he refers to a biblical passage for support: "I will restore your judges as of old. . . . After that you shall be called the city of righteousness" (Isaiah 1:26). Thus, the judges' return would preceed Redemption. Since, according to halakhic principles, "a *bet din* is not such in the full sense unless it is ordained in the Land of Israel," it is imperative to find a way to renew ordination before Redemption. For Maimonides—the rationalist exegete, philosopher, and legalist—this was a purely intellectual clarification of the halakhah that would find practical expression only at some indeterminate time in the future. However, in the eyes of a generation that saw itself at the gates of Redemption, ordination renewal became a magic key to facilitate the first human step which would provide the impetus for the remaining divine steps toward Redemption.

Graetz described the generation's readiness for messianism following the activities of Solomon Molcho (1500–1532) and noted its relevance to Berab's attempt to renew ordination. Gershom Scholem wrote at length about Abraham Halevy of Jerusalem (*Major Trends in Jewish Mysticism*, pp. 215–244), whose messianic prophecy of Redemption provides further testimony of the expectant atmosphere among the Spanish exiles who had settled in Eretz Israel. Although calculation of the End-of-Days is not mentioned in the arguments over ordination, Graetz postulates—with good reason—that 1538 was chosen for renewing ordination because it was close to Solomon Molcho's prediction of 1540 as the date of the Redemption. Joseph Caro's avid support of the renewal of ordination, coupled with his close relationship to Solomon Molcho, lends further credence to Graetz's theory. The messianic tendency in ordination renewal is also hinted at, as we shall see, in the first declaration of ordination, and is spelled out in the polemics of Berab, who undoubtedly identified his generation as that of the Messiah's appearance. One of Berab's claims against ben Habib, in fact, was that his opposition was delaying the preparation required for Redemption.

Berab was caught up in the actively expectant, mystical atmosphere of Safed, although it is almost certain that he himself was not a kabbalist. In truth, messianic activity is not dependent on mysticism, so there is no point in attributing the rivalry of Berab and ben Habib to their divergent approaches to kabbalah, as some scholars have done. The *sine qua non* for messianic activity is a particular outlook regarding the stages of Redemption. Berab acquired his concept of messianism from Maimonides, who held that the first stage of Redemption was in human hands, with the initial step being the renewal of ordination. This step was, by its very nature, a matter for those well versed in halakhah, such as Berab.

Ben Habib did not subscribe to the belief that Redemption depends on fulfilling certain conditions, and challenged the messianic outlook upon which renewing ordination depended. Indeed, he had reservations regarding any messianic concept; for him, "the future is largely concealed from everyone, even from our departed scholars." He based himself on another statement of Maimonides in his *Code* (Melakhim 12, 2), "And all these things and the like will be unknown to men until they happen; they are obscure in the sayings of the prophets, and the scholars have no received knowledge of them." (Note that these words contradict Maimonides's youthful attempt to prove the legality of renewing ordination based on a particular assumption about the order of the events in the End-of-Days.)

Ben Habib's hopes for Redemption were passive; no special action was required to accelerate it. Rather, it served as an incentive to do what is good and correct in any case—and if the meritorious deeds were more numerous, their performers would thereby earn Redemption. This practical approach is expressed in his suggestion to convene the sages of Safed and Jerusalem in order to consider the renewal of ordination.

And even if it does not succeed . . . with what strength we have at present we shall appoint fair and worthy judges throughout the Holy Land to pass judgment on all matters they have until now considered. And perhaps by virtue of this, our God will reward us, and we shall soon merit by fulfillment of this commandment the return of our judges and our Sanhedrin to their chambers.

The declaration of those who supported ordination carries a different message. While it concludes with a reference to the reinstatement of judges, it is much more abstract. The language is poetic and replete with messianic imagery and specific terms referring to Redemption. Ordination renewal is not a righteous act by virtue of which one gains Redemption, but constitutes the first stage in the process of Redemption.

The divergent positions upheld by ben Habib and Berab have each received support throughout the periods of the Exile. Entire generations followed ben Habib in anticipating Redemption; it was only necessary to fulfill the Torah commandments, the details of which were set down in halakhah and further elaborated upon and strengthened in the ethical writings. Other generations, conversely, sought to 'second-guess' the Divine Will and ascertain what special conditions were imperative for 'awakening from below' that which would be followed by 'awakening from above'. Hence, various messianic approaches developed, each delineating the different stages of Redemption.

Although Berab's generation—because of the historical circumstances following the Exile from Spain—inclined toward action based on identification with messianic conceptions, there were nonetheless individuals who espoused the passive messianic view, and who measured every step—even those that would appear to others as direct means to bring Redemption—

by the immanent standard of halakhah and morality. Ben Habib's was such a pure halakhic stance. This best explains his opposition to Berab's attempt to revive the institution of ordination.

Jacob Berab's push for ordination renewal must be seen, then, as a decision based on extrahalakhic motivations, while ben Habib passed negative judgment on the issue of ordination renewal according to pure halakhic standards. The differing approach of each protagonist is revealed in their discussions.

POSITIONS REGARDING HALAKHAH

There are essentially three issues regarding halakhah and ordination renewal upon which the two sides disagreed. The primary claim of ben Habib and de Castro was that there was insufficient halakhic ground for renewing ordination. They noted that Maimonides's argument in his *Commentary on the Mishnah*, upon which the renewers of ordination depended, was later retracted by Maimonides himself in his *Code* (Sanhedrin 4, 11) where he commences the discussion about renewal with the words "it appears to me" and concludes with "the matter requires a decision." Ben Habib argues, therefore, that Maimonides reconsidered what he had written when he was younger; for the accepted rule in determining halakhah is that a later decision overrides a former decision (a rule formulated elsewhere by Maimonides himself). All rabbinic authorities accept this rule wherever the *Code* contradicts the *Commentary on the Mishnah*.

Berab did not seek to refute this rule. However, he explained the closing words "the matter requires a decision" as referring to a different law about ordination, that is, whether the *bet din* extending ordination must be composed of three ordained persons, or whether one person who is ordained together with two unordained scholars is sufficient. Berab stuck fast to his interpretation, even though—as ben Habib argued—in the very same paragraph Maimonides clearly rules on the question of the composition of a *bet din*.

The second point of controversy was the authority of an ordained *bet din*. Here too, ben Habib's opinion is determined by halakhic reasoning, while Berab is once again influenced by external factors that compelled him to come to terms with overt contradictions in his claims. Those who favored the renewal of ordination articulated in the Ordination Declaration two areas in which an ordained *bet din* has an advantage over an ordinary *bet din*: the authority to impose penalties and fines and to mete out lashings to a penitent, thus absolving him of his fate of *karet* (being cut off), as ordained in the Bible. The matter of fines is mentioned only briefly, while the issue of lashes is discussed at length, with stress given to the need to help penitents achieve their complete absolution.

The messianic component of ordination renewal is not mentioned ex-

plicitly in the declaration, but is alluded to in its concluding passage. However, the prominence given to the practical value of ordination renewal was
an expression of the orientation toward action that was harnessed to the
messianic dream. By proving the advantage of the authority of an ordained
bet din within halakhic concepts, it was possible to contend that the establishment of such a *bet din* would be the first stage in the realization of the
messianic conception, that is, the stage of 'the return of the judges'.

In promoting the advantage of the renewed *bet din*, it was sufficient to
note its authority to impose fines, the explicit example given in talmudic
sources for the ordained *bet din's* superior authority over the common *bet
din*. There was, however, no practical need for such authority, as the *geonim*
had established substitutes for the laws of fines. Conversely, reviving the
laws of fines meant reinstatement of some Toraitic laws whose cancellation
would cause "the scholars to regret the ordination" (Maimonides). Indeed,
on this point ben Habib did not disagree with Berab, and had he found
sufficient basis for renewing ordination, he would have seen it as a return
to previous glory—without acknowledging its real need and without pin-
ning messianic hopes on that action.

Berab, however, considered reestablishment of the laws of fines suffi-
ciently important for him to link it with his messianic intentions; during the
argument he even claimed that the issue of fines was the very essence of
ordination, with the issue of lashes being incidental—an outright contradiction of the first Ordination Declaration, where the matter of lashes had
occupied the prominent place. Berab was forced into this position by the
claims of de Castro and ben Habib. They asserted that Berab was affording
his new *bet din* authority never wielded by any ordained *bet din* even during
mishnaic times. According to them, no *bet din* was empowered to impose
lashes on anyone unless he was accused by witnesses, while a penitent is
only accorded divinely ordained punishment; moreover, such lashings are
not Toraitic in source, and do not absolve one of the punishment of *karet*.
In refuting his opponents' arguments, Berab made the surprising claim that,
according to the evidence he had, even a common *bet din* could impose
upon penitents lashes stipulated in the Torah. In his second treatise Berab
elaborated that the *batei din* of his teachers in Spain had so acted; thus he
could not be blamed for affording a *bet din* new authority on questionable
halakhic grounds. If this is the case, retorted ben Habib in his decisive
answer, the new *bet din* added nothing to obtaining absolution for the
penitents, and thus could not serve as the purpose of renewing ordination.

It is difficult and indeed unnecessary to imagine that this obvious contradiction escaped Berab. His sole purpose was to prepare for Redemption;
for this end it was sufficient to add the authority of the ordained *bet din* to
impose fines. When the question of ordination renewal came up, however,
the scholars of Safed—some of whom, like R. Solomon Hazzan, were Marranos who had repented—supported it and sought to achieve total abso-

lution through the ordained *bet din*. This desire was based upon two halakhic assumptions: that someone who is lashed as a result of self-confession is absolved of *karet*, and that only an ordained *bet din* has the authority to impose lashing. These laws, however, are not spelled out in the talmudic sources; the rulings were a matter for halakhic debate and discussion.

It is understandable that the scholars of Safed would incline toward an interpretation that would help realize their aspiration of ordination. Thus Berab, who understood his colleagues' desire for absolution, assented to their wishes even though he was not totally convinced about the halakhic grounding. The issue of absolution would not determine the legality of ordination and its ultimate purpose; Berab added it to keep peace. To the charge that he was authorizing the *bet din* to do something without an absolute halakhic basis, he responded that even a regular *bet din* is authorized to impose lashes decreed in the Torah. The duality in his stance is revealed by the fact that he used this last claim in the debate with his opponents, while in his Ordination Declaration he had expressed the other side of the issue, according to which it seemed that the renewal of ordination provided a ruling answering the needs of penitent Marranos—an argument that served to convince various scholars in Safed.

A third issue within the halakhic controversy was the authority of an ordained *bet din* to proclaim the new moon and to intercalate the months. Until the institution of a permanent calendar by Hillel the Second in the fourth century c.e., these matters had been handled by an ordained *bet din*; the question was whether ordination renewal as defined by Maimonides would also restore this authority. Paradoxically, the supporters of the ordination renewal were interested in limiting the new *bet din* in this matter. This was not surprising, for undoing the fixed calendar and the order of intercalation would constitute a revolution appropriate for the coming of the Messiah; in the mundane world, though, no one would think of it.

Berab insisted that an ordained *bet din* would not have the authority to proclaim the new moon and to intercalate the months. This was so apparent to him that when he expounded upon the remaining halakhic issues before the congregation, he did not even mention it. Other scholars in Safed brought up the issue, but immediately concurred that renewing ordination had no implication for calendar order. This view was not shared by the opponents. Moses de Castro announced that an ordained *bet din* could indeed effect changes in the calendar if it had been so authorized by the Sanhedrin. He did, however, express concern that, if the number of ordained scholars increased and they established a Sanhedrin, they would ignore the doubts raised about the nature of their institution and might change the permanent calendar improperly.

Ben Habib went further; he claimed that not all commentators agreed that proclamation of the new moon was dependent on the Sanhedrin's existence. According to Nahmanides, an ordained *bet din* was quite sufficient; this court not only had the right but indeed the obligation to fix the calendar. Since the main positive commandment of setting times for festivals is fulfilled by proclaiming the new moon based on evidence, only in periods when there is no suitable *bet din* is it permissible to depend on the calendar. With the establishment of an ordained *bet din*—assuming that the ordinations were valid—the scholars of Safed were questioning the legitimacy of the existing calendar, or at least raising doubts regarding its validity, without daring to put in its stead a system of determining the festivals based on evidence.

Berab dismissed out of hand the fears arising from establishment of a new *bet din* stripped of power to deal with the calendar. Nonetheless, when he heard of these misgivings—whether from the messenger or from de Castro's letter—he related to them in absolute seriousness; his comment that the doubt was caused by the misunderstanding of a 'mistaken student' by no means disguises his seriousness. The fact is that Berab opens the Ordination Declaration with a description of what led to invalidating the proclamation of the new moon by evidence, as was explained by the Spanish astronomer Isaac Israeli in his book *Yesod Olam* (written in 1310). According to Israeli, Hillel's calendar would remain in effect until the Messiah comes.

Here ben Habib faulted Berab's logic. Israeli's book provided a historical description of events and linked the calendar's determination to an actual need, namely, that the community of Jews would not become factionalized. But, ben Habib argued, history and halakhah are two separate and distinct things; the halakhist cannot base himself on the historian's theories. Had Berab based his arguments on Maimonides and Nahmanides, said ben Habib, he would have come to the conclusion that his attempt to reestablish ordination was damaging the very basis for determining the dates of the festivals.

In addition to these three weak points in Berab's halakhic grounding, the opponents of ordination renewal found a procedural flaw serious enough to invalidate what the scholars of Safed had done. As noted, the scholars of Safed contacted their colleagues in Jerusalem only after they had ordained Berab. However, Maimonides's formulation, upon which they based themselves, explicitly stipulated "the agreement of all the scholars in the Land of Israel." It would have been logical to have gathered all the scholars together, rather than to have permitted the Safed majority to decide, on the assumption that the Jerusalem minority would agree after the fact. By turning to the Jerusalemites for their *post facto* approval, the scholars of Safed undermined the legality of their action; they revealed their opinion that the ordination's validity was dependent on the concurrence of the minority. However, such assent without prior negotiations among all the involved parties was futile.

The question was whether rectification was possible. Could all that had occurred be ignored, and negotiations now be opened? If the supporters could convince the opposition, in writing or face to face, then ordination renewal could become reality. Both de Castro and ben Habib raised this possibility. However, this was merely a gesture of appeasement on their part, so that they would not seem to turn a deaf ear to the reasoning of the opposing side. In actuality, they did not consider retracting their negative opinion. No wonder Berab ignored their suggestion. Instead of opening new negotiations, he published two treatises refuting their claims.

Apparently it had not occurred to Berab to take the Jerusalem scholars into account. He based himself on what Maimonides wrote in his *Commentary on the Mishnah* about yeshivah students gathered to ordain their rabbi; Berab ruled that "in our time the yeshivah is mainly in Safed." That this was Berab's opinion is evident from the fact that he swore the messenger not to seek the agreement of his student, de Castro. When Berab's opponents claimed that Maimonides's interpretation predicated renewed ordination on the unanimous agreement of the scholars in the Land of Israel, and that there is no effective agreement without negotiations, this claim was rejected.

Berab held that this is not a case of a *bet din* ruling based on prooftext evidence, stating that "In such a matter, there is need neither for negotiations nor a position, but only a declaration by the sages that they are in agreement." He compared this issue to the establishment of a regulation by public referendum, to which the halakhic rules applicable to the *bet din* do not apply. "And should you say" that there was indeed need for negotiations, Berab argued, the messenger who came to Jerusalem did negotiate with the scholars. This is a strange answer, for even if we consider his visit to be 'negotiating', it took place after the act of ordination by the Safed scholars. Here, as elsewhere, Berab allows his yearning for Redemption to influence halakhic considerations. Berab claimed that Maimonides's explanation in his *Commentary on the Mishnah* means that "this agreement needs only a conviction to serve the Lord, and if so there is no need for any particular convocation or even negotiations, but merely a statement of agreement." Regarding the concern about the lack of agreement on the part of the Jerusalem scholars, he said: "Who would even think of something that would delay our Redemption . . . that all who hear of it would not come with drums and dancing to subscribe to it."

AN APPRAISAL OF THE CHARACTERS

A description of the events and an analysis of the motives involved reveal that the controversy was conditioned by ambitions, states of mind, and ways of thinking prevalent at that time, and not solely by the personalities of the involved parties. However, this does not exclude the possibility that personality-based factors were involved in the development of the events.

Both of the protagonists were well-defined and vital personalities. Berab was a dynamic and authoritarian individual, driven to action and initiative—all of which gives rise to a clear sense of superiority, to the point of demanding the right of way at all times and the power of decision in every instance. In contrast, Ben Habib was a passive, almost contemplative individual. His confidence results from the lack of a need for initiated activity; he does not reveal the energy contained within him except when presented with a specific outside challenge.

These character traits were apparent in the actions of Berab and ben Habib prior to this controversy. The fact that ben Habib remained in desolate Jerusalem, "sighing bitterly, seeing the Temple ruins around" (the words he used repeatedly in signing his responsa), testifies to his wish for tranquility, even at the expense of extreme frugality. This quality is dominant in his relationship to those who pose halakhic queries; he merely responds to their doubts, without interfering in matters not under his direct authority.

In contrast to this we see Berab gallivanting from place to place—Egypt, Damascus, Jerusalem, and Safed; even if his wanderings are due only to his far-flung business dealings, they are certainly a mark of his dynamic but irritating qualities. Berab undoubtedly saw himself as the greatest scholar of his time—thus was he perceived by his students and admirers. Everywhere he went, he demanded power of decision. For this same reason he clashed with scholars who did not submit to his personal power, and thus became a factious individual, involved in controversy far and wide.

The same initiative and sense of superiority also characterize Berab's actions concerning ordination renewal. Had the undertaking succeeded, his personal authority would have been unsurpassed; perhaps such an ambition contributed to his driving nature. Nonetheless, Berab should not be viewed as desiring to establish a central institution in the Holy Land in order to impose his authority on the scattered Jews. It is possible that an ordained *bet din*—and, even more, a Sanhedrin—would have left its imprint on future generations, but that was not Berab's intention. He focused on the messianic consequences of his actions. For his generation, the hope for Redemption was based upon the expectation of sudden and radical reform. It is impossible that someone who prepared the stages of Redemption, as Berab thought to do by renewing ordination, would pin his hope on actions that could only be carried out within the existing and continuing reality. If Berab envisioned personal glory in the future, it was undoubtedly tied to the messianic conception that guided him. He undoubtedly saw himself not as one who was destined to head an institution that would function according to accepted norms, but rather as a leading actor in the messianic drama, that is, as the head of the Sanhedrin that would greet the Redeemer.

CONCLUSION

In clarifying the personal and extrapersonal motives and in recognizing the personalities of the disputants, it would seem that the historian has exhausted the possibilities of discovering the reasons for any historical dispute. Moreover, to the extent that he succeeds in understanding the opponents' personalities and motives, he becomes unable to evaluate them objectively. The conflict between these two opponents appears to have been preordained, and is not to be judged in terms of praise or criticism. The question of who is preferable—Berab, the dynamic activist who was swept up by the currents of thought and yearning of his time, or the contemplative ben Habib who, in relying on 'timeless' values of tradition and morality, disengaged himself from the historical action of his time—is almost moot. The historian should not be asked to make a value judgment between these personalities and between the spiritual and intellectual systems to which they subscribed. He should rather apply the criteria appropriate to the world of each rival and, just as they did, measure their ideals and value systems against their achievements and reality.

Occasionally, the historian finds signs of insecurity and qualms in the words of those he is scrutinizing, and by following those hints he may continue his evaluation and criticism. Berab's embarrassment when the contradictions in his claims were exposed helps us assess him. Here he himself revealed that his messianic yearning led him to utilize conflicting halakhic opinions in an attempt to achieve his goal. Nor can we ignore the fact that Berab's personal attacks on ben Habib, and the recounting of his 'old sins', were not germane. He did not dare to give explicit expression to the serious accusation about ben Habib's conversion in his youth; instead he couched it in words of self-praise ("I myself never changed my name"). Such a tactic is evidence of an emotional need to pretend that one has done nothing wrong, which is a sign of an uneasy conscience.

Ben Habib, who did not express himself with excessive sharpness, except when responding in kind, felt that in reacting to his rival tit for tat, he had sullied his own moral stance, admitting that "it would have been better in the eyes of man and God" had it not come to this.

If the historian judges Berab as taking an ambivalent intellectual stand from the outset and being compelled to employ invalid methods to defend it, and Ben Habib as abandoning his high, moral stand "in a time of anger," he may be making a moral judgment. However, he does so only by extracting testimony from the sources, and interpreting the overt and covert confessions of the litigants themselves.

I.7.23

8

BAROUH MEVORAH

Jewish Diplomatic Activities to Prevent Expulsion of the Jews from Bohemia and Moravia in 1744–45

Among the most significant characteristics of modern Jewish history is the deep sense of responsibility that communities in different countries feel toward each other, and their efforts to assist Jews in other countries in an hour of need. One of the earliest examples of such a concerted international Jewish diplomatic effort was revealed in the middle of the eighteenth century, when the Jews of Bohemia and Moravia were threatened by an expulsion decree. The history of the diplomatic efforts initiated by European Jews on their behalf is described in the following study.

Dr. Barouh Mevorah is a senior lecturer in Jewish History at The Hebrew University of Jerusalem. His studies cover early modern Jewish history and the Jewish communities in the Orient.

BACKGROUND

The expulsion of the Jews of Prague by the Habsburg Queen Maria Theresa during the years 1745–48, as well as the threat of expulsion that faced the entire Jewish community in Bohemia and Moravia in 1744–45, constitute a well-known chapter in mid-eighteenth-century Jewish history. The course of these events as they affected the Jews has been described in the historical literature. However, the intensive and wide-ranging diplomatic activities of European Jewry to save the largest Jewish community in Europe, as well

This article first appeared in Hebrew in *Zion* 28 (1963). The translation/adaptation is by Nadav Nahshon.

The International Center for University Teaching of Jewish Civilization, Jerusalem, the author of the article, and the translator/adapter grant permission to photocopy this article for teaching purposes without further permission or fee.

as the intercession of various governments and rulers on behalf of the Jews, have not been thoroughly and systematically examined.[1]

THE OCCUPATION OF PRAGUE

At the end of the summer of 1744, the armies of Frederick the Great of Prussia captured the city of Prague. It was the second time since the beginning of the War of the Austrian Succession (1740–48) that the Bohemian capital had been taken by foreign forces. The first time was in 1741–42, when combined Bavarian, French, and Saxon armies had occupied the city for over a year. Most of the nobility and leadership of Prague believed at the time that the power of the House of Habsburg was waning and they had therefore lent assistance to the enemy; many of them were tried for betraying the monarchy when the Habsburgs returned to the city. Only a few individual Jews were accused of treason, even though a group of Alsatian Jews who accompanied the French forces interceded with the occupation authorities on behalf of their coreligionists in Prague—an action that could have been viewed with suspicion.

When Prague was occupied for the second time, in the summer of 1744, the Habsburgs had managed to recover much of their strength. By the time the Prussians laid siege to the city it was already known in Prague that the Habsburg and Saxon armies were on the way to provide relief, so there was no reason for the residents to form ties with the enemy. Under these circumstances, even more than during the previous occupation, ordinary types of contact between the enemy and the city's Jews were liable to give rise to suspicion and accusations of treason. There were a few occurrences during the siege that were interpreted as favoritism toward the Jews on the part of the Prussians. This was especially the case when, shortly before the entry of the occupation forces into the city, a contingent of Prussian soldiers, accompanied by a few Jews, was sent to put down a pogrom in the Jewish quarter of Prague.[2] From that point onward, every concession granted by the occupation authorities to the Jews was considered preferential treatment. Every contact between Jews and soldiers, especially when it involved trading in items plundered from the palaces of the Bohemian nobility, increased mistrust of the Jews. A contemporary Jewish account tells of the pervasive feeling among the gentiles of Prague that the Jews had brought the Prussians to the city and were maintaining intimate contact with them.

During the occupation of Prague, rumors about Jewish collaboration with the Prussians reached the imperial court in Vienna. A newspaper article repeating the rumors appeared in Vienna in November 1744. Within the week similar articles appeared in two newspapers in Augsburg. They also reported that the idea of expelling the Jews from Prague, once the Habsburg forces recaptured the city, was being considered in Vienna.

The newspapers reached the hands of Wolf Wertheimer, the financier and son of the well-known 'court Jew' Samson Wertheimer, who had served a number of previous Habsburg rulers. Wolf Wertheimer, who was living in Augsburg in southern Germany, wrote to his son Samuel in Vienna, urging him to alert the Jewish leadership there to act quickly in order to avert a catastrophe. He suggested that a petition be sent to Queen Maria Theresa and each of her ministers, explaining that, even if a few irresponsible individuals had sinned, there was no reason to punish the entire Jewish community. Wolf Wertheimer also advised that Baron Diego D'Aguilar, a financier who had come to Vienna from Portugal where he had lived as a Marrano, should utilize his connections to influence the Dutch parliament and the King of England, and seek to have them dissuade Maria Theresa from taking drastic measures against the Jews. It is doubtful whether this first attempt to enlist international assistance for the Jews of Prague had any practical consequences.

The first widespread reaction to the travails of the Prague community came after pogroms were carried out against the Jews during the two days following the Prussian evacuation of the city (November 26–27, 1744). The rioters included soldiers from the Habsburg invasion force, Prussian deserters, and local residents. Some twenty people were killed during the disturbances and most of the members of the community sustained both physical and financial injury. For the next three weeks, until the arrival of the regular Habsburg forces, Jewish communal life was almost completely paralyzed. At the beginning of December 1744, a number of Prague Jews sent letters to their relatives and business associates in other cities, describing the troubles that had befallen them. All of the letters included requests for material assistance to the Jews of Prague, as well as a plea to spread the news of their misfortune.

The recipients of the letters did in fact disseminate the news that arrived from Prague. They made copies of the letters they received and sent them to their correspondents who, in turn, sent the information on to others. Thus the news reached Wolf Wertheimer in Augsburg via the Jewish communities in Swabia and Franconia, and he passed it on to his sons in Vienna and Munich. Similarly, knowledge of the events in Prague spread all over Germany, and even to Jewish communities in other parts of Europe, such as Italy and England.[3]

Information about the events in Prague also reached the press. A number of Jewish leaders tried to see to it that accounts sympathetic to the Jews were published in the South German press. Some Prussian newspapers reported the pogroms, apparently on their own initiative. Travelers disseminated news by word of mouth in the different Jewish communities. Such unified and coordinated methods of circulating the news, in particular the network of correspondence between the various court Jews, also proved effective later in spreading word about the edict to expel the Jews from Prague and the steps taken to prevent it.

THE DECREES OF EXPULSION

On December 18, 1744, Maria Theresa signed a decree requiring all the Jews of Prague to leave the city by the end of January 1745. In addition, the edict ordered all the Jews of Bohemia (including those who had been banished from Prague) to leave by the end of June 1745, and forbade them to resettle in any of the other Habsburg lands. Maria Theresa stated in the text of the decree that the measure was motivated by many 'very weighty' reasons, yet she did not enumerate them. The immediate impetus for the queen's decision to issue the expulsion order was almost certainly the rumors that reached her regarding the treasonous behavior of the Jews. However, even after it had been proved to her that the rumors were false, she stood by her decision. In addition, Maria Theresa issued an edict at the beginning of January 1745, expelling all of the Jews from Moravia—and they had not been involved in the war at all. It is clear, therefore, that the queen's decisions were motivated by much deeper, and less obvious, reasons.

Without doubt, the growth of the Jewish population in Prague and in Bohemia, as well as the complaints of the non-Jewish residents of Prague about Jewish economic competition, had come to the attention of generations of Habsburg rulers. The early years of the eighteenth century saw the crystallization of a conscious and consistent policy to restrict the Jewish population of Prague and Bohemia. One day before the issuance of the edict ordering the expulsion of the Jews of Prague, Graf Kinsky, the Bohemian chancellor, sent a memorandum to Maria Theresa regarding the Jews. In his opinion, the masses of poor Jews, who earned their living as middlemen, were harmful to the kingdom's economy and were robbing the Christian residents of their livelihoods. Even the organized Jewish communities were undesirable since by their very existence they facilitated Jewish solidarity, presumably directed against the interests of the Christian residents, and prevented efficient supervision of the activities of the Jews. But Graf Kinsky was also influenced by the mercantilistic outlook then prevalent in most of the courts in central Europe. In line with this theory he held the view—which the queen did not share—that not every Jew was harmful to the state. He pointed out that the wealthy Jews, who controlled most of Bohemia's foreign trade and financed most of its manufacture, benefited the state. They should be allowed, therefore, to remain in Bohemia and its capital, although their autonomous institutions should be abolished, as was then the case in Vienna. In addition, advised Kinsky, a 'hasty' expulsion of the rest of the Jews was liable to inflict harm on their Christian creditors, as well as contradict the principles of Christian compassion.

Despite Kinsky's recommendations, Maria Theresa affixed her signature to a general order expelling all the Jews from Prague and the Kingdom of Bohemia. Even afterward, the queen would not listen to arguments based on utilitarian or humanitarian considerations. It is clear that Maria Theresa's deep animosity toward the Jews, the product of her Jesuit education and devout Catholicism, motivated the expulsion order although, in the eyes of most of her courtiers and the statesmen of her day, it was not in keeping with the spirit of the times.

Word of the expulsion order, as well as the pleas to rescind it, issued simultaneously from Prague and Vienna. The leaders of the Jewish community in Prague assumed that the queen was taken in by the libels against them and that the leaders of the Vienna community had not yet succeeded in assuaging her wrath. As was customary during times of trial, the community endeavored to arouse the mercy of heaven by fasting and mourning. In addition to these measures, the secular and religious leadership of the community maintained constant consultations in order to find more down-to-earth means of relieving their distress. They sent letters to Jewish communities and leaders, both within and outside the Habsburg lands, in the hope that some of them would find ways to pressure the court in Vienna. They also sent two emissaries to the community leaders in Vienna, to apprise them of their dire situation.

While various members of the community sent their own letters describing the emergency facing the Jews of Prague, the community leadership prepared a circular letter for wide distribution, to which a copy of the expulsion order was attached. It described the serious economic situation of the community and the fact that there were many sick and impoverished people who might die if forced to leave during the height of winter, which was especially harsh that year. It went on to tell of the poor conditions of the roads, crowded with troops, and that the countries bordering Bohemia forbade Jews to settle within their territories. The circular claimed that the expulsion order was the result of lies and libels spread by the enemies of the Jews, and it contained a plea for assistance from the recipients of the letter.

The circular letter was sent from Prague to Jewish leaders and communities throughout the Holy Roman Empire immediately following the issuance of the expulsion edict. The recipients copied and forwarded the letter to other communities throughout Europe and even in the Ottoman Empire. By the first week in January 1745, the news had reached Holland, Italy, England, and Denmark. With similar expediency, letters were dispatched from Vienna. The most noteworthy of these, sent by Samuel Wertheimer to his father Wolf in Augsburg, was intended for, and received, wide distribution. It was the first in a series of reports that Wolf Wertheimer received from his son in the Habsburg capital. Samuel's letters reflected the anti-Jewish atmosphere prevailing at the court in Vienna, and the distress and apprehension that had taken hold of the leaders of the Jewish community there. During the days preceding the promulgation of the edict, several prominent Jews had approached their acquaintances among the ministers and courtiers, asking them to try to calm the queen's anger against the Jews. Maria Theresa, however, reacted so violently to any attempt to raise the Jewish issue that no one dared to mention it to her, let alone present her with a petition on the subject. Furthermore, the queen ordered that no Jew should set foot in court, thereby limiting the influence of Baron D'Aguilar and other Jews with contacts there. Following the official announcement of the expulsion order, the anxiety of the Viennese Jews grew even more intense. Samuel Wertheimer hinted in his letter of fears that new decrees would be issued affecting the Jews in other Habsburg lands.

RESPONSES TO THE EDICTS OF EXPULSION

The feeling of interdependency and solidarity among the widely scattered Jewish communities is illustrated by the scores of letters exchanged among them beginning in late December 1744. They reacted to the news of the impending expulsion of the Jewish community of Prague as if they were all limbs belonging to a single body. Especially striking is the extraordinary speed with which the news spread, considering the forms of communication available in the mid-eighteenth century. Activities aimed at obtaining diplomatic intercession on behalf of Prague Jewry began almost simultaneously in several European courts.

This offensive was initiated in six major Jewish communities at almost the same time. At the outset of the campaign most of those involved were unaware of the activities being conducted elsewhere, although they assumed that other communities were participating in the effort. Although there was no central force directing the activities of the 'court Jews' of Europe, as some historians have surmised, they used very similar, if not identical, arguments. This was true both of the arguments employed internally, to rouse Jews to action, and of those directed at the courts of Europe. Among the former, two in particular are to be found in almost every letter that has survived to the present day. First and foremost was the spontaneous expression that it was a moral imperative to come to the aid of the Prague community, the 'metropolis of Israel', a center of learning for all of Ashkenazi Jewry. The fact that Prague had one of the oldest and largest Jewish communities in Europe gave it a special place of honor. The second argument was political in nature. By the middle of the eighteenth century the practice of expelling entire Jewish communities had been generally abandoned. The Jewish leaders felt that if the Jews were expelled from Prague a very dangerous precedent would be set. They likened the act of expulsion to a contagion, and warned each other that if it were not stopped it would spread to other countries.

The letters produced their first results within a few days of their despatch. In late December 1744, one royal court after another began to send instructions to its diplomatic representatives in Vienna to intercede with the court of Maria Theresa on behalf of the Jews of Prague. The Jewish communities of Holland were the first to request intercession on the part of their government. The tolerant attitude exhibited by the Dutch government toward the Jews had given the Jewish leaders in different parts of the Holy Roman Empire and elsewhere the idea of appealing to the Jews of Holland for help. But even before these appeals arrived, Dutch Jewry had taken action—immediately after receiving word from Prague.

At the end of December, Bendit Gomperz, a banker for the Dutch government who lived in Nijmegen, Holland, received the circular letter from Prague. He immediately wrote to a relative in Amsterdam, asking him to go to The Hague and seek help from the Estates-General, the Dutch parliament. Gomperz also alerted London Jewry to the situation, asking them to seek the intervention of the King of England. In the meantime the leaders of the Amsterdam community received letters sent to them by special courier from Prague via Hanover. The leaders of the Amsterdam community, both Ashkenazim and Sephardim, announced the establishment of a fund to help the Jews of Prague. They sent a delegation to The Hague, which met on December 31 with Tobias Boas, one of the most important bankers in Holland, and emissaries from Rotterdam.

The joint delegation appeared before the Estates-General and presented a petition in which they claimed that their brethren in Prague had sworn by all that was holy to them that they had done nothing to deserve the wrath of the queen. The petition also noted that, if the edict were carried out, the Jews of Holland were liable to suffer substantial financial losses, since they were owed considerable amounts of money by their brethren in Prague and Bohemia who might be prevented from fulfilling their obligations because of the expulsion. Furthermore, it was pointed out that the ties and commercial relations between Jews in Holland and their coreligionists in Bohemia would be completely disrupted, causing irreparable harm to many Dutch Jewish families. The Estates-General was asked to take into account considerations based on justice and mercy, as well as practical arguments. The petition requested that the Dutch ambassador in Vienna be instructed to take all necessary steps to see that a commission of inquiry be appointed and the expulsion prevented.

The Estates-General sent a copy of the Jewish petition to the Dutch ambassador in Vienna and instructed him to investigate carefully the reasons for such a harsh edict. If he were to discover that the expulsion was indeed unjustified, he was to represent the interests of those residents of Holland who, "by virtue of their economic ties," had a stake in the fate of the Jews of Prague. This intercession was to be undertaken with great care and discretion, according to the instructions of the Estates-General. By the first week in January 1745, the leaders of the Dutch communities informed their counterparts in other places that they had spared no effort to obtain the diplomatic intervention of the Dutch authorities, and that they had also contacted "our brethren, who dwell in England," in order that they might plead before the king on behalf of the Jews of Prague.

Wolf Wertheimer was quick to respond to the appeals for help that reached him from Vienna and Prague in late December 1744. He was personally acquainted with most of the rulers within the Holy Roman Empire, being court factor for the House of Habsburg and the rulers of Saxony-Poland and Bavaria, as well as other royal figures. His activities involved him in the financial and the political affairs of the courts with which he was in contact.[4] Being unable to leave Augsburg, Wertheimer directed his own wide-ranging diplomatic campaign by correspondence.[5] He wrote to a number of rulers to plead the cause of Prague's Jews, but not having a great deal of faith in the power of the written word he employed another tactic as well. He wrote to court Jews in various lands, encouraging them to approach their rulers in person.

Among the letters that Wertheimer wrote was one to his brother-in-law, Rabbi Moses Kann, the head of the yeshiva in Frankfurt am Main. Wertheimer urged Kann to speak to the Archbishop of Mainz, whom Kann served as court factor. Wertheimer attached special importance to the intervention of the archbishop, who wielded a great deal of influence in the courts of the Empire—especially in the court of the House of Habsburg. A letter written by him might mitigate the queen's fury and obtain at least a postponement of the expulsion. Among the ammunition that Wertheimer proffered was the argument that it would be unjust to punish an entire community for the sins of a few individuals, especially since the matter had not been investigated at all. In addition he recalled that after the French occupation force had evacuated Prague in 1742, a commission of inquiry had not accused the Jews of treasonable behavior; rather it had placed blame on the nobility and upon many of the gentile residents of Prague. Perhaps that was why the latter now wished to slander the Jews.

Wertheimer also urged his brother-in-law to contact Tobias Boas in The Hague and ask him to seek help from the Dutch Estates-General and perhaps even from the King of England. He further advised the Frankfurt community to send a delegation to the Jewish community in Rome in order that they might jointly attempt to sway the Pope to exert his influence on Maria Theresa, whose religious zeal was well known in the courts of Europe. Wertheimer's letter to Kann is only one example of the many he wrote in his attempt to weave a web of diplomatic activity that spanned Central Europe and reached Holland, England, Denmark, and Italy. In addition to trying to enlist the aid of rulers (especially Catholics), diplomats, and prominent clergymen, it would seem that Wertheimer hoped to employ his contacts to influence members of Maria Theresa's own family.

Wolf Wertheimer worked quickly and carried out all of this activity, and much more, during approximately one week (December 28, 1744 to January

I.8.8

5, 1745). Many of his suggestions, however, reached the various Jewish leaders after they had already begun to act on their own initiative. Rabbi Moses Kann, for example, had also received the circular letter from Prague. In his reply to Wertheimer he wrote that the Frankfurt community had been profoundly shocked by the news from Prague and that ever since they had received it they had been sending urgent messages to "every place in which Jews reside."[6]

Kann had formulated his own plan to go to Mainz, and on the night of January 3, 1745 he was granted an audience with the archbishop. As Kann described the meeting in a subsequent letter to Wertheimer, he prostrated himself before the archbishop and broke into tears, arousing the compassion of the influential clergyman. According to Kann, the archbishop consulted with his ministers that very night, and the following day he voiced his protest against the expulsion order to the Habsburg ambassador in Mainz. The archbishop wrote a letter to Maria Theresa telling her that if she were to banish a group of people who had enjoyed her protection for many years and were willing to continue to serve her, a negative impression would be created in the Empire and in all of Europe. If, on the other hand, she would give the Jews an opportunity to atone for their misdeeds, she would become known as a merciful queen. Kann also received the assurance of the chancellor of Mainz, Baron Erthal, that he would try to influence the representatives of Hanover and Saxony to intercede with Vienna. Erthal kept his promise. Kann achieved all this during two days in Mainz. Immediately upon completing his mission, Kann reported to the Frankfurt leadership.

German Jewry continued to mobilize for the diplomatic offensive. The Jews of Saxony, as well as those of Altona, Hamburg, and Wandsbek, were among the many who were involved. By mid-January 1745, a number of letters pleading for the Jews had been sent to Maria Theresa, including letters from the queen's mother, and from her grandfather, the Duke of Brunswick.

Word of the expulsion edict reached the Jews of England from Holland and Hamburg. On January 8, King George II granted an audience to a delegation of London Jews. The king was presented with a petition that claimed that the expulsion of the Jews, who had been loyal to Maria Theresa and had supported her against her enemies, would be an unjust act and would "prove detrimental and prejudicial to the true interest of the common cause"—a reference, it seems, to the alliance between England and the House of Habsburg in the War of the Austrian Succession, which was still going on. According to the accounts of the delegation, the king was quite upset by what he heard and condemned the idea of punishing the entire Jewish community of Prague for the sins of a few individuals.[7] On that very day a message was sent in the name of the king to the English ambassador in Vienna, instructing him to cooperate with his Dutch colleague in trying to dissuade Maria Theresa from carrying out the expulsion. The British diplomat was also advised to hint to the Habsburg court that the expulsion would create a very bad impression in the world and, at the same time, would cause great harm to the Bohemian economy and substantially reduce the queen's income.

On the same day that the King of England received the London delegation, a group of Jews from Copenhagen submitted a petition to the King of Denmark. The Danish king sent a personal letter to Maria Theresa, in which he argued that the expulsion edict was unjust and that it would inflict financial losses on the residents of many European countries, including those of Denmark. The Jews of Italy were also active in the campaign. One of the most significant activities was the attempt to convince the Pope to intercede with Maria Theresa. The Pope, however, did not act until the end of February, at which time he instructed his representative in Vienna to try to persuade the queen to be lenient with the Jews.

By the middle of January 1745, a substantial number of letters arguing against the expulsion of the Jews from Prague had been sent to Vienna. Among those who sent letters were the Estates-General of Holland, the Kings of England and Denmark, the Archbishop of Mainz, the mother of Maria Theresa, the Duke of Brunswick, and the Venetian Senate. All this had been achieved within the space of approximately three weeks. Information regarding the various diplomatic activities was disseminated throughout the Jewish communities of Europe on an almost daily basis. The fact that the Jewish leadership was able to enlist the aid of so many courts in such a short time, despite the fact that a large-scale war was in progress, gave them the feeling that they had done everything possible to help their brethren in Prague. Now all waited to hear from the Jews of Vienna.

Most of the letters were forwarded through the Jewish leadership of Vienna to the various diplomatic representatives in the Austrian capital. The recipients of the letters were instructed to try to intercede at court on behalf of the Jews of Prague. The queen, however, was not willing to receive any petitions regarding the matter, nor were foreign diplomats able to approach her, as she was in confinement due to her pregnancy. Two of the letters were sent directly to Maria Theresa—those of the King of Denmark and the Archbishop of Mainz. To these she reacted angrily, claiming that they represented an infringement on her sovereignty.

Such was the news conveyed by the Jews of Vienna in the then relatively sparse correspondence that they maintained with the other Jewish communities in Europe. By the end of January they had nothing to report regarding the results of the various letters, even failing to acknowledge their receipt in most cases. Not surprisingly, this situation was a source of considerable consternation to the communities that had been active in obtaining the diplomatic intervention. The silence of the Jews of Vienna may be partially explained by their reluctance to send sensitive information through the mails, for fear that it might fall into the wrong hands. In any event, the vague and disjointed nature of the correspondence between the Jews of Vienna and of the other Jewish communities provides a very incomplete picture of what went on in the Habsburg capital during the winter of 1744–45.

The letters of Samuel Wertheimer have proved to be a somewhat more useful source of information. In a letter dated January 20, he wrote that the leadership of the Vienna community led by Baron D'Aguilar, as well as the emissaries sent from Prague, were continuing their diplomatic efforts. Among those contacted were friends of the queen, her husband, and her brother-in-law Charles of Lorraine. However, those who had access to the queen and attempted to raise the issue of the Jews were harshly rebuffed. Maria Theresa stated that while she was now aware that the Jews were innocent of the charges which had been leveled against them, she was nevertheless unwilling to continue tolerating them in her lands. This attitude, understandably, discouraged further entreaties.

Despite the bleak situation, the Jewish leadership of Vienna and the representatives of the Prague community continued contacting members of the diplomatic corps, as well as Graf Kinsky and others. The only tangible result of all this activity was the postponement of the expulsion until the end of February 1745. Samuel Wertheimer reported that matters were not helped by the fact that the Vienna leadership did not coordinate their actions and allowed personal vanity to interfere with the task at hand. Most of those involved were members of various families of court Jews and were not united in a single communal framework, which might have facilitated cooperation. Nevertheless they did expend a great deal of effort in their attempt to have the expulsion decree canceled. The surviving correspondence between the foreign diplomats and their governments makes it very clear that the queen was almost completely inaccessible and that most of the contacts were limited to semiofficial discussions with the ministers of the Austrian court. The best that these ministers could offer by the end of January was the hope that further postponements might be obtained.

ENFORCEMENT OF THE EDICTS

The beginning of February marked a change in the general political situation in Europe. On January 20, the emperor (the Elector of Bavaria) died. Maria Theresa now saw an opportunity to restore the crown of the Holy Roman Empire to the House of Habsburg by having her husband, Franz of Lorraine, chosen emperor. Word spread throughout the courts of Europe that, in return for the imperial crown, Maria Theresa would be willing to make substantial concessions regarding the remaining issues being contested by Austria and other European powers. Diplomats and special emissaries began negotiations in Vienna, at first with the queen's husband and her ministers and, during the second half of February (after she had given birth), with Maria Theresa herself.[8] The Jewish leadership in Vienna and in the Empire saw in the stepped-up diplomatic activity a renewed opportunity to achieve a repeal of the expulsion decree. Contact was reestablished with Baron Erthal, the chancellor of Mainz, as well as with the special emissary of the King of Poland who, in his capacity as the Elector of Saxony, played a role in choosing the new emperor.

In the third week of February, the queen finally decided to raise the issue of the Jews of Prague before her secret ministerial council (*Geheimkon ferenz*). The council formulated a uniform reply to the appeals from England, Holland, and Poland-Saxony on behalf of the Jews. In it the queen reiterated her claim of exclusive sovereignty over the matter, and stated that she had every intention of carrying out the decree. She did aver, however, that she would take into account the financial interests of those foreign nationals who might be affected by the expulsion, and stated that she would be willing to display some flexibility as far as the timing of the expulsion was concerned.

By now it was clear to all involved that a cancellation of the expulsion order was not possible. According to Samuel Wertheimer, Viennese Jewry had given up hope that salvation could be achieved by earthly means. At the end of February Samuel wrote to his father, Wolf, that he need no longer trouble himself over the issue since none of the diplomatic efforts had succeeded in swaying the queen. As if to underscore the point, a royal decree was issued which, while postponing the implementation of the decree for one more month (until the end of March 1745), stated flatly that the expulsion would be postponed no further.

By the beginning of March, most of the Jews of Prague had left the city. The additional appeals that reached the Viennese court during the first half of the month—including that of the Pope—fell on deaf ears. Especially significant were the repeated efforts of the English and Dutch governments to help the Jews. Lord Harrington, head of the British Cabinet, wrote that the King of England wished to see the terrible decree annulled by the queen, and that "her persevering in that severe and merciless resolution could not but be esteemed by all mankind as an indelible stain both in point of justice and clemency upon her hitherto moderate and equitable Government."

On the last day of March 1745, the leaders of the Prague community handed the keys of the ghetto over to the local authorities as the last Jews filed out of the city. Most of the exiles encamped temporarily in the vicinity of Prague. Others wasted little time and left the country altogether. The wealthier turned to other Jewish communities in the Empire, to Holland, and to Italy. The poor wandered in groups, most of them going to Poland, with a number emigrating to Holland. During April and the early part of May, processions of exiles could be seen passing through Saxony and Prussia, a sight that aroused the compassion of both Jews and non-Jews.

In the meantime, the date set for the expulsion of all the Jews of Bohemia and Moravia—the end of June—was drawing near. Diplomatic efforts aimed at averting the expulsion continued throughout the spring, but not at the same feverish pace that had characterized the activity of the previous January. On April 13, a special messenger from Turkey arrived in Vienna, with a message from the Sultan pleading the cause of the Jews of Bohemia and Moravia. It may be assumed that the letter was the result of Jewish diplomatic activity. The Sultan's plea, however, was no more successful than those that had preceded it.

The Jewish leadership was pessimistic, especially after the issuance of two royal decrees on April 8, containing instructions for implementation of the expulsion from Moravia. Copies of the orders were distributed among the various Jewish communities, accompanied by a warning that a major tragedy was imminent. Once again, networks of correspondence were activated and foreign governments were approached with requests to intercede on behalf of Jews facing expulsion from their homes.

On May 15, 1745, Maria Theresa issued an order indefinitely postponing the expulsion of the Jews from Bohemia and Moravia. According to the queen, the many entreaties she received convinced her that the Jews were involved in a substantial number of financial dealings with her Christian subjects, and that it would not be possible to conclude all of these affairs by the end of June. The postponement (or the cancellation, as it turned out) of the decree took both the Jews and the diplomatic representatives in Vienna completely by surprise. As soon as the news became known, letters expressing joy and relief were exchanged between Jewish communities and individuals.

CANCELLATION OF THE DECREE

What moved Maria Theresa to change her mind on an issue about which she had been so obstinate? The letters and reports of the diplomats involved in the affair do not offer even a hint as to the reason. Upon closer examination it would appear that certain general circumstances aided the diplomatic effort and contributed to its success. To begin with, since February the Habsburg court had displayed a willingness to compromise with Bavaria, with which Austria had been at war since 1741. Maria Theresa notified the Electors of Mainz and Cologne, as well as the governments of England and Holland, of her terms for peace—the cardinal condition being the 'election' of her husband as emperor. Mediation efforts were initiated immediately. In April, secret negotiations were begun in Augsburg with the participation of representatives of Austria, Bavaria, Mainz, Poland-Saxony, England, Holland, and the papal nuncio. The talks, which were moved from Augsburg to nearby Fuessen, lasted some three weeks. On May 2, less than two weeks before the signing of the order postponing the expulsion decree, a peace treaty was concluded.

The peace negotiations, which sought to determine the political future of Central and Western Europe, took place in and near Augsburg, the home of Wolf Wertheimer, one of the major protagonists in the diplomatic campaign to avert the expulsion of the Jews from Prague. The general atmosphere of conciliation surrounding the talks, as well as the presence of representatives of the most important rulers in the Empire (some of whom had tried to intercede on behalf of the Jews of Prague), provided Wertheimer with a unique opportunity to carry on his diplomatic offensive with renewed intensity. It is difficult to imagine that a man like Wertheimer, who was acquainted with most of the rulers in the Empire and maintained financial and other ties with them, would pass up such an opportunity. This assertion is, nevertheless, difficult to prove from the written record. Neither Wertheimer's name nor the issue of the expulsion appears in any of the reports regarding the negotiations, or in the text of the peace treaty. Furthermore, from the end of March until the cancellation of the expulsion decree in mid-May, Wertheimer's correspondence file contains copies of only three letters to other Jewish leaders on the subject.

Three additional memoranda written by Wertheimer during April and May 1745 are extant. One, written on May 5, was addressed to a government minister in Vienna. The other two, dating from May 11 and 14, were sent to the widow of the late emperor and to her son, the new Elector of Bavaria. The fact that Wertheimer turned to both the House of Habsburg and the Bavarian House of Wittelsbach, which had recently been at war with each other, indicates that he knew of the Peace of Fuessen even before the event had become public knowledge; otherwise his request to the Elector of Bavaria to intervene with Maria Theresa on behalf of the Jews would make no sense. Incidentally, the texts of the three memoranda are almost identical with a letter Wertheimer had addressed to the Bishop of Bamberg-Wurzburg in January. They contain no new facts or arguments.

The relative paucity of correspondence during this period may be explained by Wertheimer's preference for verbal contacts. He had been unable to leave Augsburg since the beginning of the expulsion episode, and initially had to rely on letters encouraging Jewish leaders in other locations to approach their rulers. The negotiations at Augsburg and Fuessen created a new situation. If our assumption is correct that Wertheimer took advantage of the presence of the negotiators to plead the Jewish cause, it is unlikely that he would have described contacts of such a discreet nature in letters to other Jewish leaders. The memoranda would have been meant to reinforce Wertheimer's verbal contacts, on which he placed most of his faith.

Even if Wertheimer's activity was ultimately the deciding factor, it is doubtful whether he would have succeeded without the efforts of other communities and individuals within the Empire and throughout Europe. By repeatedly raising the issue of the expulsion before ministers, diplomats, and other influential figures in Vienna, as well as before rulers and governments in other capitals, a cumulative effect was achieved, which presumably influenced the final outcome of the crisis. With the publication of the royal order of May 15, 1745, the danger of expulsion facing the major Jewish communities of Bohemia and Moravia passed. From then until the summer of 1748, when the exiles from Prague were allowed to return to the city, contacts were maintained, primarily by the exiles, with the government of Bohemia as well as with Maria Theresa.

The historical significance of this episode increases our understanding of the position of the Jews in Central and Western Europe on the threshold of the Enlightenment period. Since the end of the seventeenth century, with the growing tolerance toward the Jews of Europe, no decree had been issued that could have been expected to provoke as widespread a reaction as the Prague expulsion. One could have imagined that, as a result of this increased tolerance and the integration of certain segments of Jewish society into the surrounding culture, the feeling of Jewish solidarity would have grown weaker. However, this episode indicates that the sensitivity of Jews in various countries to the fate of their persecuted brethren had not diminished at all. Moreover, from the end of the seventeenth century until the Prague expulsion—and from that event until the Damascus affair in 1840—no single incident so focused the energies of all European Jewry toward the fulfillment of a single goal.

Jewish reaction to the expulsion edict was determined, in no small measure, by some few individuals and, particularly, by the court Jews and their associates. Toward the middle of the eighteenth century there was an increase in the number of court Jews in Central Europe, and their influence at court grew. Their position was essentially dichotomous: on the one hand they were closely connected with the ruler-patrons and readily adopted the conceptual frameworks of their courts; on the other hand they continued to be deeply attached to Judaism and often held respected positions in the leadership of the Jewish communities. The events described here reflect the unifying function which the court Jews and their circle fulfilled in Jewish society. Their proximity to the courts which, to some extent, undermined their moral authority within the community, was the factor that enabled them to act as effectively as they did on behalf of the Jews of Bohemia and Moravia. The existing network of mutual Jewish ties, which facilitated the court Jews' involvement in international trade and finance, also made possible the rapid and wide-ranging organization and exchange of information that was necessary for the intensive diplomatic campaign carried out by European Jewry.

The expulsion decree, the traditional feeling of Jewish solidarity, and the unusual historical circumstances of Central and Western European Jewry in the mid-eighteenth century, all contributed to the making of a historical drama with a unique political-diplomatic character. In its pan-Jewish scope it was hardly matched by any other event from the beginning of the modern era until the second half of the nineteenth century.

NOTES

1. S. Stern, *The Court Jew* (Philadelphia: JPS, 1950), pp. 204–207, deals briefly with the diplomatic activities surrounding this episode, and presents it as an example of the reciprocal relations that existed between the Jewish courtiers in various countries.

2. The episode occurred during the interim period between the Austrian surrender and the entry of the Prussians. The populace began to plunder the Jewish quarter, and a delegation of Jews asked the Prussian commander to protect them. The Jewish delegation accompanied the troop of soldiers sent to their aid. The chronicle continues, "And when the townspeople saw the Prussians with four Jews, they cursed roundly and could be heard saying wickedly one to the other, 'See, the Jews have brought the Prussians into the city.' " (*Jahrbuch der Judisch-Literarischen Gesellschaft* 2 [1904]: 3–66.)

3. Copies of this correspondence were kept in the archival ledgers (*pinkas*) of the various Jewish communities, many of which have been transferred to the Jewish National and University Library and to the Central Archives of the History of the Jewish People, both in Jerusalem.

4. See S. Stern, *The Court Jews*, pp. 63, 89, 92–93, 235.

5. The Central Archives of the History of the Jewish People contains a bundle of draft memos (CS85) written by Wolf Wertheimer to various rulers. Two signed memos were directed to the Bishop of Bamberg-Wurzburg and were intended to support the petitions of a delegation of Jews whom Wertheimer had requested to appear before the bishop.

6. It should be remembered that it was customary for the leaders of the Jewish communities to copy every important news item and send it to a number of correspondents, together with newspaper clippings, extracts, documents, and so on. Thus, the limited number of letters and documents found in various archives represents only a fraction of the written material that was circulating during this period.

7. " . . . as His Majesty does extremely commiserate the terrible circumstances of distress—He is most . . . earnestly desirous of procuring the repeal of it by His royal intercession."

8. See D. B. Horn, "Saxony in the War of Austrian Succession." *English Historical Review* (1929): 33–47.

SUGGESTION FOR FURTHER READING

Transactions of the Jewish Historical Society of England 22 (1970): 30–41; includes bibliographical references.

9

MICHAEL GRAETZ

On the Return of Moses Hess to Judaism: The Background to "Rome and Jerusalem"

Some of the most important Jewish thinkers who had an impact on nineteenth- and twentieth-century Jewish history arrived at their ideas after combining, in different ways, Jewish traditional culture and modern European schools of thought. Very often their attitude is characterized by ambivalence—attraction to or reaction against one or both of these frameworks—and these feelings intermingle to create the unique nature of their philosophy. Moses Hess is an example of such a dialectic combination. The following article traces the development of his thought against the background of his spiritual biography.

Michael Graetz is professor of Modern Jewish History at The Hebrew University of Jerusalem. He specializes in modern Jewish ideological movements, especially in nineteenth-century France, about which he has written a major book.

BACKGROUND

Moses Hess was a leader in the emerging European socialist movement; indeed, many historians consider him the father of German social democracy. His lifelong career as a socialist began at the University of Bonn, where he studied philosophy for two years. Hess became a left-wing Hegelian and a proponent of antibourgeois revolution.

In the early 1840s Hess was a founder, editor, and Paris correspondent

This article first appeared in Hebrew in *Zion* 45 (1980). The translation/adaptation is by Daniel Weinstein.

The International Center for University Teaching of Jewish Civilization, Jerusalem, the author of the article, and the translator/adapter grant permission to photocopy this article for teaching purposes without further permission or fee.

for the newspaper, *Rheinische Zeitung*, the first socialist daily in Cologne. He discovered Karl Marx in 1841, when Marx did not yet enjoy wide circulation. Hess had no small influence on Frederick Engels as well. He collaborated with this famous socialist duo on their book, *German Ideology*.

During the great period of revolution that swept across Europe in 1848 and 1849, Hess was living in Paris as the correspondent for a number of German-language newspapers and was witness to the overthrow of the monarchy and the tumultuous days of the Second Republic of France. He fled France in 1849, and sought refuge in Switzerland and later in Belgium. It was not until 1853 that he was able to return; thereafter with only brief interruptions, he lived in Paris until his death in 1875.

The French uprising had enormous impact throughout Europe and inspired numerous other revolts, but they proved short-lived, not only in France but in all of Europe. In the period of bitter disappointment which followed the crushing of the 1848 revolutions, Hess and Marx parted company. Each man reacted differently to the new situation and the failure of their dreams to realize a new social and economic order. Marx went on to develop his theories of communist materialism based on economic and class factors. Hess became a social democrat, ever faithful to the precepts of utopian socialism based on a vision of an ideal future social organization. While not denying the influence of social and economic realities, he stressed the importance of education and moral ethics in preparing the ground for socialism. The first book published by Hess in 1837 signaled the beginning of his lifelong fascination with a historical-philosophical theory of the development of mankind. It also reflected those sources of inspiration that characterized all of his works—the Bible, Spinoza, and socialism.

Although Hess was the product of an Orthodox upbringing, his early attitude toward Jews varied from indifference to scorn. At best, he gave Jews credit for the introduction of monotheism. Yet he felt that this contribution was negated by their rejection of the next stage in man's moral development, Christianity. Hess derisively described the Jews as a people with no future, either as a religion or a nation. Their religion had been supplanted by more advanced ideas and their national consciousness had been totally destroyed during the course of 2,000 years of exile. Moreover, Hess identified the Jews with capitalism. For all of these reasons, he claimed that the Jews resisted the flow of history and were worthy of nothing more than contempt for failing to abandon an antiquated philosophy. In his writings during the mid–1840s Hess leveled criticism of the most extreme sort against his own people.

In the early 1860s, however, *Rome and Jerusalem* appeared, whose call for a Jewish national revival firmly installed Hess as one of the most remarkable precursors of modern Zionism. In the opening pages of this book Hess wrote:

I.9.2

Here I stand once more, after twenty years of estrangement, in the midst of my people; I participate in its holy days of joy and mourning, its memories and hope, its spiritual struggles in its own house and with the civilized people among which it lives, but with which, despite 2,000 years of living and striving together, it cannot organically coalesce. A thought which I had stifled forever within my heart is again vividly present with me; the thought of my nationality, inseparable from the inheritance of my ancestors, the Holy Land and the eternal city, the birthplace of my belief in the divine unity of life and in the future brotherhood of all men. This thought, buried alive, had for years throbbed in my sealed heart, demanding outlet. But I lacked the energy necessary for the transition, from a path apparently so remote from Judaism as mine was, to that new path which appeared before me in the hazy distance and only in its general outlines.

So startling was the content of this book that in 1901 Herzl wrote in his diary "What an exalted noble spirit! Everything that we have tried is already in his book. . . . Since Spinoza, Jewry has brought forth no greater spirit than this forgotten Moses Hess."

During Hess's own time, however, *Rome and Jerusalem* met with a great deal less enthusiasm. In fact, he had difficulty finding a publisher for his strange work. The Jewish community was a full generation away from national revival and greeted his work with silence or with the greatest of reservations. Hess's socialist friends saw it as an individual aberration without wider significance.

Our major concern here is with the background to Hess's 'return' to the Jewish people. Clearly, he had undergone a major change in attitude toward Judaism. Among the reasons given for his about-face were the influence of the Italian wars of national unification fought during 1859–1860 or, as Buber thought, the influence of monotheism and a messianic yearning. This essay examines these factors and proposes new theories on why Moses Hess returned to the Jewish people.

INFLUENCES ON HESS'S THINKING

Hess himself admitted to the influence which the Italian wars had on his thinking. He was certainly enthusiastic about the sudden rebirth of the Italian spirit and drive for national unity. Since the fall of ancient Rome, Italy had been divided into a checkerboard of city-states, dukedoms, principalities, kingdoms, and papal-ruled lands. The renewed national vigor of Italians after millennia of division led Hess to write in 1860 in the French newspaper *Esperance*, "In the steps of Italian rebirth will come the turn of the peoples of the East, even of the ancient Jewish people. . . . "

Later that same year, after the efforts of the Italian national movement had been crowned with success, Hess wrote in the *Pariser Zeitung*, "They [the Italians] are rising anew, with the patience to await their appointed hour. Thus it will be for Greece and thus it will be for the ancient Jewish people. However, Jerusalem will not be rebuilt in a day." Hence it can be said that at the same time the Italian wars were being fought, Jewish nationalism burst into Hess's consciousness. However, one must be cautious not to be trapped by the temptation to see here a mechanical relationship of cause and effect. Things were not so simple.

Ferdinand Lassalle, a Jewish socialist and a friend of Hess, was also an enthusiastic follower of the national struggle of the Italian people. He, however, saw in the Italian events the sign of a much different revival, having nothing to do with Jews. Under the influence of what happened in Italy, Lassalle wrote his well-known book, *The Italian War and the Prussian Task*, in which he expressed his hope for the early unity of the German nation, also divided at that time into various sovereign states. Nowhere in Lassalle's book do we find the slightest hint of the wars for Italian national unity enticing him to return to Judaism.

Clearly, then, there must have been factors at work on Hess other than just the Italian wars. Beyond external political events, one must look into the spiritual and intellectual development of the man. Let us investigate the world view and philosophy of history which he formed a decade before the Italian upheaval.

During the 1850s Hess's alienation from Judaism began to dissipate. Jewish motifs appear more frequently in his printed articles. He begins to see Judaism as having a crucial mission in the world, as carrying an essential message. Monotheism and messianic vision, unique to the people of Israel, could advance humanity through history toward a future of happiness and harmony. In these early articles there was as yet no sign of Jewish nationalism but, beyond doubt, they represent an important turning point on the road to *Rome and Jerusalem*.

Hess began trying to come to grips with the significance of the historical continuity of the Jewish people. Here, his world view was formed through conflict with the Christian viewpoint. Christianity maintained that with the birth of Jesus the period of the Jewish mission in the world came to an end. Moreover, the very right of the Jewish people to exist ended with the ascendancy of Christianity. Jews therefore had to be pushed outside the course of world history, isolated in every possible way.

When Hess dealt with the question of the position of the Jews in history in his pre–1850 meetings, he essentially adopted the Christian attitude. The following typifies this earlier point of view. "After the Jews gave up their vision of the future and expelled Jesus from their midst, they had no form of existence aside from that of mummies, bodies without a soul." The Jewish yearning for salvation, and the belief in the coming of the Messiah were devoid of meaning because the Jews had rejected the true path found in Jesus. Theirs was, Hess continued, a barren religion as they wandered like ghosts across the face of the living world.

Only in 1855 did Hess manifest a tendency to move away from this Christian source of inspiration. He began to relate to Jews in a more positive manner. In one conceptual package, Hess wrapped together the monotheism and new social order of the coming new age with the monotheism and messianic vision of the Jews. The reintegration of the Jewish people into world history was an obvious effort to overcome the barrier erected by Christian ideology. No longer were Jews to be kept outside the course of history because of their denial of Jesus. Now Jews could aspire to play an essential and positive role in the fate of mankind.

Seven years before the publication of *Rome and Jerusalem*, the signs of a spiritual change within Hess were apparent. He now claimed that the Jews were the first to bring to the world the fundamental principles that form its spiritual and social order. No longer did Hess praise Christianity at the expense of Judaism. To him Christianity was only the geographically western side of the world's advance toward the final harmonious age; furthermore, it derived the inspiration for its basic tenets from Judaism. No longer was Judaism merely the launching point for religious development; it was now the ultimate stage in religious history.

Hess had previously considered the religious-mystical dimension of the concepts 'chosen people' and 'messianic vision'; now he maintained that they held historical and social significance as well. Messianic vision constituted the broad sweep of mankind's march through history, extending to humanity a final goal and delineating a planned path of advancement. It was Judaism's great privilege to have fathered the prophecy about the End-of-Days, and to have set in motion the wheels of history toward that end. Christianity had a role in furthering the process. Jesus was one of mankind's great moral teachers; he gave to Judaism a universal resonance. Hess appreciated the Christianity that adhered to the monotheistic basis set down by Judaism. But, stated Hess, from the days of Paul, Christianity became corrupted and lost its right to be the bearer of the messianic vision. In such a condition, Christianity could not be the final stage in universal history; an additional non-Christian stage was necessary. After Christianity's deviation from monotheism, the Jewish people became the key for historical advancement toward the messianic age. Jewish involvement in history was a precondition for the planned evolution of mankind. In order to prevent mankind from straying from the path, the Jewish people had produced a moral teacher at each turning point in history—Moses, the prophets, Jesus, Spinoza—who labored to keep mankind on the road to messianic salvation.

Hess went still further in buttressing the role of the Jewish people. The foundation of future messianic harmony was unity, deeply rooted in Jewish tradition. He identified this with the uniformity of the law of heaven and its holiness in nature and history. This Jewish principle of unity presumed not only the law of the uniform development of history but also the impossibility of dividing the spiritual and material realms that correspond to the heavens and the earth. It also established the unity of individual and collective existence.

Hess considered himself a student of Spinoza in his understanding of unity, and an opponent of the duality of Christianity. He identified duality in the Christian belief in the immortality of the soul that diminished the appreciation of life in this world by emphasizing the fruits of the world-to-come. Christian belief in the holy Trinity was further proof to Hess of the deep rift between Judaism and Christianity and the latter's inability to provide the basis for the formation of messianic harmony in the future.

The Jewish principle of unity had political and social validity. It was destined to create an earthly messianic kingdom in which the struggle between opposing forces would cease. (Hess had absorbed the theory of opposing forces, a basic premise of Hegelian philosophy, in the 1830s.) The race and class wars that had propelled history in the past would come to an end. A new form of association, unbounded in time and space, would dominate. The particularist tendencies of man would be united with the universal in perfect harmony.

Certainly, Hess's vision of such a radically reformed world order was influenced by the utopian socialists. However, Jewish philosophy, which spoke of an earthly messianic kingdom, played no small role as well. In fact, Hess identified the messianic age as a Mosaic precept. Here it must be stressed that he believed this messianic age would be realized within, and not outside, the borders of history.

The change in Hess's orientation during the 1850s was not determined solely by a yearning for a reformed world order styled on utopian socialism. He had already embarked on that quest during his youth; nor was the messianic vision new to him. The metamorphosis was gradual. In Hess's time it was usually claimed that it was Christianity that established happiness, freedom, and justice as the goals of universal development. However, during the 1850s, Hess came to see Judaism as a legitimate source for the socialist utopia. This new and favorable interpretation that he gave to basic Jewish concepts was compatible with the European notion of a philosophy of history; it represented the beginning of his return to the Jewish people.

SOCIAL AND IDEOLOGICAL INFLUENCES

The social and ideological forces that set into motion the dynamics of Hess's return to Judaism require further analysis. The revolution of 1848 was a traumatic experience for all the revolutionary fighters, liberals or radicals, Christians or Jews. All of them were, to a greater or lesser extent, deeply affected by the failure of their messianic expectations. The messianic age had been proclaimed to be just around the corner. Yet, when the corner was turned, they found nothing but brutal counterrevolutionary repression.

Such apocalyptic tension followed by terrible disappointment inevitably led to frustration. To seek release from this condition, one could move in two possible directions. One would be to take fresh stock of the conditions that led to the failure. This was the course taken by Marx, who returned to the socialist world with a new analysis of the situation. A nonrational hardening of old positions characterized the second reaction; the stubborn refusal to renounce the messianic vision was the path chosen by Hess.

After 1848 Hess sought to combat despair by expressing a continuing faith in an imminent revolution. The title of his first book in this period, *Jugement dernier du vieux monde sociale* (1857), illustrates Hess's belief that he was living on the doorstep of the great revolutionary transition to the new age. The epic struggle he described as being waged between the democratic forces of light and the antidemocratic forces of darkness were not far removed from the imagery of the apocalyptic war between Gog and Magog mentioned in the Bible. Revolution, Hess contended, was the unavoidable conclusion to the final tension that would propel the world from disharmony to harmony. It was characteristic of his obstinate approach that Hess added no new elements to prove the historical logic of his claim that the troops of democracy, the proletariat, the republic, and socialism, would soon vanquish their opposition. With the anticipation of Judgment Day and the messianic era at the very heart of his philosophy of history, no further proof was needed for his predictions. In Hess's own words, "We have arrived at the end of one world and are the eyewitnesses to the birth of another."

Nowhere in those troubled days following the defeat of 1848 did Hess proceed to a new analysis of his central concepts of class war and revolution. He believed the messianic vision to be an immediate reality. This total orientation toward the future buoyed up his confidence, his optimism, and his will to act. Rather than fall into passive contemplation or destructive criticism of the past, he directed his efforts toward formulating an ideal future world order. Hess criticized Marx for his lack of future orientation, and maintained that Marx's negativism was not at all conducive to social revolution. "In order to succeed in organizing the workers, we are in need of a different sort of human being." Hess's contempt for Marx spilled over on all radical Germans. "Germany . . . has had within it the talent to criticize the dead past, but not the past which is likely to show humanity the way to a living future."

THE INFLUENCE OF UTOPIAN SOCIALISM

Hess found the positive force he was seeking in utopian socialism. He had formed a close friendship with this school upon his arrival in France, where it was particularly strong. The peak of this movement's influence

and creativity had already passed; the most noteworthy of the French utopian socialists were either in exile in London (Blanc and Raspail) or in North
America (Cabet, Considerant, and Leroux). Others such as Buchez, La-
mennais, Vidal, and Pecqueur ceased all political activity after 1848 due to
their profound feelings of disappointment and frustration. Hence, what
Hess joined ranks with was a rather marginal group of French utopian
socialists who were on the fringes of French society and European socialism.
They were a group without new ideas who were content repeating the
sayings of the 'fathers'. The utopians stubbornly refused to admit that these
teachings had proved lacking during the decisive events of 1848. Although
history had written finis to their movement, they continued with publications, organizations, and fellowship.

Hess joined these utopians for both ideological and emotional reasons.
He shared their denial of messianic failure. Cabet's journal, *Le Populaire*,
reflected this refusal to accept reality and greatly attracted Hess during this
crucial period. *The Great Judgment Day* was published in installments in that
journal. In sharp contrast to his remarks about Marx, Hess praised Cabet's
constructive point of view: "In order to organize we need men in the mold
of Cabet." He became convinced that the forces capable of building the
exemplary future society would arise in France.

At the same time Karl Marx wrote that because of objective political and
economic circumstances the chances for immediate revolutionary change
were growing weaker, *Le Populaire*'s banner headline was that the Great
Judgment Day was approaching. Marx derided this utopian messianism
with its absence of objective analysis. The total incompatibility of approaches
finally caused a definitive rift between Marx and Hess in 1850.

A. Guepin, a physician and republican activist, was a member of the *Le
Populaire* group. In the past he had been a follower of Saint-Simon, the
founder of French socialism, and had earned his militant reputation by his
untiring support of the 1848 Second Republic. Hess praised Guepin and his
works as reflecting the best of French socialism. Guepin shared Hess's
orientation toward the future, and his belief that the solidarity of all religions
and peoples would pave the way to a realization of socialism. They both
maintained a strong belief in moral principles and relied on the wisdom of
man and his ability to profit by education. Hence they believed the future
order would be based on scientific thought and moral values.

This philosophy of history was unacceptable to Marx for two primary
reasons. First and foremost, Marx rejected the mixing of religious and moral
arguments with socialist theory. Second, Marx dismissed the overemphasis
on a utopian vision of the future, preferring an empirical analysis of past
and present social and economic liberations.

Hess and Guepin did not, however, find Marx's ideas unattractive; the
utopians simply pursued different paths of inquiry. Most notably they
sought to discover the one true universal law that would explain the evo-

lutionary processes that functioned on three levels: the universe, the natural world, and human history. In this quest Guepin shared Hess's conviction that the ideal social and political order had already been sketched in the laws of nature. Thus, it was within the grasp of man's intellect to unlock the secrets of the reformed world of the future. As Hess wrote in *The Great Judgment Day*,

In order to understand the movement taking place today within human society, we must discern the fundamental law of nature, according to which organic life, all organisms and all organized systems are divided into periods of antagonism and periods of harmony, separated by the revolution of birth.

This broad concept, which Hess found in utopian socialism, became during the 1850s the leitmotif for all of his writings. Eventually it was to find its way into *Rome and Jerusalem*. Starting in 1853, Hess took up the study of natural science in order to flesh out his theory of an all-encompassing, uniform law. He and his friends hoped to gain greater authority in their battle with the established order by basing their radical social theory on the laws of nature.

The circle of utopian socialists provided a suitable social and intellectual framework for Hess. Overt anti-Semitism was to a great extent absent from utopian circles; this had not been the case with his friends from an earlier period, the left-wing young Hegelians. Hess had disagreements with his non-Jewish utopian comrades, but they were not destined to lead to either a social or intellectual split between them. He would retain the utopian socialists' fundamental, universal messianic vision, elaborating it to include particularistic Jewish concerns. Hess never, even in his youth, denied the justice of the Jewish struggle for equal civil rights. He believed that his contemporaries' new universal and rational value system would justify this struggle.

One of Hess's disagreements with the utopian socialists sprang from the fact that they drew a great deal of inspiration from the social function of Christian religious values. The utopians saw Christianity playing a positive role at various stages in human development. Out of both internal conviction and a desire to find an attentive ear within French society at large, the utopians frequently wove certain Christian motifs into their works. Ironically, even anti-Church republicans such as Hess's friend Guepin had, on occasion, recourse to flaunt his praise of the Early Church as a model of the coming socialist order. Christian brotherhood, it was claimed, would be the basis of social order during the messianic age. Some utopians even went so far as to repeat the old indictment that Jews were the enemies of mankind. There can be no doubt that these Christian themes and occasional expressions of anti-Semitism on the part of his close friends were an irritant to Moses Hess.

I.9.9

There were, however, other voices within utopian socialism that were quite sympathetic to Jews. Prior to 1848, C. Pecqueur was one of the early central figures in French socialism. He often seemed to rank Judaism above Christianity. According to him the Jewish lawgiver Moses was "the first to declare the oneness of God, which meant one thing: there is a natural equality of all men." Pecqueur recounted the impact that Jewish religious teachings had on society at large, even noting the value of the jubilee year and the apportioning of the land to the tribes of Israel. The freeing of the slaves in the jubilee year signified that Moses aspired to the universal brotherhood of man; a just apportionment of the land validated the notion of collective ownership of property. Hess repeated Pecqueur's praise in his own book, *Rome and Jerusalem*.

To fully appreciate the exceptional nature of Pecqueur's positive view of Judaism, we must bear in mind that, while he was writing in the early 1840s, the standard attitude of the Christian world was that the Torah of Moses was nothing more than the basis for useless commentaries and barren legalism. In sharp contrast, Pecqueur's *Theorie Nouvelle D'economie Sociale et Politique* contained none of the traditional Christian accusations against Judaism. Instead, he portrayed the Jewish people and Jewish law as a model for the new reformed society of the future.

Cabet, another of the more notable French utopian socialists, joined Pecqueur in an uphill battle against the negative evaluation of Judaism then dominant in Christian society. He, too, underscored the link between the ancient Jewish republic and the Law of Nature. Jewish law, which had been for so many centuries the target of Christian scorn, was transformed into a source of inspiration and encouragement. Cabet found therein the principles of brotherhood, equality, democracy, and collective ownership.

P. Leroux was another French utopian who assigned the Jews a place of honor in humanity's march toward salvation. The Jews, he wrote, not only gave the world the idea of the messianic age, but defined the characteristics of that new age as well. According to Leroux, Moses was the first to bridge the gap between heaven and earth and to translate metaphysical-religious truths into human and national language. He recognized the Sabbath as the ultimate Jewish contribution to the new age. In the laws of Sabbath the Jews succeeded in uniting the Eternal with earthly social realities. In his view this was the essence of the Jewish messianic vision. Hess later incorporated Leroux's thesis into *Rome and Jerusalem*.

In espousing a favorable attitude toward the Jews, Leroux was apparently trying to remain faithful to the historical model proposed by G. Lessing, the eighteenth-century German philosopher, in his *Education of Mankind*. Lessing's philosophy of history contained two assumptions that inspired Leroux's rehabilitation of Judaism. First, Moses and the Jews were participants in the advancement of world history. They set it into motion and established its moral guidelines; the seeds of the subsequent stages of de-

I.9.10

velopment were in their teachings. The development of Christianity did not represent a major split with Judaism; it was but a transition stage on the road to the 'third age' of messianic times. Second, the laws of Moses, that is to say the social and political system of the ancient 'Hebrew State', were the means for educating mankind.

Leroux, Pecqueur, and Cabet all generated an image of Judaism worthy of positive mention in the works of Christian socialists. In turn, this strengthened the tiny flame of Hess's positive Jewish self-awareness. On the other hand, this socialist world view also contained the seeds of the tension and division that eventually stirred Hess to formulate a theory placing even greater emphasis on the Jewish role in the social redemption of the world.

In the mid–1850s, Hess's friends who had published *Le Populaire* became active in producing the journal *La Revue Philosophique et Religieuse*. They continued their positive assessment of Judaism but nonetheless assigned a dominant role to Christianity in the quest toward utopian socialism. They believed the teachings of Jesus represented a higher stage in the evolution toward a reformed world order, and turned to early Christianity for the foundations of the 'third age'. As they focused on the need for universal brotherhood they saw themselves as the offspring of the early Christians, and not of the Jews who preceded them.

As the utopian socialists disputed the origins and basis of their philosophy, the ancient Jewish-Christian antagonism found its way into Hess's peer group. Sensing discrimination in the elevation of the role of Christianity, Hess reacted by raising the banner of Judaism. He juxtaposed the ancient selection of the People of Israel against the newly found birthright of Christianity. Nevertheless, he did not make a full break with socialism and abandon its universal vision. He managed to synthesize Judaism and socialism through a restrained and moderate process that took on the characteristics of a dialogue between two forces.

Hess saw a possibility of correcting the deviation of the French socialists who had not completely negated Jewish values, but had assigned Judaism only a minor role in the universal vision. He wanted to stake out a wider claim for the Jewish mission in history. He came to see Jewish national revival as the precondition for the establishment of a reformed social order among all the people of the world. Hess nonetheless harbored no hopes for a fruitful dialogue with the members of Marx's communist alliance, who called on the Jews to assimilate fully and then join the socialist cause.

Thus the driving force behind Hess's return to the Jewish people came from the French utopian socialists. A small group on the fringes of both Christian and Jewish society, they were a microcosmic source of norms and values which allowed Hess to form a world view that, in the end, did not overlap with that of Christians or of Jews who were outside the miniworld of utopian socialism. Hess's link with that group proved to be exceedingly stable and to withstand the test of time.

I.9.11

The macrocosmic framework of French and European society was not, of course, without influence on Hess and the utopians. The political and social events as well as the norms and values of the outside world left an indelible imprint on Hess's utopian group—perhaps the greatest of those outside influences being the Italian wars, the revolts of the Poles against Russian domination, and the process of Jewish emancipation.

HESS'S REVISED PHILOSOPHY OF HISTORY

The publication of *Rome and Jerusalem*, with its call for national revival, was rejected by the Jewish public. Never in Hess's lifetime was he granted a position of honor within the Jewish community. Until the day of his death it was the circle of utopian socialist survivors of 1848 who formed Hess's closest social and intellectual relationships.

Nor did the surrounding society appreciate the significance of his work. Hess's fate matched that of the seventeenth-century Jewish philosopher Baruch Spinoza, whom he cited above all others. His regard for Spinoza extended back to 1837 when he subtitled his first book, 'by a student of Spinoza'. In Spinoza's philosophy Hess discovered the means of joining together those two seemingly disparate worlds—heaven and earth, mechanical materialism and the spiritual strength of the philosopher who can build a bridge to the future, thereby saving man's free choice from the blind determinism of the eternal laws of nature. Spinoza pointed to the possibility of mediating between apparently opposite systems of belief, he himself having mediated between modern science and Jewish monotheism. Hess reevaluated Spinoza, emphasizing the Jewish nature of his philosophy. Spinoza's work guided Hess's faith in the ability to unite Jewish particularism and encompassing universalism. Included in his own struggle to reconcile these two concepts were the arguments on the oneness of God, the Jewish messianic vision, and all other elements that would lead to the national revival of his people.

Hess now saw history as developing along two lines: the line of general history evolving through the French revolution toward socialism, and the Jewish continuum leading through emancipation toward national revival. Inevitably the two lines would unite in the harmony of the End-of-Days. Hess gave credit to Spinoza for planting the seeds of the solution to final peace between races, peoples, and religions.

Hess's transformation of Spinoza into a symbol of the essential Jewish spirit was the result of a polemic whose consequences were considerable. He labored to use Spinoza to contradict the anti-Jewish prejudices of his socialist comrades. Spinoza served as absolute proof that it was folly to portray Judaism as barren, totally lacking in creative power, and standing outside the course of human history. Indeed it was the Jews—Moses, the prophets, and Spinoza—who showed the way to an exemplary social and political order without conflict between races, classes, and religions.

The antecedents of *Rome and Jerusalem* are not inscrutable. The developments within Hess's world caused him to undergo a slow internal evolution, which led to what the uninitiated might term an inexplicable return to the Jewish people. Hess was a most exceptional figure in his own time. However, as he called for Jewish national revival, he remained a voice crying in the wilderness. His book *Rome and Jerusalem* came a full generation before the Jewish national movement took on mass dimensions. He was certainly one of those rare visionaries who was able to sense coming events.

The macrocosmic background of Hess's turning from alienation to identification with the Jewish national cause included the Italian wars of national unity as well as the movement toward emancipation within the Jewish communities of Central and Western Europe. Microcosmically speaking, the turning point was the profound impression created when Hess, an educated Jew, came into contact with a group of gentile messianic seekers who allowed him to feel total participation and belonging, thanks to their apparently common socialist vision of salvation. This sense of belonging contributed to Hess's universalist orientation that was not shaken even when the ancient Christian-Jewish antagonism reared its head. However, when his utopian friends redefined Jesus as a social radical, the first socialist in history, Hess recoiled and reacted by formulating a world view in which Judaism had a past, present, and future. In response to the Christian particularism of his friends, Hess adopted an outlook that returned the Jewish people to a central place in world history, even after the birth of Jesus. Many of the specifics of Hess's new master plan of human events were added later by other German Jewish scholars, most notably under the influence of Heinrich Graetz (1817–1891). However, as we have seen, Hess had already drawn up the general outline of his revised philosophy of history some seven years before the publication in 1862 of *Rome and Jerusalem*.

SUGGESTIONS FOR FURTHER READING

Berlin, Isaiah, *The Life and Opinions of Moses Hess*. Cambridge: Jewish Historical Society of England, 1959.

Avineri, Shlomo, *Moses Hess: A Prophet of Communism and Zionism*. New York: NYU Press, 1985.

10

URIEL TAL

The 'Kulturkampf' and the Jews of Germany

Nineteenth-century Jewish communities in Western and Central Europe were engaged in a major struggle to achieve equal rights with their non-Jewish compatriots, and to become integrated within the framework of the European nation-states. This effort necessarily obligated them to relate to some of the major historical and cultural conflicts which rent the societies in which they lived. One of these important involvements is studied in the following article—the attitudes of the Jews in Germany toward the 'Kulturkampf' in the second half of the nineteenth century.

Uriel Tal was, until his untimely death in 1984, a professor of Modern Jewish History at Tel-Aviv University. He published many articles and books on Jewish history, especially of the Jews in Central Europe during the nineteenth and twentieth centuries. He focused in particular on the cultural upheavals which characterize that period. His penetrating analyses of ideological trends are models of historical treatment of such problems.

BACKGROUND

During the 1880s the term *Kulturkampf* (literally, culture struggle) began to proliferate in German writings dealing with contemporary history. At the end of the nineteenth century and during the twentieth, the term became a rather common one in Western culture. While originally it referred to the

---

This article first appeared in Hebrew in *Zion* 29 (1964). The translation/adaptation is by Nadav Nahshon.

The International Center for University Teaching of Jewish Civilization, Jerusalem, the literary estate of the author of the article, and the translator/adapter grant permission to photocopy this article for teaching purposes without further permission or fee.

struggle between the German state and the Roman Catholic Church during the time of Bismarck, it has since become identified with the political and spiritual struggle to separate church and state, in a general sense. Liberals have even extended the concept, applying it to the effort to effect a separation between religion and society, science and culture.

Modern historiography has pointed out that the struggle to separate church and state was only one aspect of the *Kulturkampf* waged during the first two decades of the German Second Reich, that is, in the 1870s and 1880s. Both sides, state and church, endeavored to strengthen their positions in terms of ideological arguments and public support, tried to extend their influence over one another, and even attempted to renew mutual understanding and the division of political tasks between them. In this vein some recent historians, including Friedrich Sell, Hajo Holborn, Heinrich Bornkamm, and Fritz Stern, have argued that the *Kulturkampf* in Germany was not only aimed at liberating the state from the authority of the church and of religion, but was also a struggle waged by particularistic social and religious forces for independence and even for the very right of existence in the face of the egalitarian tendencies of the modern *Kulturstaat*.[1]

This study, while adopting the historical approach described, will examine a facet of the subject hitherto almost totally unexplored, namely, the relationship between the *Kulturkampf* and the Jews of Germany. From the primary sources at our disposal it is clear that the major protagonists in the *Kulturkampf*—the liberals, the Protestants, and the Catholics, representing different shades of opinion—considered the status of the Jews one of the criteria to be reviewed when evaluating the political and moral ramifications of that struggle.

SIGNIFICANCE OF THE *KULTURKAMPF*

The term *Kulturkampf* was coined by Rudolf Virchow, an eminent scientist and a member of the Progressive Party, in a speech delivered in the Prussian Diet in January 1873. In a subsequent address he argued that the historical significance of the *Kulturkampf* was not limited to the efforts of Bismarck and the liberals to weaken the particularistic power base of the ultramontane Catholics (i.e., those who supported papal supremacy in German Catholic affairs). Rather, declared Virchow, the *Kulturkampf* had a double meaning: On the one hand it was intended to liberate religion from the rule of the Church and to emancipate culture from the yoke of religion; on the other hand it was the duty of the state to force this emancipation on the entire nation. Therefore a *Kulturkampf* was required—a struggle for the sake of culture to be waged even at the cost of a "ministerial dictatorship."

Eugen Richter, one of the leaders of the Progressive Party, commented that Virchow's ambivalent definition reflected the dilemma that German liberalism had been faced with from the day that it attained power. In theory the Progressives represented the classic positions of 'Manchester Liberalism', including the principle that the state should not interfere in the lives of the individual and the society in the economic and cultural spheres, and in matters of education and religion. In classic liberalism this principle was the sole guarantee for the achievement of spiritual and political freedom for the individual. In practice, however, the liberals could no longer make do with the naive assumption, espoused by the early spokesmen of liberalism and the Enlightenment, that progress would occur naturally and spontaneously. Some kind of intervention was required, according to Richter, in order to free the monarchy from the grip of the clergy—and that intervention must come from the state.

During the *Kulturkampf*, which began in 1872 and ended officially with the declarations issued by Bismarck and Pope Leo XIII in 1887, the historic dilemma of the liberals took on an added dimension. Among the liberal intelligentsia in Germany the notion spread that human freedom does not materialize in a formal, rational vacuum; rather it develops in the context of a historic national-political entity. That entity was identified with the Protestant Prussian monarchy, which was perceived as the symbol and focal point of nationalism in the Reich. Historic nationalism and historic state were considered a continuation of the Lutheran tradition in which the church was not separate from the state but subordinate to it. Therefore the Lutheran Church, which had become one of the symbols of renascent German nationalism, was integrated into the monarchical regime.

As the *Kulturkampf* intensified, the National Liberals became more persistent in their efforts to replace the concept of *Rechstaat*, the government founded on law and built on rational and universal foundations, with the concept of *Kulturstaat*, the state whose foundations are historic and national. The major ideologists of the National Liberals, including Rudolf von Gneist and Theodor Mommsen, saw the *Kulturkampf* as a decisive historic turning point, following which the German nation would attain self-awareness and freedom. As a function of this freedom the nation-state would implement the historic principle of the sovereignty of the state over the church.

The political ideology current among German liberals during the 1870s and 1880s was diametrically opposed to the views held by many of Germany's Jews at that time. Most of the Jewish public in Germany, including the local and national leadership, rabbis, educators, intellectuals, and students, still clung to the old ideas of the Enlightenment and classic or 'Manchester Liberalism', as it was then called. These concepts posited that a rational and moral harmony existed in potentiality and was gradually materializing in economic and political activity, in the development of each child as he grew up and was educated, and in the everyday relationships between people. The realization of this harmony would signal the separation of church and state as well as the attainment of social equality for the Jews of Germany. Thus the last 'irrational' obstacles on the road to the full integration of Germany's Jews would be removed. To many non-Jewish German liberals, however, these were considered antiquated ideas that inhibited the development of German statehood.

The contradiction which existed between the concrete and the abstract, between reality and aspirations, and between the formal emancipation granted to the Jews in 1869 and the *Kulturkampf* which began two or three years later, penetrated the consciousness of many Jewish leaders as the changes in the attitudes of Catholics toward Jews and Judaism became apparent.[2]

CATHOLIC INFLUENCES ON THE *KULTURKAMPF*

During the *Kulturkampf* the Catholic stance toward the Jews was molded by the major political and ideological issue occupying the attention of the Catholic public, especially the politicians, clergy, and intellectuals among them—emancipation. They were concerned with the meaning of emancipation as a general human phenomenon: the emancipation of the worker, the woman, the intellectual, the farmer; the emancipation of man in modern society and culture; and emancipation from the burden of tradition and authority.

This problem had engaged German Catholic thinkers and politicians since the beginning of the nineteenth century. The advent of rationalism and secularism, the French Revolution and the Napoleonic conquests, the awakening of nationalism and romanticism, and the rise of liberalism and humanism in the days of Humboldt and Hardenberg—all this forced German Catholicism to seek a way to resolve the conflicts between the traditions of the Roman Catholic Church and the political legacy of the Peace of Westphalia which concluded the Thirty Years' War in 1648, and modern culture which based itself upon the 'emancipation of the spirit'. This latter concept of emancipation was elaborated even further when Rudolf Virchow declared that the goal of the *Kulturkampf* legislation was to bring about the 'emancipation of the state'.

Ludwig Windthorst and Hermann von Malinckrodt, leaders of the Catholic Center Party, claimed that emancipation of this kind was nothing other than the enforced secularization of the state. The process of secularization would impose materialism, egoism, immorality, and narrow self-interest on German public and cultural life. The inevitable result would be a general avoidance of civic and public duty and this, in turn, would lead to the 'deification' of the state which was, after all, the objective of those who instigated the *Kulturkampf* in the first place.

In fact the Catholics had assigned a double meaning to the concept 'emancipation' since the Napoleonic Wars, and this was the case during the *Kulturkampf* in particular. On the one hand emancipation was considered to mean the attainment of equal civil rights; as such it was a political and social goal of the Catholic public, especially in the Protestant states of Germany. As the persecutions of the Catholics intensified during the *Kulturkampf*, the ultramontanists and the supporters of the Center Party became even more ideologically convinced that the historic and moral mission of Catholicism was to struggle for the realization of political emancipation.

At the same time, however, 'emancipation' was perceived to be a characteristic condition of modern man undermining the Catholic principle of obedience. The emancipation of modern man conflicted with the theological, religious, and communal status of the traditional Catholic and was a force that destroyed the moral-spiritual fiber and emotional stability of the individual. This emancipation from tradition was leading to the disintegration of the family, of the organic social framework, and even of the traditional religious foundations upon which the authority of the state and the church were based.

According to this interpretation, emancipation was seen not as the attainment of equal rights or even as a release from traditional or irrational forces, but rather as a severance from the source of religious authority—the Church. Emancipation was thus viewed as a process through which man was cut off from the source of traditional truth and from the faith that bestowed upon the believer the theological certainty of his salvation. The *Kulturkampf* was interpreted as being a punishment from heaven for the sin of casting off traditional authority. This sin found political and social expression in the emancipation of the woman from the authority of her husband, of the farmer from his landlord, and of the believer from his church, leading to the notion that modern man was abandoning the historic process of salvation.

In the general context of these two seemingly irreconcilable meanings of emancipation, the Catholic attitude toward the Jews also acquired an ambivalent character which not infrequently showed signs of internal contradictions. In the view of the liberals in the Center Party, the status of the Jews was one criterion for evaluating the emancipation of religious and national minorities in Germany. Here, emancipation was taken to mean equal civil rights. In the eyes of the conservative Catholics, however, the emancipation of the Jews was an indicator of the corroding influence of emancipation in its broader sense, that is, the process of modern man's denial of the religious validity of tradition, discipline, and obedience to authority.

The contradictory nature of both general and Jewish emancipation set the tone for the Catholic position against the Jews that gathered momentum during the *Kulturkampf*. Many Catholics tried to distinguish between their anti-Jewish stance and contemporary racist and political anti-Semitism. The spokesmen of the conservative Catholics, including the Bishop of Paderborn, Konrad Martin, and the theologian Professor Joseph Rebbert, eschewed the discriminatory political stance as 'anti-Christian anti-Semitism'.

I.10.5

By this they meant that their political and economic views were not those of the anti-Semitic parties and that from an ideological and religious standpoint their opposition to Judaism stemmed from the historic Jewish position that obstinately rejected the principles of the Catholic faith: the belief in Jesus as the Messiah and the acceptance of the authority of the Church as the Kingdom of Heaven-on-earth. The term 'anti-Semitism' as such did not gain currency among the Catholic public until the end of the nineteenth century, when the anti-Semitic political parties were in decline.

The Catholic position vis-a-vis the Jews was a continuation of the views expressed by some of the leading conservative Catholic clergy in the mid-nineteenth century. Catholic opposition to the granting of civil rights to the Jews and, later, to the informal, social emancipation of the Jews, derived from a rejection of the rationalism upon which emancipation was based. The leaders of the conservative Catholics repudiated the humanistic assumption of the emancipation that all men were of equal worth by virtue of natural law. They felt that this idea, when put into practice in political and cultural life, destroyed the traditional structures of the family, the economy, the society, and the community. The cause of this liberal deterioration was Judaism as a religion, the Jews as a people, and the Jew as a symbol of a defective and dangerous human nature.

In 1848 Bishop Konrad Martin, along with the prelate Sebastian Brunner, published an article warning against 'talmudic anti-Christianity'. They claimed that the root of this phenomenon was the age-old stubbornness that prevented the Jews from admitting the truth of Christian salvation and the church. This, as well as their economic power, political cunning, and moral turpitude, were capable of destroying Christian life. According to Brunner and Martin, the danger facing the economy, society, state, and Christian culture would increase immeasurably if the Jews were granted legal emancipation and their historic liabilities were expunged.

In 1876, during the height of the *Kulturkampf,* the article written by Martin and Brunner almost twenty years earlier was reissued in pamphlet form by Professor Joseph Rebbert and entitled *A Look at Talmudic Judaism.* The pamphlet contained the traditional arguments against what Rebbert described as the corrupt practices that were dictated to the Jews by their laws dealing with economic, social, and political transactions involving gentiles. This time the well-used arguments were employed as political propaganda directed against Bismarck and the Liberals who, according to ultramontane circles in Westphalia and the political anti-Semites, waged the *Kulturkampf* for the sake of the Jews.

In reaction to the pamphlet, the *Deutsch-Israelitischer Gemeindebund* (Union of German Jewish Communities) prevailed upon the Prussian attorney-general to prosecute Rebbert and his publisher. When the *Gemeindebund* won the case, a group of conservative Protestants wrote an open letter to the general secretary of the organization stating, *inter alia:* "In this trial against Christians you have won as Jews, but you were defeated as liberals since, against your will, you demonstrated that there is no religious freedom unless it is enforced by the might of the state."

During the years when the *Kulturkampf* reached its climax, and especially during the reactionary backlash against the *Kulturkampf* (1877 through the end of the 1880s), anti-Jewish sentiment spread among the Catholic public all over Germany. Rebbert summarized the Catholic anti-Jewish position thus: "Our struggle against talmudic Judaism is simply self-defense. . . . In these days of *Kulturkampf*, the Jewish emancipation is liable to contaminate the Christians, and the Jews might even bring about the emancipation of the Christian from Christianity."

A variety of social, political, and ideological elements played roles in the emerging anti-Jewish position espoused by many of the conservative and ultramontane Catholics. As early as 1874, the theologian and popular writer, Professor Alban Stolz, declared that the Catholics must learn a lesson from the harsh Prussian 'May Laws' of 1873. At stake was the need to limit the destabilizing influence of liberalism and Judaism on Christian life, traditional social institutions, and the civic morality of the German Christian citizen. Stolz's attacks were followed by various diatribes against the Talmud and the *Shulhan Arukh*, followed by claims that the German economy, culture, press, and, in particular, the policies of the Bismarck government and the liberals were dominated by the Jews.

Among the voices heard in the growing barrage of anti-Jewish sentiment were those of Ludwig Erler, the disciple and successor of Wilhelm von Ketteler, Bishop of Mainz, and of Professor Georg Ratzinger, the economist and member of the Bavarian parliament. While these leaders used different tactics, they shared a basic view of what they considered to be the character and historical essence of the Jews. They contended that the Jews had revealed their true nature from the beginning of their exile. Then, as now, they brought destruction and ruin; they swindled and victimized their 'hosts', like parasites; and they deceived and betrayed anyone who was not of their faith. Furthermore, many of the Roman persecutions of the early Christians could be traced back to Jewish treachery; and had not the Jews betrayed and murdered Christ? In similar fashion the persecutions of the Catholics by the Prussian authorities was nothing more than a reflection of the insidious rule of the Jews in Germany.

The argument regarding the historic character of Judaism and the Jews was bolstered by a survey of the economic role played by the Jews in history. Until the 1870s German historiography had generally tended to speak of the Jews as having made a contribution to the growth of European cities and the development of mercantilistic and industrial economies. Now, under the influence of the *Kulturkampf* and perhaps of the economic crash of 1873, emphasis was transferred to descriptions of the economic and moral mayhem the Jews supposedly wreaked. In 1862 the Catholics had attacked

I.10.7

what they referred to as the destructive impact of capitalism, industriali-
zation, and the Jews on the economy, family, and public morality. They
believed this to be especially true in the case of the workers and the lower
middle class. Ten years later, during the period of the political and economic
ascendancy of the liberals, it was declared that the Jews had attained so
much power that the very 'German essence' (*das deutsche Wesen*) was determined by them. The combination of scorn for the Jews and, at the same
time, fear of their power, was endemic to the development of anti-Semitism
in general during the Second Reich and of the anti-Jewish position of the
Catholics in particular.

In their polemic against the Jews, the Catholic spokesmen tended to
buttress their arguments with examples from the history of the Roman
Catholic Church; for example, the Council of Elvira (306), which forbade
the Christians to share meals or intermarry with Jews, and the Council of
Macon (583), which prohibited the appointment of Jews to judicial offices
in order that they might never be in the position to judge or punish Christians.

The evolution of the Catholic position against the Jews was tied to the
fundamental changes that took place in the political outlook of the ultramontanists at the close of the 1870s, which marked the completion of the
Kulturkampf legislation. A basic change was the shift from the position favoring a monarchy headed by the Catholic Austrian House of Habsburg,
to a nationalistic and patriotic German stance. In addition, strict political
and theological subordination to Rome in matters of education and politics
was replaced by an independent posture, especially following the council
of German Catholics in Breslau in 1886. The fragmentation that had characterized the Catholic public, which comprised groups with different and
even conflicting interests, had coalesced into a unified (although by no
means uniform) front represented by the all-Catholic Center Party.

The transition was, in short, from a position which did not look favorably
upon the Reich, its nationalism, or centralistic tendencies, to a more active,
even central role in German political life. Modern German historiography
correctly claims that the indisputable political result of the *Kulturkampf* was
the ascendancy of the Christian parties over the liberals. With the decisive
denouement of the struggle itself at the end of the 1880s, the Center Party
became a political and social force with which every coalition had to reckon
in order to succeed in the government of the Second Reich.

The gradual integration of the ultramontane Catholics into the national
political system of the Reich was a key factor in creating the new political
balance. The ideological momentum for this change was the encyclical of
Pope Leo XIII dated December 28, 1878. The encyclical was followed by a
declaration from the Center Party stating the need to reinforce the conservative social and moral foundations of Germany. In the spirit of the papal
document, the party leaders emphasized the corrupting effect that social

democracy, liberalism, and materialism could have on the Christian faith. They embraced the conciliatory policy of Leo XIII and exploited this opportunity to move in the direction of even greater political self-reliance and independence from Rome. Bismarck's alliance with the conservative political forces in 1877–78 set the stage for the progressive integration of the Catholics into the Second Reich. This process created a need among the ultramontane Catholics for an anti-Jewish platform, to bridge the gap between the Catholics who had supported the House of Habsburg and the vision of a 'Greater Germany' (*Grossdeutschland*), and the Protestant public and the masses.

POSITIONS OF JEWISH LEADERS DURING THE *KULTURKAMPF*

As early as the initial stage of the *Kulturkampf*, during 1871–75, the positions of the Jewish leadership in Germany vacillated between two poles. There was a feeling of identification with the goals of the *Kulturkampf* in theory, yet there were also reservations about the violent course of the struggle in reality. There was support for the liberal camp which sided with Bismarck as the leader of the *Kulturkampf*, as well as apprehension about the centrist tendencies developing in that circle. There was a belief in the policy of maintaining a separation between church and state, but it was qualified by the fear that such a policy would result in the separation of religion from society, thereby undermining the basic premise upon which post-emancipation Jewish life rested.

Most of the Jewish leadership, professionals, and intellectuals supported Bismarck in the early stages of the *Kulturkampf*. They approved of the Prussian decrees enacted against the ultramontanists in 1871–72, and were especially in favor of the law of July 4, 1872, which banned the Jesuit and other Catholic orders. The appointment of Adalbert Falk, in 1872, to the post of Prussian Minister of Ecclesiastical Affairs and Education was also welcomed, as it was perceived as being a sign of the beginning of a genuinely liberal government policy.

At the end of 1872, the Union of German Jewish Communities issued a series of public declarations in support of the law of December 10, 1871 which forbade the ultramontane clergy from dismissing teachers and priests who associated themselves with German nationalism. The law also prohibited the dismissal of liberally inclined Catholic clergymen and teachers who refused to accept the doctrine of papal infallibility which had been invoked by the Vatican Council in 1870. The Union's proclamations aroused sharp criticism from some well-known non-Orthodox rabbis, including Rabbi Manuel Joel. These rabbis argued that the state had neither a legal nor a moral right to intervene in the internal affairs of religious associations in the Reich. It was certainly inappropriate, they claimed, for the central representative body of German Jewry to condone the government's anti-liberal policies.

The Jews, as members of a religious minority, stood to lose the most from these policies.

For the time being these criticisms reflected the views of only a small number of German Jews. Jewish public opinion, to the extent that it was given overt expression, was explicitly in favor of the first measures enacted by the government against the ultramontane Catholics. This support grew in the wake of the Prussian May laws of 1873. These laws inaugurated an aggressive, and even violent, stage of the struggle being waged by Bismarck and Falk. The May laws increased secular government supervision of the educational system and the training of teachers and clergy. Strict censorship was imposed on Catholic clergymen, teachers, writers, and even statesmen who were categorized as ultramontanists. The government established a secular supreme court for ecclesiastical affairs, and monitored national and regional church organizations. Catholics who were suspected of disloyalty to the German national movement had to face persecutions and expulsions. The spokesmen for the major German Jewish communities considered these steps "measures taken in the defense of liberalism, nationalism, and scientific progress—measures which were forced upon us by the ultramontanists."

During the first four years of the *Kulturkampf*, the conflict generated a great deal of interest in the Jewish communities in Germany. It was a subject of deliberation in both private and public forums at all levels of Jewish society. It came up in day-to-day conversations and served as a subject for humor and satire in the local and national Jewish press. It was a topic for discussion in private homes during leisure hours, and was one of the important issues on the agenda of major Jewish community councils.

The various primary sources available to us lead to a number of conclusions about the way German Jewry perceived the *Kulturkampf* during its early years. To begin with, it was viewed as both a political and spiritual struggle against the ultramontane Catholics. In the eyes of German Jewry, the ultramontanists negated the rational and universal principles of liberalism. They opposed the concept which served as the basis for Jewish emancipation—that human freedom must find expression in spiritual and intellectual autonomy. They rejected the new symbols of German nationalism—which was also the nationalism of Germany's Jews—and they were essentially opposed to the entire concept of nationhood, at least as it was understood by German Jewry. The concept itself derived from the theories advanced by Moritz Lazarus and Hermann Heymann Steinthal regarding what they called the 'psychology of nations'. According to this school of thought, the nation did not develop in a strictly organic fashion, as postulated by nineteenth-century romanticism. Rather, it was an entity which could be attained only by exertion of willpower, self-awareness, and conscious identification, with the aid of intellectual tools, such as linguistic expression and spiritual and aesthetic creativity. Since the fulfillment of

Jewish emancipation in Germany depended upon the realization of those liberal and humanistic principles to which the ultramontanists were opposed—so went the argument—the Jews of Germany had a genuine stake in a liberal victory in the *Kulturkampf*.

Another claim was that German nationalism included, as part of its traditional system of values, the principle of religious toleration. It was said that this notion had even found expression as far back as 1648 in the Peace of Westphalia; in other words, before the rise of liberalism and modern science. The historic foundations of toleration were strengthened and developed during the enlightened reign of Frederick the Great (1740–1786), preceding, and even contrasting with, the French Revolution. This development continued during the struggle for Jewish emancipation and reached fruition in the 1860s. In accepting this line of thinking, German Jewry was following the lead of the National Liberals and both the conservative and liberal Protestants. These groups, who were the backbone of German nationalism, imbued their national ideology with German historical elements, as opposed to rationalistic principles which were deprecatingly referred to as 'French'.

Since it was now being claimed that German nationalism had deep historic roots, which even included irrational romantic elements, the Lutheran Reformation was also evaluated in a new light. It, rather than the rationalistic revolution initiated by the Enlightenment, was defined as the source of individual freedom and civil liberties in the modern nation-state. The 'heritage of Luther', and not classical rationalism, was claimed to be the most important element of liberalism. The essence of Luther's heritage, according to the liberal Protestant view, was the transference of the source of religious and political authority from the church to the consciousness of the individual.

The leaders of German Jewry were now faced with a dilemma. On the one hand, the increase in the use of Lutheran symbols in German nationalism corroborated their conviction that Jewish emancipation would be achieved only if the granting of civil liberties were based on liberal and rationalistic principles. On the other hand, as the *Kulturkampf* progressed, German Jews became increasingly critical of the secular rationalistic foundations of the Enlightenment and the French Revolution. Secularism and rationalism militated against the aggrandizement of a Jewish public, since the singularity of that public, according to the prevailing definition, was based on its being a strictly religious grouping. This view was reflected in the label 'Germans of the Mosaic persuasion', which many Jews adopted for themselves. In light of their fears and in accordance with the ideology of conservative and even some liberal Protestants, German Jewish leaders took pains to emphasize the 'historical' foundations of the Enlightenment and the emancipation, rather than their rational and secular aspects.

Nevertheless, during the first years of the *Kulturkampf*, the Jews of Germany felt that their future depended on the fate of rationalism and liberalism. As a result, their criticism of the ultramontane Catholics largely centered around what they perceived as the latter's opposition to toleration, liberty, equality, and liberalism. In 1873, Hermann Steinthal claimed that the ultramontanists even denied the historical development which maintained that toleration was an 'organic' and binding German national treasure. Steinthal's criticism of Catholicism was seconded by Rabbi Manuel Joel who brought forward, as a historical example, the papal bull *Zelo Domus Dei* of 1648, in which the pope negated the principle of toleration as delineated in the Peace of Westphalia of that same year.

Following the enactment of the harsh 'May laws' of 1873, which were directed against the ultramontanists, the leaders of the Union of German Jewish Communities contacted local communities, teachers' organizations, and rabbis, suggesting that they explain to the Jewish public what the leaders of the Union called the antiliberal and irrational attitude of Catholicism. They were to cite examples from documents issued by the Roman Catholic Church, including the encyclical of July 8, 1864, and the *Syllabus Erorum Nostri Tempi* (A List of the Errors of Our Times), in which Pope Pius IX attacked the principle of toleration.

The ensuing public outrage was systematic and apparently well orchestrated. The *Syllabus* was attacked by the Jewish leadership—in rabbis' sermons, teachers' classrooms, and on the pages of the Jewish press—for what were called inhuman, illiberal, and anti-intellectual ideas advanced by the pope. The *Syllabus* was assailed not only for its content, but also for the fact that it, as well as other 'lists', was blindly accepted by supposedly intellectual and enlightened people.

In the context of the polemic surrounding the papal 'list of errors' during 1871–1873, a group of Jewish economists and jurists belonging to the Progressive Party attempted to link the theoretical elements of the 'list' with the political and economic views of the conservative wing in the Catholic Center Party. In the progressives' opinion, the economic outlook of the ultramontanists was in conflict with the ideals of laissez-faire, free trade, and economic competition. The Catholics were said to be in favor of protective tariffs and maintaining the irrational character of traditional social groupings and methods of production. Their conclusion was that the general world view of the ultramontanists, in keeping with the spirit of the 'list of errors' and papal encyclicals, was one in which religious, social, and economic tradition had turned into rigid dogmas. Since dogmatism was an obstacle to fulfilling the vision of liberalism, it would also be a hindrance to achieving full equality for Germany's Jews.

This evaluation of the German Catholics' economic views was not entirely objective. While, as early as the second half of the 1870s, the Center Party lent consistent support to Bismarck's protective tariff policy (and thus took the first step in defusing the *Kulturkampf*), the spectrum of economic views of the Catholic public was much more complex and not altogether antiliberal. Be that as it may, the socioeconomic unity of the Center Party derived from the fact that it attracted social classes and pressure groups with diverse, even antagonistic, interests. The Center Party encompassed a labor movement with a Christian-social ideology founded by Bishop von Ketteler, members of the lower middle class and the urban proletariat, professionals, intellectuals, farmers, titled landowners, and other groups as well. To paraphrase one contemporary observer, the phenomenon of the Center Party destroyed the illusion fostered by classic liberalism that 'enlightened society' was composed of enlightened, autonomous individuals and, at the same time, exploded the myth held by the socialists which maintained that people form groups purely on the basis of materialistic considerations.

The success of the Center Party in uniting such diverse social and political interests was not lost on the liberals and the Jews of Germany. In fact, their criticism of the Catholics took on an ideological tone that focused on the supposedly reactionary nature of Catholicism as reflected by the Center Party. German Jewry did not perceive the *Kulturkampf* solely as a struggle against a political adversary; it was a continuation of an old historic rivalry against Catholicism, the opponent of Jews and Judaism throughout the ages.

OPPOSITION TO THE *KULTURKAMPF*

As mentioned earlier, not all of the opinions voiced by the German Jewish public were in favor of the *Kulturkampf*. For the most part, however, the negative opinions did not reflect a polarization within the Jewish public but, rather, a situation wherein the Jewish leadership tended to express multiple views that were inconsistent if not contradictory. This discordancy seems to have stemmed from the basic dilemma which faced the entire liberal camp, namely, the need to choose between the ideals of freedom and governmental nonintervention in the private lives of the citizens, and a reality in which the ever-growing power of the state was aimed at forcing these very same ideals down the throats of its citizens.

The outset of the general public debate during the early stage of the *Kulturkampf* centered around an edict adopted by the Reichstag in March 1871, called the *Kanzelparagraph*. The new regulation sought to prohibit what was vaguely defined as improper use of the religious sermon for political purposes. While an earlier version of the edict had, ironically, been adopted in Bavaria in order to prevent liberal Catholic and Protestant clergy from preaching against the conservative Bavarian regime, the *Kanzelparagraph* was clearly aimed against the ultramontane clergy in most of the states of the Reich.

For the most part, the new policy was welcomed by the Jewish public, since its official rationale was to ensure the separation of church and state. However, a few voices did rise up in opposition to the measure, such as

I.10.13

that of Emil Lehmann, a leader of Reform Judaism in Germany and an active member of the Dresden City Council. Lehmann claimed that the law was the first step toward an 'omnipotent' state.

The doubts and criticisms of German Jewry about the *Kulturkampf* increased in the wake of the public debate waged between the leaders of the Center Party and the spokesmen of the National Liberals, most notably the historian Heinrich von Treitschke and his followers, and Rudolf von Bennigsen, the founder of the National Liberal Party and leader of the German Protestant Union. The polemic began in earnest surrounding the issue of the *Kanzelparagraph*. The leaders of the National Liberals claimed that the law was not aimed at separating all churches from the state, as the Progressives, 'Manchester Liberals', and Jews believed. It was only designed to disengage the state from the ultramontane Catholic Church, whereas the Protestant Church was a historic and organic part of the state. The National Liberal spokesmen denied that the *Kanzelparagraph* contradicted the principles of freedom of religion. On the contrary they claimed that, by prohibiting ultramontane sermons directed against the state, the Reich was making it easier for the citizen to fully identify with his state and reach an informed decision to accept its authority. According to Bennigsen, the Reich would not be safe from the ultramontanists until the state succeeded in ensuring its sovereignty over the nation and over religion.

The National Liberals also contested the Catholic view that the source of the state's authority was not to be found on the political plane at all, but rather in the context of transcendental values. Treitschke argued that the ultramontanists sought to infuse alien elements into German culture, whereas the National Liberals fixed the source of the state's authority within itself and within the *Volkgeist* (national spirit). Giving a romantic interpretation to the Hegelian concept of statehood, Treitschke declared that the *Volkgeist* was the historic inner essence of the nation, achieving its full freedom, fulfillment, and power through the state and for the state. Another important liberal leader, Eduard Lasker, reached conclusions similar to those of Treitschke, even though many of his basic premises differed considerably. Lasker believed that the moral authority of the state to rule actually derived from the emancipation of the state from all external metaphysical systems; only in the context of the state could man be released from the bond of alien elements and achieve full freedom.

The Center Party spokesmen presented counterarguments during 1871–1875. They contended that the National Liberals had transformed the state into an omnipotent power, and that every addition to the *Kulturkampf* legislation augmented the all-encompassing authority of the government and moved in the direction of the deification of the state. They also claimed that the popularized materialistic philosophies disseminated by the liberals in the universities, schools, and press would lead to total secularism and spiritual deprivation, repudiation of religion, and rejection of authority. This would necessarily lead to the enslavement of the citizen to the state, since no individual or community could survive without some form of authority. The result of this process would be the *Machstaat*, the state based on sheer power, which would lead in turn to the oppression of every national, religious, and cultural minority in the Reich. As Ludwig Windthorst put it in an address before the Prussian Diet in 1872, a state without God would end up by deifying itself.

The ongoing debate between the National Liberals and Progressives and the Catholics presented a new dilemma for German Jewry. Many German Jews considered themselves political and even ideological allies of the liberals. Yet the views professed by some of the leaders of National Liberalism, such as Treitschke, Bennigsen, Lasker, and Virchow (despite the differences among them), raised doubts and even outright opposition among the leadership of the Union of German Jewish Communities, rabbis, teachers, and students. They argued that the policy pursued by the liberals during the *Kulturkampf* would not result in the emancipation of the state from the grip of the church, with ensuing spiritual and cultural freedom, including the freedom to be different.[3] Instead, spiritual and cultural conformity would be the order of the day.

The so-called 'scientific liberalism' of Rudolf Virchow was criticized as forcing uniformity on the spiritual life of Germany, with the help of secular rationalism and religious indifference. The Jewish historian Martin Philippson maintained that the 'spiritual unification' demanded by Virchow was a provocation against Judaism, Catholicism, and all other minority groups which sought to maintain their individuality. Treitschke and Bennigsen were attacked for interpreting the *Kulturkampf* as a struggle to mold the Reich in the image of the historic Protestant state.

The major weekly periodical of German Jewry, the *Allgemeine Zeitung des Judentums*, systematically, openly, and emphatically encouraged this criticism. As early as 1872, the paper declared its rejection of the equalizing and conformist tendencies that the secular National Liberals were trying to impose on the Jews and other religious and social minority groups in the Reich. This 'egalitarianism' was seen to be nothing other than a fear of any vigorous display of individualism and a suspicion of all nonconformist religious phenomena. According to the *Allgemeine Zeitung*, German Jewry's mission was to maintain its existence as a unique religious community, thereby affirming the principles of individualism and freedom. The individualism of the Jews was described as being cultural-religious in nature, possessing both existential vitality and historical validity. If German liberalism could not tolerate this kind of individualism, which did not in any way conflict with political and social liberalism, there was nothing left for the *Allgemeine Zeitung* to do but express its sorrow and part ways.

I.10.15

NEW LAWS RESULTING FROM THE *KULTURKAMPF*

As the *Kulturkampf* progressed, some of the Jewish leadership modified their evaluation of German liberalism. The public and legal status of the Jewish communities in Germany changed as well. These changes occurred in the wake of *Kulturkampf* legislation passed during 1873–1876 in Prussia and, to a certain degree, throughout the Reich. The new laws were designed to redefine the legal rights and, in some cases, the public status of church and communal organizations.

In March 1873, the National Liberals and the Prussian Minister of Ecclesiastical Affairs and Education, Adalbert Falk, initiated a proposal to annul some sections of the Prussian constitution of 1850. One target was section 15 which stated that the Evangelical and Roman Catholic churches, as well as all other religious organizations, could arrange and manage their affairs in an independent manner. They could also administer funds and collect dues for the maintenance of their internal religious, cultural, educational, and social welfare institutions. The intention of the liberals making this proposal was to further erode the power of the Catholic clergy and to establish 'uniform' government control in the state. In this way, Bismarck and the National Liberals hoped to strengthen the authority of the state in the realms of religion, culture, and education. The proposal was ratified in May 1873, and turned out to be one of the most decisive steps in escalating the *Kulturkampf*.

One reaction to the new measure was a polemical article published by the leaders of the Magdeburg Jewish community, criticizing the law and arguing that it was liable to blunt the special character of the Jewish communities and undermine the already weakened influence of the community leadership. Moreover, the erosion of the particularistic powers of the communities would destroy their ability to collect dues for the maintenance of communal institutions and services, and would endanger the continued existence of the Jewish communities.

In 1875, during renewed debate over the abrogation of section 15, the *Allgemeine Zeitung* printed a harsh criticism of 'the new step in church policy'. The attack was directed against the measures undertaken by the National Liberals in the context of the *Kulturkampf*. The newspaper asserted that these measures destroyed the public force of religion around which social and cultural groups coalesced. Among the laws criticized were the regulations regarding civil marriages, the replacement of church supervision of religious administration by government control, and a law called the *Austrittsgesetz* (see below). According to the *Allgemeine Zeitung*, the laws reflected a policy that would remove the legal authority of the religious communities and reduce them to the level of private organizations, thus threatening the continued existence of the Jewish communities. This policy was the result of a confusion of concepts within German liberalism. The paper agreed that there was a need to limit the political power of the church, but this did not mean that the church and religion were identical and that the status of religion should be demoted.

THE SECESSION LAW

During the debate over the annulment of section 15 in the constitution of 1850, a measure called the *Austrittsgesetz* (secession law) was adopted by the Prussian Diet. It comprised the fourth of the well-known "May laws" which became the juristic and ideological nucleus of the *Kulturkampf* legislation. The *Austrittsgesetz* stated that henceforth a Protestant or a Catholic could leave the church to which he belonged without being regarded as having abandoned Christianity or any particular denomination within Christianity. Like all the *Kulturkampf* legislation, this law sought to attenuate the consolidated strength of Catholicism. Under the new law, liberal-minded or nationalistic Catholics could leave existing conservative church institutions and set up new ones, without having to bear the onus of officially leaving the Roman Catholic religion.

According to the original version of the law, the status of Jews was different from that of Christians. While Catholics and Protestants were now allowed to terminate their membership in their churches and other religious institutions without these acts being legally interpreted as breaking the bond with Christianity, a Jew who left his religious community was legally considered to have terminated his association with Judaism. In the eyes of the law, a lapsed Jew was considered an atheist or an agnostic.

During the early deliberations on the proposed law, in March 1873, Eduard Lasker claimed that the law was discriminatory, and that it imposed moral constraints on those Jews who did not wish to remain part of their officially constituted communities for reasons of conscience, yet did not want to relinquish their legal association with Judaism. Orthodox Jewry pressured Lasker and other liberal members of the Diet to extend the *Austrittsgesetz* to include the Jews. Eminent Orthodox rabbis, including Samson Raphael Hirsch and Azriel Hildesheimer, complained that the law prevented Orthodox Jews from leaving communal organizations which were not to their liking and forced them to remain members of communities dominated by liberal and reform elements.

The desire expressed by Orthodox Jewish leaders to extend the law to include the Jewish communities did not reflect a consensus among the German Jewish leadership. In fact, the non-Orthodox leadership emphatically disagreed with the views expressed by Orthodox figures such as Hirsch and Hildesheimer. Immediately following the adoption of the original law in May 1873, the representatives of the major non-Orthodox Jewish communities, including rabbis, teachers, and communal officials, met in Leipzig to discuss the ramifications of the law on Jewish public life. Many

I.10.17

participants in the conference held that the law, nominally intended to put an end to government intervention in the religious and cultural life of the citizens, would, if extended to include the Jews, actually constitute serious interference in Jewish life. Removal of the obligation to be a member of the Jewish community, so the argument went, would result in many Jews ending their affiliation with it. Few would leave in order to found Orthodox communities; most of those who left would shirk off all sense of responsibility toward the community because of religious indifference, or apathy toward Jewish tradition and the Jewish people. The fear was expressed that there would be a mass exodus and, as a result, the income of the communities from dues and contributions would drop drastically. Hence, many communities would no longer be able to maintain basic services, such as synagogues, schools, and social welfare programs. Even Jewish cemeteries might fall into neglect due to lack of funds.

From the end of 1873 and during 1874, Jewish communal leaders, including Martin Philippson and his father Ludwig Philippson (who was the founder and editor of the *Allgemeine Zeitung des Judentums*), intensified their efforts to convince the Prussian government to maintain the obligation of community membership for Jews. In a series of petitions submitted in 1874 to the Prussian Diet, to Eduard Lasker, and to the leadership of the National Liberal and Progressive parties, leaders of the non-Orthodox Jewish public urged refraining from further legislation that would, in their view, result in the total disintegration of the Jewish communities.

In a memorandum presented by the Union of German Jewish Communities to the Prussian Diet in 1874, a claim was made that the Orthodox Jews were similar in nature to the ultramontane Catholics, the main opponents of the *Kulturkampf*. This similarity was apparent in their intolerance, dogmatism, and devotion to medieval tradition. The memorandum also argued that some of the Orthodox leaders like Hirsch and Hildesheimer felt a spiritual, and perhaps even political attachment toward previous places of residence, such as Hungary and Moravia—and what were these places if not centers of ultramontanism in Jewish garb? Orthodox Jews even resembled the ultramontanists in maintaining allegiance to the 'homeland' outside the borders of Germany—namely, Palestine.

Thus, Orthodox Jewry was accused of endangering the continued existence of the organized Jewish community in Germany. They were said to be concerned only with themselves and with maintaining a separate existence from the rest of the Jewish public, in order to achieve a broader version of the *Austrittsgesetz*. In so doing, they were undermining the legal authority of the Jewish community. Without that authority, most of the non-Orthodox Jewish leadership feared an increase in intermarriage or apostasy.

Despite the vociferous opposition of the Union of German Jewish Communities and other institutions and personalities representing major segments of German Jewry, a revised version of the *Austrittsgesetz* was adopted in May 1876, extending the regulation to include the Jewish communities. The change in the law was a direct result of the active intervention by Lasker and other liberal deputies, as well as the lobbying efforts of Orthodox Jewry.

Until then, Jews had been required to maintain membership in their local communities, according to the 1847 'law governing the status of Jews'. Nonpayment of dues and a failure to fulfill other communal obligations were legally considered departure from Judaism. In terms of the laws which regulated civil status in Prussia, a Jew was anyone who was a member of an officially recognized Jewish community; there was no other legal way to maintain affiliation with Judaism. The revised version of the *Austrittsgesetz* imparted a new legal and public status to the Jews. Now a Jew could terminate his membership in a Jewish community, or abstain from joining altogether, yet still enjoy the legal status of remaining a Jew.

Among those who reacted against the law in its new form was Ludwig Philippson. He complained against what he called the intervention of the state in the lives and the freedom of conscience of its citizens. The law reflected a distortion of the principles of liberalism upon which the 'May laws' had been based. Those who had supported the *Kulturkampf* had done so not to witness the dismemberment of the Jewish and Christian religious communities, but rather to promote their independence and freedom.

CONCLUSION

This study has attempted to investigate the interrelationship between the *Kulturkampf* and the status of the Jews in the Second Reich. By examining some of the crucial historical issues which arose during the *Kulturkampf*, we may be able to cast some light on the status of religion and religious institutions in the modern state in general, and on the status of the Jews as a minority group in particular. Despite the declarations by Bismarck and the liberals, the *Kulturkampf* was not solely a struggle to make the state independent of the church, or to ensure more of a separation between religion and German society and culture. It also embodied the struggle of the church to stave off the intervention of the state into its affairs. It also expressed the quest of religious groups—both Catholic and Jewish—to obtain political and economic conditions and a spiritual and educational climate that would allow them to practice their religion and preserve their unique character within the context of the nation-state, with its modern culture and industrialized society.

At the outset of the *Kulturkampf*, the German state represented, at least in theory, the goals of liberalism, especially the principles of civic equality and spiritual and religious freedom. However, as the *Kulturkampf* intensified, the liberals became an instrument of a government which sought to enforce these very same principles on the public through means of propaganda, police measures, and economic and political pressure. Freedom

I.10.19

was twisted into forced 'egalitarianism'; civil liberties were made conditional upon national commitment; spiritual freedom was exchanged for cultural uniformity.

The ultramontane Catholics held conservative, antiliberal, and antinationalist positions at the inception of the *Kulturkampf*. Yet, the more they were persecuted by the government, the more they were transformed into one of the foremost public champions of self-determination for all groups within the Reich. This new-found 'liberalism' was not unlimited, however. For one thing, it was advocated only in areas where the Catholics were a minority among a Protestant majority. Moreover, it was abandoned during the second half of the 1880s, following the integration of the Catholics into the political life and nationalist ambiance of the Reich.

The ideological shift which took place had an impact on how the sources of political and religious authority were perceived. The rational basis of political authority was deemphasized, while traditional, romantic, and mythical elements received greater attention. In religion, on the other hand, rational and liberal ideas were strengthened at the expense of traditional and historical sources. As a result, liberalism paradoxically became a conservative force, while Catholicism assumed the liberal role.

The Jews occupied a unique position within the dynamic historic context of the *Kulturkampf*. Initially, the Jews by and large strongly supported the liberal camp. Within the framework of liberalism the Jews of Germany hoped to find the social, political, economic, and spiritual conditions conducive to full emancipation. Most German Jews endowed emancipation with a double meaning. It meant the achievement of total integration in the Christian environment, including full social involvement on a daily basis. It also meant that they could remain unique in terms of their Jewish faith, even though they functioned as German citizens in all respects. However, the more intense the *Kulturkampf* became, the more obstacles arose in the path of realizing this twofold quest. The egalitarian tendencies of the liberals made it difficult for the Jews to fulfill their aspirations; the basically anti-Jewish stance of the Catholics deepened as they increasingly integrated into German political life.

As a consequence of these trends, some of the leaders and scholars among the Jews became convinced that the historic mission of Judaism was to promote the preservation of the minority as a positive value and even as an ideal expressing the moral obligation of the citizen in the modern nation-state. It was incumbent upon every citizen to struggle to preserve one's individuality, even while adapting oneself to the surrounding society. The special position occupied by the Jews was likened by some liberals to a barometer that measured the extent to which the liberals and Christians adhered to their ideals—the liberal principles of equality and freedom, and the Christian teachings of love and toleration.

We may conclude, therefore, that even in the modern nation-state the existence of the Jews as a political and social minority served as a stimulus, spurring the Christians to introspection and self-examination. By the very fact of their presence, the Jews aroused awareness of flaws in their host countries' systems of government, ideologies, and ways of life. It is possible, perhaps, that this public exposé was one of the root causes of the long history of Christian-Jewish antagonism.

NOTES

1. See Fritz Stern, "The Political Consequences of the Unpolitical Germans," *History* 3 (1960): 106ff.

2. The primary sources upon which this article is based were found in the Central Archives for the History of the Jewish People, Jerusalem; the Bundesarchiv, Koblenz, West Germany; and the library and archives of the Loccum monastery near Hanover, West Germany. This archival material made possible a comparative study of Jewish and Christian source documents.

3. A small group of Jewish leaders and scholars of Jewish thought emphasized the historical, political, and ethical uniqueness of German Jewry; their opinions are reflected in the source material at the historian's disposal. One may assume, however, that during the *Kulturkampf* period most of the Jewish intellectuals, members of the free professions and of the upper middle class, were not involved in Jewish communal life. It is unlikely that they shared the views of the leaders of the organized Jewish community.

SUGGESTIONS FOR FURTHER READING

Schorsch, Ismar, *The Jewish Reactions to German Anti-Semitism, 1870–1914*. New York: Columbia University Press, 1972.

Tal, Uriel, *Christians and Jews in Germany: Religion, Politics, and Ideology in the Second Reich, 1870–1914*. Ithaca: Cornell University Press, 1975.

ABOUT THE EDITOR

JOSEPH DAN (born 1935) is Gershom Scholem Professor of Kabbalah at The Hebrew University of Jerusalem. In 1966–67 and again in 1977–78, he was a visiting professor of Judaic studies at the University of California. In 1984–85 he was Director of the Jewish National and University Library and, since 1979, he has been on the board of directors of the World Union of Jewish Studies. In addition to editing *Jerusalem Studies in Jewish Thought*, he has published numerous books and articles. His books in English include *The Teachings of Hasidism, Jewish Mysticism and Jewish Ethics, The Early Kabbalah*, and *Gershom Scholem and the Mystical Dimension in Jewish History*.